Refugee Support and Moral Practice in Slovakia

Refugee Support and Moral Practice in Slovakia

An Ethnographic Study

Eva-Maria Walther

ANTHEM PRESS

Anthem Press
An imprint of Wimbledon Publishing Company
www.anthempress.com

This edition first published in UK and USA 2024
by ANTHEM PRESS
75–76 Blackfriars Road, London SE1 8HA, UK
or PO Box 9779, London SW19 7ZG, UK
and
244 Madison Ave #116, New York, NY 10016, USA

Supported by Schroubek Fonds Östliches Europa, a German foundation that supports
research projects and scholarly publications on Eastern Europe.

British Library Cataloguing-in-Publication Data
A catalogue record for this book is available from the British Library.

Library of Congress Cataloging-in-Publication Data: 2024930882
A catalog record for this book has been requested.

ISBN-13: 978-1-83999-124-0 (Hbk)
ISBN-10: 1-83999-124-0 (Hbk)

Cover Credit: Kvet Nguyen

This title is also available as an e-book.

CONTENTS

ACKNOWLEDGMENTS*

What am I actually looking at? A substance of a strange shape without a specific indication. I need to define, I need to classify, I need to know what or who is on the other side. Are you like me? Or are you someone else? What group do you belong to? Do you belong to me or are you external?

This is the text accompanying the photography series *Mutual Otherness*, which includes the cover image of this book by Slovak-Vietnamese photographer Kvet Nguyen. It engages with the ambivalent feelings connected with encountering the 'Other': Even though we live in a globalized age and are seemingly accustomed to a world of difference, the 'Other' retains an uncanniness and a fascination. The urge to categorize, to schematize, to familiarize is comprehensive. The photo series seeks to undermine these instincts through "a process of creation and extinction of forms, but also an event that places forms on the border of visible and invisible, known and unknown, present and absent."

This book engages with a lot of 'Otherness'—with those dimensions of difference that are visible and expectable when talking about asylum and migration: culture, origin, religion, but also vastly different biographies with varying experiences of suffering and resilience. It belongs to the magic of ethnography that differences, demarcations and distinctions, upon closer scrutiny, almost always appear less pronounced than a first glance of the amorphous 'Other' might suggest. However, throughout my anthropological training, I have also learned that every encounter is an encounter across difference. Every human contains multitudes, every being is a world of life experience apart from the other.

Reaching out into the unknown and tackling this difference can be a scary and a transformative experience for both sides. The ethnographic fieldwork for this book has certainly been both of these things for me, and it would not have been possible if it had not been for the many individuals who were willing to reveal to me small parts of what it means to be them: the employees of the three NGOs I conducted fieldwork in, the employees of the Migration Office, the people who support refugees as volunteers, teachers, priests, and interpreters, the refugees who started a new life in Slovakia, and my landlady in Bratislava. I am eternally grateful that they were willing to talk to me, acknowledging our mutual otherness (and sameness), receiving very little in return. This book is dedicated to them.

---

* This book is based on a doctoral dissertation accepted by the Faculty of Philosophy, Art History, History and Humanities of the University of Regensburg in 2021.

I also want to thank my Slovak colleagues Miroslava Hlinčíková, PhD, Miriama Bošelová, Prof. Michal Kozubík, Elena Gallová Kriglerová, and Alena Chudžíková for encouraging me, for sharing their expertise and offering incredibly much in terms of practical and ideological support for this project.

The Graduate School for East and Southeast European Studies has been a truly inspiring and supportive environment for completing my PhD, thanks mainly to Prof. Ulf Brunnbauer, Prof. Martin Schulze Wessel and Dr. Heidrun Hamersky who have crafted a focused, well-structured, and welcoming atmosphere. I also want to thank Dr. Daniela Mathuber, Daniel Schrader, Dr. Andrey Vozyanov, Dr. Kathleen Beger, Drivalda Delia, Frederik Lange, Dr. Dora Vúk, Dr. Jaqueline Nießer, and the other colleagues from the Graduate School for their advice and companionship along the way.

Many people have read one or several chapters of my work and provided valuable commentary: Prof. Rainer Liedke, Prof. Andreas Renner, Prof. Marie-Janine Calic, Prof. Caitlin Murdoch, Prof. Monique Scheer, Dr. Tilman Heil, Dr. Katerina Rozakou, and Hana Antal. Their insights have helped develop ideas further and, in many cases, make them take shape in the first place. I especially thank Vita Zelenska and Anton Liavitski for being particularly attentive and belligerent readers, and much more. My dear friends Marion Krall and Lisa Kappmeyer have shared thoughts and insights from behind my anthropological bubble, for which I am very grateful. And there have been so many more encounters I have benefited from tremendously as a scholar of Slovakia, of migration and as a clueless young academic: with Prof. Čarna Brković, Prof. Heath Cabot, Dr. Marek Mikuš, Prof. Melanie Arndt, Prof. Steven Jobbitt, and Dr. Kai-Olaf Lang. I also thank Prof. Tatjana Thelen for her highly knowledgeable and differentiated input as head assessor of the thesis.

Thanks to the professional and friendly team of Anthem Press; preparing this book has been a pleasant and inspiring experience. The same is true for the two reviews that have contained a lot of constructive in-depth feedback. I want to thank the anonymous reviewers for taking the time for a close reading of the book; it is very much appreciated. And thanks to Kvet Nguyen for the beautiful cover photo.

I have had the privilege to work with two supervisors who have both been everything a PhD student could wish for: Helena Tužinská, whose guidance through the 'messy,' rules, conditions, and interdependencies of Slovak refugee care was invaluable for me. Despite the gravity of the issue, her vigor and enthusiasm for the topics she cares about have been truly contagious.

And Prof. Ger Duijzings, who is such an inspiring scholar and ethnographer and a wonderful mentor. I want to thank him for his presence, for the recommendations, the opportunities offered to me, and for always taking the time to discuss the intellectual and other challenges of doing a PhD.

Finally, I want to thank Matej, my parents, Annalena, Ben, and Toni for their endless love and support.

Fulda, 08.01.2024.

Chapter 1

INTRODUCTION

Is It Enough?

"You know, it is a strange feeling when refugees leave the Slovak reception facilities and travel on to Austria or Germany. I mean, we are trying our best here, is it not enough?" Peter, a social worker from the Slovak Migration Office, told me with a mixture of disappointment and irritation. He had just shown me a housing facility for refugees awaiting their asylum trial, about 35 kilometers northeast of Bratislava. A significant amount of asylum seekers leaves Slovakia before their trial, trying to apply for asylum somewhere else—even though they know they might get transferred back, Slovakia being the first country in the EU they registered in. Slovaks who support refugees in their country as social workers, translators, language teachers, lawyers, or volunteers often feel outright heartbroken about these premature departures. They are the dramatic conclusions of encounters with high emotional and moral stakes. The tensions that complicate these encounters are manifold: they encompass disagreements between state and non-state actors in refugee care and reach into the intimate realms of interpersonal relationships.

Slovakia is not a typical destination for refugees or migrants. They are more likely to join kinship networks or diaspora groups which have already established themselves abroad, usually in Western Europe. The Central and East European countries that are EU member states now, but used to lie behind the Iron Curtain, do not belong to the most desired target countries—due to their reputation of being less accommodating toward strangers, and due to being less affluent. Indeed, Western Europe is an attractive destination for Slovak and other Central and Eastern European emigrants, as well, and refugees' allegedly easy access to the German or Austrian labor markets increases reservations against them (Hann 2015). At the same time, the continually small numbers of people arriving in Slovakia from abroad serve as an excuse for political stakeholders not to develop a more comprehensive integration program or a more welcoming attitude.[1] Hence, refugees avoiding Slovakia and politicians delaying overdue reforms are forming a vicious circle. In public discourse, refugees are arguably the least desired migrants, and their 'premature departures' (to wealthier EU member

---

1. Theoretically, other EU countries could send asylum seekers back to Slovakia if they first applied for asylum there, and back to their countries of origin if they had failed to do so: the fact that so many will accept this risk and leave Slovakia shortly after registering there is telling.

states) are believed to demonstrate the illegitimacy of their asylum pleas, not the inefficacy of the Slovak asylum system.

There is a relatively small group of individuals who defy the negative attitude toward refugees that dominates public opinion and political rhetoric. Not only do they call on Slovakia to fulfill its obligation as an EU member state and accept more refugees—they actively support those individuals who are—due to Dublin Regulation and predominantly opposed to their original plans—stranded on Slovak territory. They are the protagonists of this book. Since this group encompasses professional NGO workers as well as volunteers, I employ for them the open and general term 'refugee supporters.' The attribute 'supportive' applies to this group in both its meanings, as in having a political opinion that endorses or approves of the presence of refugees in the country, and as in offering them concrete help or care.

For refugees, refugee supporters can be a friendly face and helping hand amid rejection and hostility, and tender relationships of mutual respect and appreciation may and do emerge. On the other hand, being the primary points of contact with their new Slovak surroundings, refugee supporters come to stand for all adversities and difficulties this life presents: they help refugees to settle into a life they probably never wanted, they are the most immediate representatives of an unwelcoming bureaucracy, they relate to refugees in ways that appear, depending on individual needs, patronizing and overbearing or detached and neglectful.

Refugee supporters thus experience gratitude but are also confronted with frustration, fatigue, and hostility. Given the time and effort they invest not only in helping refugees but also in trying to resist or negotiate restrictive policies to their best abilities, refugee supporters often feel torn, upset, burned out, even betrayed when applicants leave Slovakia before or after their asylum trial.

Conflicts multiply as part of the confrontation with the third category of actors in the triad, those that relate to refugees and migration not primarily in a supportive but a regulating sense (although, as we shall see, the boundaries between categories are sometimes fluid). These are administrative units like states or the EU as well as border guards, the police, courts, and migration authorities—actors who impose the interests of receiving communities which are often in conflict with those of people on the move. In this study, they are mainly represented by the *Migračný úrad* (Migration Office), a department of the Slovak Ministry of the Interior that supervises refugees' arrival and integration from the state's side. As a state authority, the Migration Office has a very different approach to refugees and vastly different goals and intentions. However, the way that refugee care is organized in Slovakia necessitates close and daily cooperation between state and non-state actors. The Migration Office nominates and partly finances NGOs that assume responsibilities of control and supervision on behalf of the state. Without knowing the specifics of the Slovak case, one would certainly assume that the clash of state and non-state actors matches a juxtaposition of liberal and non-liberal philosophies. We will see that this distinction can only partly account for individual attitudes and actions, but by and large, this is the fundamental disagreement in which many conflicts originate: refugee supporters often embrace ideas that are labeled as 'liberal' in the Slovak context, such as an appreciation for diversity and an obligation to protect minority and marginalized groups, while politicians and state actors often act on decidedly more conservative, protectionist, and nationalist motives.

The corner points in this triangle between refugees, supporters, and the state are in perpetual tension. Refugee care in Slovakia is thus an ideal stage for "social drama" (Turner 1974), those kinds of intense eruptions of conflict that punctuate the orderliness of everyday sociality. Amid the battle lines, I, as a German researcher, also took on an ambiguous role: I was expected to look down upon refugee supporters' struggles, coming from a country that had allegedly figured out refugee integration. This assumed condescension was perceived as arrogant or cynical. After all, Germany is considerably wealthier than Slovakia and has had a several decades-long head start to being an immigration society. Refugees, for their part, asked me countless times how to get to Germany and find a job, making me a part of their 'betrayal.'

The "Is it not enough?" Peter uttered to me was not a purely rhetorical question: he looked into the rearview mirror, driving away from the refugee camp we had just visited, as if evaluating the impressions he must have had countless times before, trying to make an objective judgment. *Was* it enough? The former military barrack has more than enough room for the nine refugees accommodated there at the time, but they are forced to sleep in the same room (in steel bunk beds) to make the maintenance of the building as easy as possible; the canteen serves three meals daily, but it is almost always chicken, caterers being unable to cook other pork-free foods; a kitchen is at disposal, but residents receive only forty cents pocket money per day and can hardly afford their own groceries; there is a library, a prayer room, a stock of donated clothes, a Slovak language class, and even the opportunity to participate in field trips to one of the many Slovak mountains or castles from time to time; but there is also a frightening amount of nothingness while awaiting an asylum decision that will probably be negative. All of this represents something, doubtlessly, but is it enough?

If the decision in asylum court, against the odds, turns out positive, and asylum seekers receive asylum or subsidiary protection status, they are still stuck between 'better than nothing' and 'not enough': refugees receive financial support that allows for just a humble subsistence for six months, after that a struggle over cuts and prolongations, sanctions and special benefits begins. How much is enough? There is a constant lack of Slovak language teaching, and thus most language tutoring is done by volunteers without linguistic or pedagogical training. Is it enough? Could it be better? Refugee supporters accompany refugees to the authorities, schools, doctors, or anywhere where their linguistic assistance as well as cultural interpretation is direly needed to help newcomers make sense of the way of doing things. How often, for how long should these services be provided? How can the scarce resources be used to accommodate the needs of refugees adequately?

Studying Messiness

These questions engage refugee supporters in a truly holistic sense: they strive to provide not just good enough, but 'good' refugee care. They do so to show that they are competent workers or volunteers, to express their values and political opinions regarding refugees and asylum, to honor their relationships with individual refugees, to try and change a faulty system from within, and also to practice self-improvement, becoming more and more of the person they want to be. Consequently, refugee supporters are very invested in finding appropriate solutions. The contradictory expectations from refugees, the state and other authorities, their organizations' mission statement, and—last but not least—their own ideals make it hard for them to reach satisfactory results, and what is more: they constantly contest, shift, and upend their benchmarks for satisfactoriness. In short, refugee care challenges those who engage with it morally and emotionally.

In this book, I want to focus on the 'mess' that refugee care seems to represent in Slovakia and beyond. How do actors in refugee care maintain their capability to act despite contradictory appeals to their emotional and moral makeup? I will examine messiness as a conglomerate of ideas about morality and emotional dispositions and analyze which practices refugee supporters develop to navigate the simultaneity of these seemingly incompatible impulses.

"It's messy" is not just the judgment of an outsider like me. Refugee supporters commonly use metaphors of chaos and disorientation to describe their activities and their discontent with the situation. They would sink into their chairs after a challenging encounter or explaining a complicated procedure, and sigh something like *je to bordel* (it's a mess). A loan word from the German term for a brothel, the word *bordel* means just that but is also commonly used to refer to situations of man-made disorder. This double meaning adds a strong normative and moral judgment to the word: whoever diagnoses something as being a bordel casts disorder as an undesired, but allegedly temporary state, expressing a moral impulse to get to the bottom of it and re-establish a lasting order. I use *bordel* as an emic term which has great significance for refugee supporters' conceptualization of their own reality.

Joanna Kusiak has offered a perceptive critique of using chaos as a theoretical concept, her main criticism being that what is denoted as chaos by researchers in such accounts is often really "a conglomerate of multiple pockets of order regulated by non-transparent power relations that only appear to be arbitrary" (Kusiak 2012, 294). She also maintains that there is a "cunning" (ibid.) to chaos, making those who suffer from chaotic circumstances believe that their misery is accidental and meaningless rather than caused by consciously obscured power struggles.[2] "Pockets of order" (ibid.) are indubitably an important part of the situation I am describing here. There are logic, intentions, and goals behind the maintenance of chaos that work against refugees and refugee supporters, and a lot of space in this book will be dedicated to disentangling these constraints.

---

2. Her critique pertains to a trend, especially in urban studies, to theorize 'chaos' with the intention of coming to terms with highly complex social structures and celebrating the creativity and adaptability of individuals exposed to them. She maintains that since such conceptualizations are often developed by European scholars looking at localities in the Global South or the postsocialist world, identifying 'chaos' is often a remnant of a colonial gaze, the result of incomplete understanding or romanization of what might be the result of oppression and scarcity.

But differently from what Kusiak observes, my protagonists are not unaware of these forces. They acknowledge that refugee policy in Slovakia is—I'm paraphrasing their utterances—chaos by design, and even identify as its constituents, if not the most influential ones. I see mess not (just) as hidden structures of oppression. Rather, messiness is a condition that is inseparable from those who engage with it: they are active and indelible parts of it, and it resides in them. Therefore, in my analysis of chaotic circumstances, I integrate individual agency, respectively the clash of individual agencies within human relationships or even within the same mind. Rather than the drama on the social scene, I will hence focus on the dramatic trials and contestations on an individual level.

The mode of engagement with this kind of mess is encapsulated in the word *riešiť*—the word commonly used to refer to refugee supporters' activities. *Riešiť* means to solve, but different from the English language, in which the usage of the verb is restricted to a definite set of nouns, like 'problem' and 'riddle,' in Slovak you can combine *riešiť* with everything—*Riešim ZTP* (I am dealing with disability certificates) or *ešte musíme riešiť klienta X* (We still need to solve/discuss (the case of) client X), or even on its own: *Celý deň iba riešim, nemá to koniec* (I am hustling/working/solving problems the whole day, there's no end in sight). This broad usage of the word suggests that although actors are constantly looking for solutions, it is sometimes tricky for them to discern *what* exactly these solutions pertain to. The word *riešiť* epitomizes the clash of open-endedness and processuality, sometimes reminiscing futility, with a desire for permanent resolution. *Riešiť*, in some moments, mobilizes the human ingenuity, playfulness, and adaptability anthropologists and ethnologists have explored with such concepts as "bricolage" (Lévi-Strauss 1966), "making do" (Certeau 1984), "homo ludens" (Huizinga 2016 [1955]), or "variegation" (Ong 2004). But other moments spell resignation before external and internal expectations and obligations. To operationalize the interplay of riešiť and bordel theoretically, I envision bordel as the conflicting and contradictory moral imperatives of living a life, and riešiť as the efforts or "practices" (Reckwitz 2002) that are applied in order to act within them—either through conscious reflection and decision for one out of several options or through a more piecemeal, intuitive process of trial and error. I will elaborate on these two practices as "moral breakdown" and "moral laboratory" in the theory section of the book.

The structural and individual dimensions of the messiness are of course difficult to tell apart in the everyday practice of refugee care. In the ethnographic segment of this book, I will scrutinize the clashes, intersections, and unexpected synergies that emerge. Nonetheless, to start with a broad overview of both aspects, I will do my best to explore the structural conditions and individual foundations of messiness separately and in this order.

In the second chapter, "A Deeply Divided Country," I present the political and social roots of controversy on refugees as the context of my research. I discuss the imaginary of the 'rift' that runs through Slovak society—between progressive and conservative, tolerant and nationalist, 'liberal elites' and 'decent people.' Before this background, the topic of migration appears as polarizing and identity-defining issue, and the specific political circumstances in 2015–2016 have boosted it to unprecedented levels of public attention. If looking more closely at the beliefs and convictions of refugee supporters and opponents, the demarcations become blurrier, and similarities in lines of reasoning get easily overlooked. In the third chapter, "Moralities and Emotions," I will introduce my theoretical framework, a practice theory approach to emotion and morality. I describe both emotion and individual morality as part cognitive, part beyond the realm of conscious control: they are embodied appraisals, which means they procure evaluations that are informed by bodily reactions and internalized knowledge. In the moment of appraisal, morality and emotion merge in translating a normative judgment into practice. I also show that judgments are by definition ephemeral and not necessarily congruent with previous evaluations, causing refugee supporters' activities to discord with values and ideals they, in theory, subscribe to.

The subsequent four chapters engage extensively with my ethnographic material and are each dedicated to one prominent dilemma in refugee supporters' work. Chapter 4, "Formality and Improvisation," describes refugee care as being caught between (insufficient) laws and regulations, and (good enough) informal improvisations. The refugee supporters I accompanied wanted to provide the best possible care despite lacking institutionalized solutions. The state institutions, keeping efforts and expenses at a minimum, depend on non-state actors' disproportionate efforts to solve clients' problems individually. Through their cunning and creative solutions, refugee supporters knowingly, but unwillingly conceal the urgency of political reform. I also show how this forges close bonds among the network of refugee supporters and endows its members with feelings of purpose, community, and pride. Chapter 5, "Acceptance and Adaptation," explores how refugee supporters manage (cultural) difference over the course of their relationships with refugees. The dilemma that presents itself concerning this task is that refugee supporters approve of refugees' own cultural identities while also feeling obliged to teach them to be 'Slovak' enough to handle life in Slovakia. Refugee supporters often understand themselves as hosts and refugees as their guests, the framework of hospitality not only offering an instinctively moral way of relating to 'strangers' but also circumscribing a domain of influence and control. As refugees and refugee supporters get to know each other better and forge friendships, their readiness to intervene in their clients' lives, urging them to adapt, may even increase. Chapter 6, "Trust and Mistrust" builds on the observation that there is a comprehensive imperative to distrust refugees, even though refugee supporters strive to be their clients' confidants. I show how while working together, refugees and refugee supporters do not move from mistrust to trust in a linear fashion. Rather, they constantly investigate and question each other's trustworthiness and adopt a strategic ambiguity, leaving one's counterparts guessing whether they are being trusted or not. One reason for this balancing act lies in how trust is created: mistrust is a cognitive operation and hence often the precautionary result of incomplete knowledge. At the same time, trust is an emotional state that draws on the entirety of a person's experiences, fears, grudges, and so on, and can thus be extended or withheld despite 'better knowledge'—exemplifying how structural-political and deeply personal influences interplay in shaping refugee care. Chapter 7, "Emancipation and Paternalization," shows how refugee supporters are torn between affectionate care and tough love. They believe helping refugees to become independent quickly is the morally superior approach to integration, but they still often find themselves offering comprehensive (in their own eyes) even excessive support. The ethical conundrum offers the opportunity to reflect on the concept of integration, concluding that common critiques of integration do not fully account for the interpersonal dimension of integration encounters, and underestimate both the need to help and the need to be helped. In the "Conclusion," I review recent shifts in asylum policy beyond Slovakia and summarize the political recommendations that emerge from my study as well as its potential analytical contribution to refugee (care) studies and related fields.

Themes and Topics in Recent Research on Refugee Care

The specificities of the 'mess' I examine in this book emerge in the unique historical and geopolitical setting of Slovakia in the 2010s, but it is embedded in global dynamics. The topics of refugee and asylum have stirred political controversies and received a lot of scholarly attention, especially in the European context.[3] I want to briefly summarize the main conversations and conceptual frameworks in recent research on refugee care in anthropology and neighboring disciplines before specifying the parameters and contributions of my study. The body of anthropological literature on migration is too large for me to even begin to recapitulate it, but one focal point of the last decade has been the emergence and maintenance of forced migration management, also entailing my subject matter, refugee care.

The premise that has emerged for this kind of scholarship in the last decade is that refugee defense and refugee acceptance are inextricably entangled, they are performed simultaneously, sometimes by the same actors. Hence, efforts to control, restrict, revert, redirect, or stop the arrival of refugees need to be studied together with efforts to offer legal, administrative, financial, psychological, educational, and practical support. This is the categorical tension that shapes the interaction between state actors, refugees, and refugee support organizations. Arguably, refugee care and refugee deterrence or deportation have always been closely linked. Scholarly interest in the frictions and conflicts arising between different actors in this social drama spiked most recently in the aftermath of 2015. During the *Long Summer of Migration* (Kasparek and Speer 2015), rapidly growing numbers of refugees were making their way into EU territory, leading to several unprecedented political measures like the temporary suspension of the Dublin Regulation. Publics and politicians soon unanimously referred to the situation as a "crisis" (Hess et al. 2017; Rajaram 2016). In Chapter 2, I analyze how the situation was widely

---

3. The anthropological interest in flight and asylum may have peaked in the aftermath of the "long summer of migration" in 2015 (Kasparek and Speer 2015), but migrants and refugees have been at the center of anthropological interest for at least two decades. If I focus this brief review, for reasons of space and clarity, mainly on studies in Europe that emerged in the last twenty years, these are of course somewhat arbitrary demarcations; obviously, patterns and dynamics of mobility today take shape in a globalized world and connect remote localities and movements to an unprecedented extent. I also acknowledge that some dynamics we observe today are by no means new but either upgrades of established structures or outcomes of long-term developments.

and actively interpreted as a crisis even in Slovakia, although there were hardly any refugees in the country. Social scientists, referring to Agamben (2005) and Calhoun (2004), acknowledge the phenomenology of the crisis, respectively emergency, as a cosmopolitan imaginary that evokes particular sets of political action. Declaring a "state of exception" endows power holders with greater leverage for taking comprehensive measures. At the same time, extending a helping hand to victims of an acute crisis automatically takes on traits of a generous gesture, even if no more is done than conforming to binding national legislation or international agreements, like the Geneva Convention. Misery and suffering get detached from their geopolitical sources, and structural inequality is recast as individual misfortune (Lisle and Johnson 2018; Garelli and Taziolli 2013). "The so-called European refugee crisis is a moral issue before it is a demographic one," Didier Fassin argued in his essay "From rights to favor" (2016). Looking at ethical arguments in the refugee debate, one can identify a perpetual tension between the moral imperative to relieve suffering and support 'helpless victims,' and the consensus of countries in the Global North to classify migration, if it can be labeled as 'irregular,' as a moral transgression, as a wrong to be fixed.

Scholars in the critical border studies and related autonomy of migration schools of thought have examined how the irresolvable tensions between actors with different interests shape the diffusion of power in forced migration management. The term "autonomy of migration" has been coined to denote how migration worlds are made from below and are influenced but never determined by political decisions and events that will come to be thought of as "big history" (Transit Migration Forschungsgruppe 2007; De Genova, Garelli and Taziolli 2018; De Genova 2017). Scholars of the influential Transit Migration Research group have defined "migration regimes" as an ensemble of social structures and actions, containing discourses, subjects, and state rhetoric and practices as important components. These are not arranged into a fixed constellation but react flexibly to the questions posed by dynamic elements and processes (Karakayali and Tsianos 2007, 14; see also Tazzioli 2019; Pott et al. 2018; Mavelli 2017). Although I do not test or develop the regime vocabulary further, I think it provides an apt characterization of the confrontations and efforts surrounding migration management globally. The dynamics of migration regulation in Slovakia fit into the same scheme: there is a pronounced coercive effort from authorities to impede access in the shape of residence and entitlements in the form of benefits or participation (see Chapter 6). But because various actors have different agencies, the range reaching from slightly divergent to diametrically opposed, access is never negotiated in absolute terms but in minute gradings of constraint or freedom. The imprint on individual freedom ranges from the biopolitics regulating all aspects of everyday life in refugee camps to different residential statuses that encode different degrees of belonging and access to host societies. Casas-Cortes et al. call this "differential inclusion": "These systems tend to multiply and increasingly stratify the legal statuses of subjects inhabiting the same political space" (Casas-Cortes et al. 2014, 68–69; see also Mezzadra and Neilson 2012).

Processes of opening and closure are most tangible at the borders, and thus special attention has been paid to the border as the focal point of migration regimes (Pott et al. 2018; Transit Migration Forschungsgruppe 2007; Mezzadra and Neilson 2013;

Dijstelbloem and Veer 2019; De Genova 2017). Borders, in a regime imaginary, are conceptualized not only as geographical demarcations but as social spaces that are shaped by various actors competing for rights and political participation. They are constantly reconfigured or reinstated through performative enactment (Hess et al. 2014, 18). In a global mediascape, the material and symbolic meanings of borders have merged to form a persuasive and widespread imaginary of bordering as indissolubly linked to the need for regulation—which is also how it appears in the Slovak discourse. The images from the Mediterranean or the Balkan route are ubiquitous in Slovakia, and mobilized, in the public consciousness, as an allegory of migration per se (Chudžíková 2016; Borárosová and Filipec 2017). Although the geographical borders of the Slovak Republic are rarely a focus of attention, a figurative border that is imagined as demarcating a precious possession (Slovak culture, identity, community) and as needy of protection from outsiders is at the core of the Slovak refugee discourse.

Most of the aforementioned authors maintain that those who are invested in co-constructing migration regimes view refugees themselves largely with ethical indifference. Thom Davies, Arshad Isakjee, and Surindar Desi have summarized the state authorities' efforts to minimize responsibility for the protection of refugees, especially on their own territory, as "violent inaction" (2017, 1263)—manifesting itself in a deliberate abandonment of refugees in border camps or transit countries. A broad segment of literature focusing on migrant subjectivities confirms that although refugee biographies and experiences are naturally very diverse, the indifferent or actively hostile attitudes of receiving countries almost invariably play a part in them.

These accounts document the adversities migrants are faced with, from the symbolic or physical violence committed by smugglers and border guards or encountered in refugee camps, detention centers, and deportation flights (Holmes 2013; Andersson 2014; De Genova 2002; Vries and Guild 2019) to the claustrophobic subjectivities produced by impenetrable bureaucracy and its manifestation in waiting, insecurity, precarity, and illegality (Graham 2002; Dunn 2018; Haas 2017). At the same time, studies that adopt migrants' standpoints portray instances of autonomy, resilience and community, for example, Syrian refugees in Belgium building informal networks of mutual support and creating sociable occasions in which a sense of memory and belonging is fostered while sharing familiar food and drinks (Vandevoordt 2017). They thus argue that people are never truly reduced to a *homo sacer*-like existence and that spaces for individual agency and recalcitrance exist even in the most difficult circumstances (Brković 2017).[4]

This segment of the literature shows that the range of experiences is broad, and this holds for refugees in Slovakia, too. However, the structural forces outlined above

---

4. Within this literature, there is a move toward giving refugees a platform not only to tell their own stories but also, wherever possible, for them to maintain the sovereignty of interpretation over their own experiences. Many anthropologists have chosen the medium of ethnographic film to deliver such accounts, such as in *The Land Between* (Fedele 2014), *Other Europe/Altra Europa* (Schillaci 2011), *Hotel Splendid* (Bucci 2016), and *A Song for Mursal* (Nicolaysen 2016). Others choose the path of autoethnographies, like *"Illegal" Traveller* by Shahram Khosravi (2010).

concern everyone, even if to varying degrees. What unites the individual accounts of refugees in Slovakia is, according to the conversations I had, that they experience the arrival as no less onerous than the departure. The ordeal of the asylum trial, jungles of red tape, racism and discrimination, loneliness, and lack of perspective often concur with the resurfacing of suppressed trauma. Some refugees overcame these initial hardships and settled into a safe and relatively happy existence, while others perceived their life in Slovakia as an ongoing uphill battle or submitted to apathy.

The question of how organizations whose purpose is to help refugees feature in these structures has received a lot of scholarly attention. In the tripartite constellation with refugees and regulating authorities, they are the ones most likely and able to fight for refugees' interests and reduce "the costs necessary to overcome boundaries" (both literally and figuratively) (Faist 2014, 42). This is due to their supposed altruistic or humanitarian motivations (de Jong 2011).

Contemporary scholarship, inspired by William Fisher's scrutiny in how far humanitarians' work does or does not amount to "doing good" (Fisher 1997) puts question marks behind the characterization of humanitarians as influential idealists. In refugee studies, a fundamental distinction is made between humanitarian and activist actors. Solidarity activists stand up for concrete political demands and work actively to change structures for refugees' benefit. They strive for a relationship on eye level and thus often refrain from offering concrete help (Rozakou 2016).

Humanitarianism, by contrast, is often defined as apolitical with the primary goal of providing essential goods and services. However, as many critical scholarly investigations have pointed out, humanitarian refugee help organizations that operate on a national or international scale and have established structures of management and accountability are arguably equally involved in "governing" migrant populations and building "regimes" that are, if not supportive of, then at least compatible with state policies (Fassin 2011; Geiger and Pécoud 2013). Indeed, NGOs oftentimes allow states to abdicate their responsibility for migrant populations. This perpetuates dependence on makeshift, projectized, and precarious NGO work (Cabot 2014, 86). Another major point of criticism is that NGO moralities often build upon an assessment of neediness and entitlement, in which access to help is determined by the degree of "vulnerability," thus favoring certain groups like children and women and reinforcing a paternalistic approach to humanitarian care (Ticktin 2017; Chouliaraki 2010).

Small-scale, local and community-based initiatives of refugee support challenge the analytical distinction between humanitarianism and activism (Rosenberger and Winkler 2014; Cuttitta 2017). Numerous new civic initiatives and semi-organized associations rushed to help struggling authorities in 2015, for instance in Germany, where the phenomenon soon received the name *Willkommenskultur* (Hamann and Karakayali 2016; Karakayali and Kleist 2015; Sutter 2017; Holmes and Castaneda 2016). This trend urged scholars to introduce a hybrid type commonly referred to as "subversive humanitarianism" (Pries 2018, 11). Ludger Pries points out that "organizations related to refugee protection" (Pries 2018, 3) across Europe since 2015 developed a new international and critical consciousness based on an unprecedented public awareness for refugee matters as a global problem and a new reliance on civic actors like them to make up for state authorities' "organized irresponsibility" (Beck 1995 [1988], 32; see also Perl and Strasser 2018). Volunteers in Western European countries, working with refugees and witnessing the precarious environments of refugee reception at close range, sometimes turn from do-gooders who "only want to help" into adamant spokespersons for more humane refugee policies (Sutter 2017; Sandri 2018). Volunteers in Hungary, on the other hand, were often already anchored in oppositional movements (specially to Prime Minister Victor Orbán's administration) and framed their support for refugees as applied critique of Fidesz' politics of abandoning and scapegoating socially marginalized groups in general (Feischmidt and Zachariás 2019).

The present book fits into the scholarly conversation on forced migration management and refugee support and contributes to the exploration of the (power) dynamics between state actors, NGOs, and refugees. The characteristics of my field site introduce perspectives to this field of study that either expand or destabilize some of its broad lines of reasoning.

Firstly, the organizations I examine go against the grain of the distinction between state-critical activists and state-complicit humanitarians. There is no refugee solidarity movement in Slovakia as there is, for instance, in Greece, not even a politically constituted humanitarianism as in Hungary. Two of the organizations I am describing here (Pomoc a Nádej and Refúgium) enter a purpose alliance with the Slovak state authorities in which they also 'govern' migrants in the ways outlined above while providing nonprofit care. Those who support refugees as NGO employees or as volunteers in Slovakia certainly understand themselves as providers of welfare rather than as activists with a political agenda. But the organizations occasionally operate politically on a local level, and two of them (Obývačka and Pomoc a Nádej) are compassionate grassroots responses to the 2015 momentum. All of them are decidedly critical of official policies and speak out publicly for refugees' interests. Cooperation and criticism, charity and advocacy, all are realized by the same actors in the same organizations at similar times. By focusing not on how organizations, but how individuals are chafed between incompatible missions and allegiances, I provide not a characterization of a certain type of humanitarianism but show the inherent pitfalls of humanitarian subjectivity in a particular setting.

Secondly, my perspective offers a rare look at the *longue durée* of supporting refugees. As mentioned above, the border is the site where migration is most visible and regimes are most elaborate, which is why we know a lot about migratory projects from departure until engagement with the (material and administrative) barrier. The literature acknowledges that migration is often not a one-time act that concludes with the crossing of a border, but that migrants dwell in administrative limbo, in detention, camps, or residential statuses that denote a 'neither in nor out' position.

However, a long-term, processual perspective is under-represented in the literature on refugees. Being a refugee does not end with the attainment of an official status. Bureaucratic procedures single out non-national residents when it comes to health care, job markets, accommodation, and many other situations. It takes time to come to grips with new realities and acquire some of the basic skills necessary to navigate life in a strange country. Individuals may be confronted with discrimination based on a non-European appearance and foreign accent their entire lives. Focusing on organizations that accompany refugees throughout all these difficulties allows me to study the long-term trajectories and the slow unfolding of subjectivities in encounters between refugees and citizens. The clients my interlocutors worked with had all received a positive decision on their requests for asylum, some of them as long as 16 years ago, but their identities and everyday lives continued to be deeply affected by them being refugees. They still demanded and received help from humanitarian actors. Also, "differential access" remained a problem for them—individuals with subsidiary protection are disadvantaged compared to acknowledged refugees in many respects, and it is almost impossible to switch status.

Thirdly, in many of the studies of the past decade, especially those focusing on the dissemination of the powers and influences that shape refugees' fates, refugee helpers are usually regarded as less deserving of an individualizing, inquiring approach than refugees. This is despite studies that focus on the incentives, experiences, and struggles of do-gooders have helped expand the understanding of humanitarianism and arrive at a broader picture of encounters between the 'needy' and the 'needed.' A good example is Liisa Malkki's study on Red Cross humanitarians' "need to help," pledging to take seriously "the frequent weakness, neediness, and non-universality of the 'benefactor'— the giver who, no less than the receiver, always sets out from a social and existential position both specific and precarious" (Malkki 2015, 8). By focusing on NGO workers, their biographies, their motivations, and their everyday practice of working with refugees, I analyze how individual morality and emotional dispositions intersect with policies in shaping the shared reality of individuals with Slovak citizenship and those with asylum status in Slovakia. This focus contributes to the depolarization of the humanitarian sphere between either selfless (liberal) justice warriors or morally indifferent (non-liberal) government cronies.

Finally, studying refugee care *in Slovakia* not only fills in a blind spot in refugee studies, but the particularities of the setting also offer a new and diverging perspective on some of the key problems in this field. My field site is slightly removed from the epicenters of refugee scholarship. Although the existing literature has covered a wealth of geographies, perspectives, and analytic approaches, most studies engage either with Southern European countries at the margin of the Schengen zone, where the highly visible 'hot spots' and refugee camps are located (Italy and Greece), or with the Western/Northern European countries that accept most asylum seekers (Germany, Sweden, France, and the Netherlands).

The so-called Visegrád states did play a prominent role in the public narrative of the 'refugee crisis': the Czech Republic, Slovakia, Poland, and Hungary allied to reject a redistribution of refugees across EU member states regulated by predefined quotas, and soon advanced to be the most outspoken critics of the EU's handling of the so-called crisis. But they have barely been a focus of refugee scholarship. Migrant experiences, as well as migration regimes and policies and practices of refugee care in these countries, have not attracted much scholarly attention. Karolina Follis, in her ethnography *Building Fortress Europe*, has explored the 'rebordering' of the border between Poland and Ukraine after Poland's accession to the EU and the tacit toleration of illicit migration of Ukrainians into Poland which is, nevertheless, subject to a complex, part formal, part informal border regime. There is also a segment of literature on the topic for the Visegrád Four, often projects carried out by local researchers in the respective country's language with the explicit mission to advise and consult public authorities from municipalities to national governments (see Chapters 4 and 7).[5] Even after a close reading of these works, there remains a lack of qualitative approaches and thick descriptions of the complex and intricate relationships between refugees, state, and non-state actors as is available for the southern and north-western countries.

This is an omission because Slovakia differs from the most common settings for studies of refugee help in significant ways. The analyses of power structures in refugee studies often revolve around a disbalance of wealth and influence between the Northern and Southern hemispheres; they discuss the inequalities forged by capitalist modes of distribution (exploitation of resources and cheap labor force in the Global South, arms exports, subsidized trade of EU goods, climate change) as constitutive of migration and migration regimes—all at the benefit of rich Western industry nations. Recently, there has been an increased effort to "examine possible connections between the rationalities, technologies and programs of migration governance and the histories of colonialism" (Walters 2015, 11, see also Qadim 2014; Fiddian-Qasmiyeh 2016). This endeavor aims at breaking up the Eurocentric framing of the debate, which may convey the impression that migrants are only prey to the heavyweight interests of governments in the Global North. A postcolonial critique may provide an antidote for the way migrant voices are either silenced or fetishized as the sole source of authenticity (Mayblin and Turner 2020).

Slovakia, although located in the center of Europe, does not fully fit the profile of the (post)colonizers implied in such critiques. It has technically never been involved in any colonial project; it did not emerge as an independent state before 1992, except for a short intermezzo as a fascist (Nazi puppet-)state between 1939 and 1945. Having been at the receiving end of colonizing processes under Ottoman and Habsburg rule and, in a milder form, even in the decades of the Czech-Slovak 'Union,' Slovaks usually identify with the side of the colonized rather than the colonizers and reject any historical guilt regarding the colonial era. Contemporary Slovaks often live under the impression of being part of a 'second-class' Europe. After the late industrialization of the Slovak part of Czechoslovakia and, of course, over four decades of socialist rule, living standards were in arrears compared to the west of the continent.

In the phase of economic transition, the formerly socialist countries were a European laboratory for neoliberalization, deregulation, and austerity policy, which exacerbated some discrepancies rather than removing them (Ther 2014). Surveys show that Slovaks tend to be dissatisfied with public services such as the health and education systems,

---

5. For overviews on the respective countries in English, see: Hungary: Rajaram 2016; Speer 2016; Czech Republic: Jelínková 2019; Burnett 2015; Hanzelka and Schmidt 2017; Poland: Krzyżanowski 2018; Górák-Sosnowska 2016; Slovakia: Tužinská 2019; Borárosová and Filipec 2017.

state welfare and salaries (Vigoda-Gadot, Shoham and Vashdi 2010; Pažitný et al. 2014; Bosáková et al. 2020; Krajčová 2015). In 2015, the governments of the Visegrád states argued that it was only logical and morally appropriate that Western European states, being both more affluent and more blameworthy for the causes of flight, take a larger share of responsibility for refugees.

Dissenting voices argued that Slovakia is now a comparatively wealthy and free country in the Global North with obligations toward its fellow EU states. These voices urge Slovakia to abandon its 'victim role' and acknowledge that the country appears as a peaceful safe haven if compared to refugees' countries of origin.

Both standpoints structure encounters between refugees and Slovak refugee supporters daily. It is by taking these conversations into account that the present study can be read as an interjection from the gallery into the important debate on postcolonial approaches to global migration. Putting these geopolitical specifics aside, one could also argue that the differences between European countries' response to refugees have been fading: since 2015, hostility toward refugees has resurged everywhere, leading to a more defensive redesign of national asylum policies and accelerating the rise of right-wing, extreme right, and neo-fascist parties. Arguments that still seemed extreme and specific for the Central European countries in 2015 have thus spread far beyond the Visegrád Four (see Conclusion).

Between Investment and Observation

When working with groups that are structurally disadvantaged or exposed to hostility and violence, like refugees, the question of research ethics poses itself with acute urgency. Many scholars working on refugee-related topics have opted for various forms of applied anthropology, advocacy, or activist/militant research. Throughout my PhD, in conferences, workshops and summer schools, situations abounded in which the researcher's identification with the refugees' cause was either taken for granted or explicitly promoted as a duty and debt of the "ethnographer/witness" (Scheper-Hughes 1995, 419). I admire the astuteness and dedication with which some anthropologists have raised awareness for injustice and oppression and have fought for positive change, yet I do not choose an activist standpoint for my dissertation. I concur with the proponents of militant research insofar as assuming a subjugated position yields epistemological benefits and can help disrupt hegemonic systems of knowledge. But there are two seminal limitations to this approach which led me to refrain from it and which, I find, are not always satisfactorily addressed in the pertinent literature.

Glenda Garelli and Martina Tazziolli developed a much-cited proposal for militant research in migration studies where "knowledges and day-to-day actions are deliberately brought to bear on one another, and where their interactions and frictions are constantly interrogated" (2013, 245), thus countering the "depoliticization of migration" (ibid., 246) but also the "paradigm of an all-encompassing governance" (ibid., 248). They see this approach in the tradition of a researcher-companionship which crafts political epistemologies "stripped of the comfort of 'critical distance'" (ibid., 246).

Essentially, they are making a plea to apply standpoint theory to refugee studies, urging researchers to 'see' from the standpoint of refugees. Admitting that all knowledge is located, embedded and partial is a tried and tested epistemological strategy. Feminist scholars have preferred subjugated perspectives to dismantle the wealth of assumptions and power structures hiding behind common notions of objectivity and to offer "more adequate, sustained, objective, transforming accounts of the world" (ibid., 579). While seeing this partial knowledge as a benefit, the work of feminists like Donna Haraway exemplifies that it is crucial to take great care to avoid the pitfalls, like exempting subjugated perspectives from critical scrutiny and romanticizing or appropriating the position. What is most complicated is that one must accumulate the skill, language, practices, and so on, to assume the position in an adequate manner (Haraway 1988, 585).

Realistically speaking, I lack the skill and language proficiency, as well as the time and resources, to see from a subjugated position—which equals, according to militant researchers, the refugee perspective—in my field in a manner that is adequate for scientific inquiry. Without any doubt, it would be worthwhile and insightful to attempt such a study in the Slovak setting—for a person equipped with the vantage point and skillset I lack. That would be, for instance, someone with the experience of coming to Slovakia as a foreigner from outside the EU to live there permanently. While I cannot see from a subjugated position, I am still very much able to acknowledge how this position is precarious and understand how an external ethnographic gaze may produce a lopsided image or even cause harm to those under study. This awareness has guided me in appropriating my research and writing to accept my ethical responsibility to my more vulnerable participants. Much more than the refugee supporters, refugees may have an interest in not making their stories heard or public—be it due to trauma or to real dangers that could emerge for them in their current or former surroundings. Hence, I never asked about refugees' backstories, and of those that were shared with me voluntarily, I repeat only those aspects that are necessary to understand the ethnographic context of my arguments. I have also changed the names and some biographical details of all refugees that appear in this text to protect their anonymity.

Of course, a different dimension of imbalance remains, which arguably resembles a constellation of subjugated and superordinate: the fact that I am doing fieldwork in a formerly socialist country while not being from there. I agree with Chris Hann, Katherine Verdery, Caroline Humphrey and others that the approaches of anthropologists born and trained in Western Europe or America coming to Central and Eastern Europe have been problematic, especially since they have tended to construct first a socialist, then a postsocialist 'other' (Hann, Humphrey and Verdery 2001, 9). I hope, with Chris Hann, that "the foreigner may on occasion come up with insights that escape and surprise the native" (Hann 2012, 47)—or that she can afford to insist on critical points which local scholars can only make at significant risk because it could cause repercussions, damage their reputation, or restrict their access to their field sites. Following Hann's advice, I can only attenuate the remaining disbalance by being reflective of my own biases and the limits to my immersion which *not being a local* imposes, and by engaging intellectually as well as personally with scholars who are rooted in Slovakia.

In this book, I choose a standpoint I feel competent to account for: that of Slovak refugee supporters and their interpersonal relationships with refugees. I embrace this perspective to the best of my abilities and ask the questions that I deem relevant in this constellation. Their names have also been changed to ensure a degree of anonymity long-term, even though the entire fieldwork took place and is now being published with all participants' consent.

The knowledge I can access is of course also situated, but it allows a glimpse of realities which would be impossible to see from a subjugated position. In parts of the militant research in refugee studies, the differentiation of agencies, motivations, and subject positions of the party endorsed is much more developed than that of the 'opponents.' The widely used regime terminology is designed to allow critical accounts of the structures in place—structures that are seminally shaped by state policies and humanitarian activity (Transit Migration Forschungsgruppe 2007; Mezzadra and Neilson 2013). Thus, both categories of actors appear primarily in their function of disciplining migrant agencies. Assuming that there is a "system of knowledge" to be disrupted, like that of "all-encompassing governance," is a normative evaluation that should ideally be based on deep familiarity and empirical evidence. From my standpoint, I saw not so much a rigid "system of knowledge," but practices of refugee care that are *inherently* contingent, messy, and punctured. Acknowledging the "primacy of the ethical" (Scheper-Hughes 1995, 419), in the specificities of my research site, means *not* taking sides, avoiding premature interpretations and refraining from identification with political or scientific commonplaces. I endorse neither refugees nor helpers a priori and am very careful in identifying abuse or potential for improvement. I already concede that despite great caution, I am not always successful in this endeavor. My positionality or sympathy might transpire by the choice of wording or the selection of material presented. The way I approach the representation of my collocutors in a field that is politically charged and fraught with strong opinions is by providing a fine-grained ethnographic context that may perhaps seem excessive to some readers. It serves to portray situations with the same gradients, ruptures, and blanks as they presented themselves to me.

Although I try my best to balance my accounts and provide a differentiated picture, I declare here for full disclosure that my sympathy goes to all sides. Representatives of state authorities like Peter, whom I mentioned in the beginning, were sincerely concerned about refugees' well-being, and voiced suggestions for structural change. It must be mentioned that those employees of state authorities who agreed to talk to me were implementing state policies rather than designing those. Much like the "street level bureaucrats" in Michael Lipsky's study (1980), they are often faced with an immense caseload and inadequate resources, and the responsibility to make decisions of considerable importance for individuals who they often came to genuinely care about. The Migration Office officials viewed the policy they were asked to implement ambiguously, sometimes criticizing it and taking the side of NGO workers, matching or surpassing their caring efforts for refugee clients. On this individual level, the non-state liberal versus state non-liberal juxtaposition already begins to crumble.

It has also been a privilege to get to know refugees from many different countries. The circumstances for starting a new life as a refugee are extraordinarily difficult everywhere, and in Slovakia especially so, for reasons I will elaborate. I was struck time and again by the bravery, patience, and grace of the men, women, and children I met. At the same time, I got a close look at how challenging and straining work in refugee care is. The refugee supporters I met were genuinely invested in their work; they often sacrificed evenings and weekends, spending less time with family and friends, and often going beyond the borders of exhaustion to do their job in a manner that is satisfactory to them. I am deeply humbled by their poise, endurance, and ingenuity.

Field and Method

Throughout my ethnographic fieldwork, I led and recorded almost forty interviews with persons dealing with refugees in their professional or private lives: four priests, one Imam, three teachers, three migration officers, one journalist, one photographer, five researchers, five volunteers, two interpreters, 11 employees working in antiracism or migrant advocacy outside my three field sites, and four persons formerly involved in refugee care. Some of these actors were refugees themselves, and I engaged in countless informal conversations with refugees inside and outside of organizational settings. I also visited several dozen public and semi-public events on topics related to migration, integration, minorities, and anti-extremism.

The core and catalyst of my analysis, however, comprise ten months of participant observation, roughly divided between three organizations: Refúgium, an NGO based in Košice, executing the official state-sponsored integration program, Obývačka (Living room), a civic initiative working with volunteers and offering mainly leisure and socializing activities in three Slovak cities, and Pomoc a Nádej (Help and Hope), an organization dealing with the largest refugee 'cohort' entering Slovakia together, a group of Iraqi Christian refugees, in a one-off project which started in 2015.[6] The organizations differ regarding their staff, funding, target groups, relationship with state organizations, relationship with the churches, and their understanding of what refugee care should ideally look like. I will point to these differences whenever it is relevant or interesting. However, the purpose of this study is not a systematic comparison of organizations. Rather, I chose these three field sites to offer a broad overview of refugee care in Slovakia as a whole. With only about 600 people in their care at the time of my fieldwork, the scene of refugee help is a compact microcosm. The three organizations, spread across the country, with different funding schemes and political sympathies, account for most of the work that is being done in Slovak refugee care. They are the primary and, most times, also the only actors working in their area of expertise, providing welfare and mentorship for refugees after their asylum trial, while they start a life in Slovakia.[7] They

---

6. The names of the organizations have been changed.
7. There are more NGOs that work primarily with refugees, albeit delivering different types of services: *Slovenská Humanitná Rada* (Slovak Humanitarian Council) runs the reception facilities in which refugees undergo quarantine and asylum interviews, and *Liga za ľudské práva* (Human Rights League) offers refugees free-of-charge legal representation. These two organizations are mainly active in a different temporal trajectory than what I am looking at—first aid and

know each other very well and even work together. The few Slovaks who engage for refugees form a scene or community based on this shared concern, exchanging favors and creating resources for everyone to use. In Chapter 2, "A Deeply Divided Country," I describe this 'bubble' in more detail. My ethnography explores this milieu rather than distinct organizations.

While the organizations represent refugee care in Slovakia in an exemplary manner, one cannot say that they constitute it, since the field is very impermanent. The NGO scene in this field is volatile, and organizations cease to exist or have to switch their field of activity due to the availability of funding. Quite a few persons have worked with refugees for many years and have changed employers several times to be able to continue working in this field—but the fluctuation of staff is also very high. Like any ethnographic project, my study is thus a snapshot of a fragile network of organizations and actors at a particular point in time. I have changed their names to support anonymity and also to stress that rather than particular organizations, the object of the study is dynamics and processes that could easily take place elsewhere. Yet, the shortcomings of the system—the parameters for the 'mess'—are remarkably long-lived, and structures that were meant to be provisional become cemented into the fabric of refugee care in Slovakia (see Chapter 4).

For the participant observation part of my fieldwork, I spent my days at the workplace of my collocutors over the entire span of their working hours. I witnessed meetings with clients as well as calls and office talk. When social workers accompanied clients in running errands or tending to bureaucratic tasks, I often joined them. I also participated in team meetings and free-time activities organized for the target group, and I occasionally joined off-work socializing too. Fieldwork in organizations usually means doing ethnography in office environments, which makes it necessary to attune the method to the space it is set in and the uncommitting character of social relationships within it. As Ulf Hannerz (2003) proclaimed for the increasingly common ethnography of modern workspaces, the ethnographer must adopt a style of socializing that resembles the one practiced in the field to gain a certain degree of trust and viable information even in less intimate relationships. Peter Loizos classified research relationships into "distant observer," "just good friends" and "negotiated trust" (94, 40–41), the latter signifying situations in which both sides approach each other cautiously but on eye level. The ethnographer, in this setting, must acknowledge that trust is not a given, but needs to

---

orientation rather than long-term integrating activities. Refúgium has a partner organization, ASPR (name changed), in Bratislava that engages in the same activities as those in the western part of the country; the two organizations are involved in the same project and communicate frequently, which is why I achieved a sound grasp of their work although not doing participant observation in their premises. There are also organizations that are of relevance for refugees, although they have a broader target group and a bigger profile of activities—the Slovak IOM (International Organization for Migration), the state institution *Migračný úrad* (Migration Office), and an organization that has previously been active in refugee integration, the Catholic Charitas. I conducted interviews with several members of all these other refugee-related organizations and attended one of their platform meetings as well as the public events and conferences they organized.

be earned and has its limitations. As Loizos suggests, my relationships were structured by complex "transactional norms" (Loizos 1994, 41)—dynamics which I aim to make transparent throughout the text as far as possible.

I find an approach that is interested, open and sympathetic, but honest about the standards of scientific impartiality I hold myself to, to be the fairest. If this is not communicated clearly, friendliness can easily be mistaken for endorsement or solidarity. Gaining access to the organizations was relatively easy, and I often had the impression that I rather had to caution interlocutors of the exposure their conversations with me could bring rather than relieving their skepticism and reservations (possibly my gender and age endowed me with a certain aura of harmlessness).

But still, if my fieldwork consisted largely of a tightrope walk between cooperation and openness on one hand and a critical distance on the other, it is only logical to assume my collocutors to strategize in the same way. It is essential to consider the incentives actors may have to trust the ethnographer and grant her access she might not otherwise have. My position was made much easier by the fact that all my collocutors, most of them having received higher education, acknowledged the existence of free and independent scholarship as an end in itself. Most of them stated that feedback from an unpartisan third could be a potential benefit for them, without suggesting it as the basis of a quid pro quo exchange. Having made sure that self-serving interests do not distort the results of the research disproportionately (a slight contortion is inevitable), I do believe that good research ethics in anthropology should go beyond 'doing no harm.' If possible, one should explore appropriate ways to show gratitude and respect for the time and effort spent on interacting with the researcher. After a period of evaluation, I thus conducted focus group discussions in all organizations to allow them to comment on preliminary findings and share observations and remarks I thought might be of use. The participants genuinely welcomed this intervention, the consideration and appreciation of their work expressed in it, and my voice as a 'corrective' from outside which confirmed many of their evaluations while challenging others.

I will now introduce each organization with a short ethnographic vignette. There are several reasons for this: I believe that episodes, anecdotes, and vignettes can introduce a place more efficiently and vividly than an enumeration of descriptive facts. For the remainder of the book, I hope that it supports readability and evokes what the respective localities look, smell, and sound like. Further, I think it will highlight the differences between the organizations; each has its distinctive personnel, explicit and implicit rules, affective grammar, and moral economy. As mentioned above, in the rest of the book more space will be dedicated to the commonalities, to patterns that recur, or topics that connect all localities. It is certainly helpful to retain the background information about the unique backgrounds of these organizations to better evaluate the coming material.

The Three Fieldsites

Obývačka

The community center is glowing with lights and a busy hustle; candles and lighting chains are lining walls and shelves; the promising scent of frying oil penetrates every corner of the half-parterre flat in the Bratislava center. Today is the Christmas celebration of Obývačka, a civic association that helps refugees make Slovakia their home and offers possibilities to mingle with locals. An eventful year comes to a close: the young organization officially registered as a civic association and opened its crowd-funded community center. Obývačka emerged from a civil initiative that was launched in 2015, when a few activists set out to convince the government to accept one hundred refugee families. They aimed to find one thousand volunteers who could stem the expected workload. After a few weeks, they had already found two thousand Slovaks who were willing to help.

The government remained unimpressed and did not comply with their demands, but the initiators kept looking for ways to put the potential they discovered to use. They asked organizations that were already working with refugees whether they needed help with anything. The result: language training and free-time activities were lacking the most. So, they reinvented themselves and launched a program with three pillars: they are training volunteers to help refugees and other foreigners stand on their own feet in Slovakia; they organize courses that provide useful skills, like language, sewing, IT, and job application training; and they organize community activities aimed at making newcomers and locals mingle and have a good time together. Next to offering help, they are also very serious about meeting their protégés on an equal footing: they strictly wanted to avoid being another player in the migration regime disciplining refugees by offering patronizing help or telling them what was good for them. Refugees offer their own courses or activities and present their country in cultural and culinary ways.

Food takes a central place in Obývačka's philosophy. It has the potential to bring people together and learn something about the others' culture in an uncontroversial, low-threshold way. Therefore, Obývačka's foreign friends are called to contribute their favorite food to Sunday brunches or theme evenings. The fact that Obývačka's team is cooking for their foreign guests today is an exception, a gesture of gratitude toward their loyal friends: "Many of you have been with Obývačka for long and helped us a lot during this year. We will thank you by serving you the traditional Slovak Christmas dinner," Martina welcomes them. Martina is the association's leader, and this is very much her project: having studied international relations in London and run an English bookshop in Jordan, building her own nonprofit project in her home country was a long-held dream of hers.

Many accepted the invitation and gathered around the long table in the main room: Aysha, an Afghan mother of three, who recently started her own kebab enterprise to support her family; Olga, who left Donetsk, aged 67, and is eagerly learning Slovak and English to become a tour guide through Bratislava; Mahmud, who is under threat in his home country Afghanistan because he served as a translator for the American military; Manuel, a Coptic Christian from Egypt, who came all the way from the refugee camp in Rohovce where he is waiting for his asylum plea to be decided in court; and many more.

Helena cuts an apple into two halves horizontally and shows the seeds forming a star to the dinner party—a forecast of good luck and health for the year to come. As a starter, Martina presents the curious Slovak Christmas combination: *oplatky*, thin, crispy, sweet wafers with honey and garlic, symbolizing abundance and health. The next course is the ultimate Slovak Christmas classic: *kapustnica*, the cabbage soup that contains half of the pantry, from hand-picked mushrooms to sausage and dried plums. To be as inclusive as possible, the team decided on a vegetarian version with soy and tofu 'meat.' The sour taste of this national dish is not for everybody. Mahmud exclaims after the first spoon: "I can make better soup!" He has been in Slovakia for five years and works as a chef in a Slovak restaurant.

The main dish consists of potato salad and carp fillet. Martina tells the bewildered audience that many Slovak families buy a live carp, put it into the bathtub for a few days, befriend it, and then kill it on Christmas day to have fresh fish. Meanwhile, behind the scenes, community manager Lukáš is juggling pans, breading and frying quadratic pieces of deep-frozen carp. Lukáš is a self-declared left-liberal and corresponding to the cliché, as he readily confesses, has spent most of his working life in various Bratislava-based NGOs. His views and lifestyle defy Slovak societal norms in many ways, manifested not least in the fact that in a country with one of the highest rates of homeownership, he is 'still' living in a rented flat in his late thirties. His carp is a true crowd pleaser: the fillets and the salad are gone in a heartbeat. Later, Slovak and non-Slovak dinner guests debate whether *opekance*, the obligatory holiday dessert made from a kind of bread dumpling with powdered sugar and poppy seeds, is the necessary evil or the crowning glory of the Christmas protocol. True to Obývačka's participative concept, the whole event reaches beyond the realm of cultural representation and invites guests into the realm of cultural intimacy (Herzfeld 1997): they experience Slovak traditions not in their tourist brochure version but as strange and lovable peculiarities. The most intimate cultural characteristics can be shameful, embarrassing, or questionable, and permission to debate or make fun of them resembles an initiation rite.

The contentious *opekance* concludes the official part of the evening—the tables are now pushed aside to make space for more guests, friends, and Slovak volunteers who helped Obývačka along the way. The volunteers who start surging into the community room are mostly students and some young professionals seeking a social counterweight to their "disgusting corporate jobs," as one told me. Some elderly women are looking for a good use of their time in retirement. Only very few are men. Most of them meet with refugees to teach them Slovak and to socialize; some help children keep up in school. Sometimes, volunteers forge close relationships and help their 'partner' in every aspect of everyday life in Slovakia. Sometimes, the pairings do not know what to do with each other and quit the program after a few visits.

The children receive their presents now, nicely wrapped and name-tagged Lego sets. They are used items or donations from Obývačka's sympathizers. While the first part of the evening was completely alcohol-free, now a big pot of punch is being brought in, accompanied by various kinds of Christmas cookies the volunteers brought with them. The Christmas tree, which Aysha's kids and Manuel decorated earlier, is lending the room a festive gleam. The kids play with their new toys, the foreign guests chat with each other or with the volunteers, American Christmas songs sound from the speakers. Mahmud is engaged in a deep conversation with his Slovak volunteer Iva. He complains that he does not always experience this kind of hospitality in Slovakia. He has got used to the long stares and skeptical expressions on public transport. What upsets him the most is when people ask him whether he expects a terrorist attack on a Slovak Christmas market—as if being a Muslim made him a terrorism expert. But the closer the Christmas holidays draw, the nicer Slovaks seem to get toward him as well as to other groups who are usually met with disdain, and the more eager they seem to share their national culture in the shape of hectoliters of kapustnica. Cultural intimacy in Slovakia has a sour taste, one way or another.

Refúgium

Sofia gets her calculator out of her drawer, puts her papers into a neat stack, and counts the money one more time. Then she waits for the clients to arrive. It is the first Monday of the month, which means it is payday and all clients who are entitled to financial benefits are supposed to stop by and get their envelope of cash that is supposed to last them another month. While waiting for the clients to arrive, Sofia looks out of the window. The office of the NGO is located in a large office building right on the central square of the old town, probably originating from socialist times. There is a music school in a different part of the building. A jolly wave of atonality washes into the office over the whole span of office hours.

Sofia is the project manager of Refúgium, an NGO that was founded in the early 2000s to support (unspecified) marginalized groups. Refugees have been their main target group for at least ten years, and currently, they are realizing project *Step II*, which means they have been appointed by the state to 'integrate' refugees residing in Košice. That means they are the primary contact for issues like finding work and housing, organizing their papers on residence and health insurance, helping navigate schools and education, and providing a crash course in everyday life in the wild and strange country called Slovakia. Sofia is not only the manager of the Košice branch of Refúgium but also the only full-time employee who runs the show. Her closest colleague is Lucia, a part-time social worker who is sitting in the little back room separated from the main office with a door, brooding over some difficult bureaucratic paperwork. Part-time social worker Nina has her day off, and psychologist Linda and lawyer Dušan have difficulties even meeting the hours specified in their contracts: they offer their services only upon request. If they do all convene, at their regular team meetings or after the first encounter with a new client which requires everyone's presence, they like to go for a beer or attend one of the countless public festivals in summer on the main square right outside the door.

The first client is, like always, Paolo. He struggles with mental illness—that is, he suffers not so much from the disease as from the threat of losing his marginal employment as a maintenance guy in a local commercial center. Sofia swears him into taking his pills regularly and informs him that they have started the process of applying for a handicap ID for him, which would grant him advantaged access to cultural activities. Paolo is an avid dancer and concertgoer. He receives his envelope of cash, signs, and leaves. "He has been here for 10 years, he knows everything about Slovakia. He knows it better than me!" Sofia laughs. She adds that he would be an "easy client" if it was not for his health problems.

The next in line is Aila, a young woman who started studying medicine shortly after arriving in Slovakia, determined to become a gynecologist. Sofia is genuinely impressed by her dedication. She praises her recent progress in Slovak language proficiency, adding with a sigh, "I wish I had learned more English while working in the UK as an au pair," upon which Aila compliments her English—they speak a mixture of both languages during their encounters. Sameera has been in Slovakia for five years now and is considering applying for citizenship. Sofia informs her that although as a student she does not have to be insured, having public health insurance at the time of application is a requirement for citizenship. Sixty euros per month is a huge financial burden for the full-time student. "But I'm very confident that it will go well. You will easily find a job as a doctor, Slovakia needs you here," Sofia adds with a reassuring smile.

Slowly more clients drop in, and a little queue forms outside the office in the hallway. Salma tells Sofia that she has only five days of holiday left for the year. It is early June. Sofia is surprised: "Did you already take so many days off?" "The children were sick," Salma replies. "In that case, you don't take a holiday! You take a leave for *ošetrovanie člena rodiny* (treatment of a family member)," she explains patiently. Unfortunately, this cannot be done in hindsight, but Sofia informs her that there is always the option of *neplatné voľno* (unpaid holidays).

Sofia treats everyone with the same neutral and focused expression, always engaging in some small talk and inquiring about the health and well-being of family members. This friendliness is a tightrope walk, because with the next sentence she might have to tell someone that they are not going to pay their medication anymore or that if they continue to skip Slovak lessons, their financial support will be cut. She has to keep everything in mind because payday is the one occasion clients never miss, and it might take a month until she sees them again. Some clients require extensive consultation on school or health-related matters, others just grab their envelope and leave the office no more than two minutes after entering it.

Sofia never forgets to explain to those who live in social flats that they will subtract the fees for garbage disposal from their benefits from now on. Tina is overwhelmed when she hears the amount of thirty-six euros for the entire family. "Thirty-six? That's little!" she rejoices in basic Slovak. "Yes, we negotiated with the city, that's the lowest fee category," Sofia replies proudly. But Tina seems a bit overenthusiastic, she repeats the sum again and again with a big smile, and Sofia grows suspicious. She finally understands that Tina thought she would only have to pay thirty-six euros monthly rent for their flat. After the misunderstanding is cleared up, her mood swings in the opposite direction. "It hurts here!" Tina points to her chest. She was sick and had kids to feed. Sofia reminds her that two of her sons earned their own money, and that still paying her benefits after nine years in the country was actually a big sign of goodwill toward her. For the first time, you can hear a slight annoyance in her tone.

A big part of Sofia's work requires translation into a language she does not speak— both literally and figuratively. Language barriers are a big challenge, and interpreters are not always at hand, which urges her to develop her own lingua franca comprised of the easiest possible Slovak, scraps of English, and hands and feet. But she also engages in cultural translation without fluency in any of her clients' backgrounds. Slovakia is a much more bureaucratic country than most refugees' countries of origin. How to translate the concept of technocratic governance without knowing what to compare it to, what points of reference, and what experiential horizons clients have in dealing with public administration? How to design a language without a shared pool of experience and knowledge? Let alone the subtleties of her own criticisms and endorsements of the procedures she is trying to explain. Tina parts in a contrite atmosphere. Throughout their relationship, both women have had to acquire the skill to endure question marks, puzzles, even outrageousness, and perceive any understanding as preliminary. These understandings count until further notice, but their revocation is not experienced as a rupture. Translation, in Refúgium's office, is not a transformation of enigma into understanding but rather a slow gradual movement producing obscurity and clarity at the same pace.

Pomoc a Nádej

The air is cool and heavy with incense in the small, dimly lit chapel on the second floor of the theological college. Visitors greet each other on all sides, children run between the benches, some are sitting motionless in silent prayer. It is time for the Holy Mass of the Iraqi community. 149 Iraqi Christian refugees were resettled into the Central Slovak small town of Nitra in 2015, in what was a unique shared effort between the state and the Catholic Church. They had been forced to leave their hometowns, where they were targeted by Daesh (ISIS) for their faith and had been living in an overcrowded Iraqi refugee camp for months or even years before being offered to come to Slovakia. As Christians in the Middle East (most of them belong to the Syriac Catholic Church), their Christian heritage dates back much longer than anyone's in Central Europe. The town they landed in, however, is also quite proud of its religious standing: despite its small size, it was significant enough for Pope John Paul II to pay a visit in 1995—his larger-than-life statue was erected in the courtyard of the castle to commemorate this event.

An NGO, founded by a priest and his circle of friends, has been taking care of the Iraqi newcomers. Enabling them to practice their faith freely and without fear has been a priority from the start. Each week, they meet with their Slovak priest for a mass that is specifically designed for them: the readings are both in Slovak and Aramaic, and the Slovak sermon is interpreted simultaneously by a junior community member with good command of both languages. These religious occasions are also a meaningful forum for personal encounters and interaction: framing religion as the connecting point between the locals and the 'strangers,' many NGO workers and other community members visit the mass from time to time as an expression of their solidarity and unity in one faith.

Obviously, religion is key in this field site, as the genius loci is very much influenced by the omnipresence of religious acts and symbols. The office of the NGO is located in a building belonging to the local branch of the *Slovenská Katolícka Charita*, the largest Catholic welfare organization in Slovakia, and this is also where some Iraqis were first accommodated after coming to Slovakia. The employees do not eat meat on Fridays and pray before every meal—except for social worker Uršuľa, who is, in her own words, "deeply spiritual" but "skeptical of organized religion." The NGO is not a religious one per se—it was founded under the impression of the suffering of refugees in 2015 and found its explicitly Christian target group by coincidence rather than intent. The founding members had not quite decided what to do with their new civic association when the Slovak Migration Office approached them and offered them the coordination and management of the recent deal with an Iraqi archbishop. They quickly cast a team of social workers (none of whom had been employed in social work before), a financial manager, and a secretary for administrative issues. A colossal task lay ahead of the new organization, but the Slovaks from the NGO project were confident that it would be manageable to integrate the Iraqis into Slovak society. Them being Christians, they assumed, meant they had similar lifestyles, values, and goals to the Slovak majority. It definitely helped boost acceptance by the local community—the inhabitants of Nitra were very skeptical when they first heard that refugees from the Middle East were to be settled in their town. Some assumed they were Muslims pretending to be Christians as a plot to 'infiltrate' Slovakia and turn it into a "multicultural" society like Germany or Sweden—a horror scenario for those who voiced such concerns. But meanwhile, the project manager Jakub reported, the little town had grown accustomed to their presence, the genuineness of their Christianity was uncontested, and there had never been any incidents of violence.

But the expectations of similarity were exaggerated. According to the Pomoc, a Nádej staff, the Iraqis still have big trouble adapting to life in Slovakia. They still feel disoriented, helpless, and homesick. They still have difficulties learning Slovak or finding jobs, and even though they "have been saved," they show a lot of frustration and discontent with life in Slovakia. After two years, almost half of them had returned to their hometowns which had meanwhile been recaptured from the Daesh but where were still far from secure. It had emerged that the shared faith, although providing a common ground, does not spare Iraqis and Slovak NGO workers the arduous, never complete process of making oneself understood to the other. Sometimes, half-jokingly, half bitter, the employees wonder out loud whether the newcomers had got the Christian ethical principles of humbleness and gratitude entirely right? But this is not to say that the social workers quail in the face of the bigger-than-anticipated challenge: much to the contrary, they spend their free time and weekends touring construction markets and comparing prices, packing moving boxes, picking up kids from schools, giving women private lessons in computer literacy, setting up bank accounts and changing car license plates, to the point that Uršuľa mocked her coworkers for their Christian overeagerness to "serve" people in need unconditionally. Jakub, who had joined the team as project leader one year after the Iraqis' arrival, also saw an acute need to tone down the team's efforts and release clients into independence. A former teacher and scholar at the Prešov University Engineering Department, he knows a bit about pedagogics and how to convince others of his approach.

In the chapel, the priest contemplates the iconic presentation of Jesus lifting a little cross over his head, symbolizing triumph over burdens that seem almost impossible to bear. "All of you have overcome difficulties. You managed a further year in Slovakia. It was hard sometimes, but in the end, you can say you made it. And you will go on overcoming things." The Iraqi refugees had indeed accomplished astonishingly much in little time, by popular standards: after two years in Slovakia, most teenagers attended *gymnázium*, the most prestigious school type in the Slovak education system; most families owned a car, and some had even taken out loans and bought houses in Nitra's surrounding villages. But it seems as if these successful emplacements into the Slovak present tense are in constant tension with forms of displacement and misplacement— the feeling of misplacing efforts from the NGO's side, the feeling of being out of place, or in the wrong place, from the Iraqis' side.

The Iraqi community was used to an entirely different religious protocol than the cute community service in the seminary chapel. The services back home followed a liturgical order that is closer to that of the Orthodox rite. One middle-aged man confessed that he missed the festive and serene atmosphere of their several hours-long masses. A younger community member was homesick for the numerous pilgrimage sites around their hometown they used to visit even at minor religious occasions. Štefan, the Slovak priest of the community, told me that he uses incense in his services wherever permissible to make his congregation feel a little more at home. Pertaining to deeply felt, almost primordial scripts for purpose and belonging, religious rituals and their embodiment can perform acts of inclusion and "homing" (Brah 1996, 197), whereas even slight displacements of the familiar routines or elements produce intense estrangement. Hence, it was possibly on the much-cited 'common ground' of religion that Iraqis felt most displaced.

***

I hope that these vignettes have transmitted a sense of the contrasts that shape refugee support in Slovakia: the closeness and conflict, the intimacy and misunderstandings, the flexibility and rigidity. The encounters connect human beings as individuals and with the social embeddedness they bring with them. What these vignettes share, despite all their differences, is that the public perception and political objectification of refugee care take deep roots in the relationship between refugees and their supporters. They reflect the ways cultural and religious difference, the legitimacy of asylum as a concept and the legitimacy of refugees based on their individual 'contribution' to host societies are talked about in public discourse. There are no innocent encounters, and every conversation references—directly or obliquely—a deeply polarized and oftentimes aggressive political confrontation. In the following chapter, I will take a closer look at the public and political negotiations of refugees in Slovakia and asylum and ask why the divisions over this issue are so compelling.

Chapter 2

A DEEPLY DIVIDED COUNTRY

When I started doing fieldwork in Slovakia in the summer of 2017, two years after the events usually referred to as 'refugee crisis,' refugees and asylum were still ubiquitous topics of conversation, causing emotional discussions wherever I went. Three days into my stay in Bratislava's eastern district of Ružinov, seemingly out of nowhere, my landlady Sára suddenly burst into a long, agitated monologue on the refugee situation. She was convinced that the recent 'exodus' was being controlled by someone with an agenda, maybe destabilizing Europe. She did not believe that all refugees were threatened by war, and even if they were, they should rather stay where they were and fight for their country. "A man who abandons his family is not a man in my eyes," she declared resolutely. "When there was war in Slovakia, no one left, we all stayed here. Indeed, we had the Slovak National Uprising!" she added with pathos.[1]

I was stumped by the raw animosity in her words. Sára was a skilled potter in her mid-sixties with Jewish roots. She had told me that when anti-communist protests started taking place in her hometown in 1989, she stood in the front row. I had got to know her as a passionate democrat and an astute observer of national and international politics. Yet she went into a downright tirade of derogatory and generalizing comments on how "the Muslims" were ungrateful and incompatible with "our" advanced and civilized European culture.

Reacting to my acute discomfort, she contained her rage. Almost apologetically, she explained that her fear and skepticism came from her life experience and her experience of Slovakia as a nation. Slovaks were hostile toward Muslims almost innately; this was because Ottoman rule in the sixteenth and seventeenth centuries came with so much violence and deprivation for an innocent population.[2]

---

1. The Slovak National Uprising was a joint effort of scattered Jewish, bourgeois, and Communist partisan groups as well as insurgent soldiers, formed in 1943 and crushed by German and Slovak troops in 1944. Their goal was to defeat the fascist regime led by Catholic priest Jozef Tiso, a client state to Nazi Germany which had created the first independent Republic of Slovakia in 1939. Further, there were plans to help the Soviet army invade the country. After the failed uprising, Slovakia lost its autonomy as Germany occupied the entire country (Zückert et al. 2017).

2. Contemporary historical evidence partly corroborates and partly complicates these claims: the Ottoman rule was connected to significant suffering for the civic population, particularly along and around the border (*pohraničí*) of the Ottoman Empire which ran through Slovak territory from 1526 to 1699 and was the site of notorious military confrontations as well as raids, lootings, and also kidnappings.

   On the other hand, Ottoman and Hungarian governance coexisted and overlapped in the respective regions, most of which belong to nowadays' Hungary; there were many instances of opportunistic collaboration; trade with the Balkans gave local economies a

Sára's argument against refugees, and my queasy reaction, shows the emotional capacity of the issue: it touches upon essential expressions of personhood—individual and national identity, and (collective) memory—and upon core values such as safety, continuity, and justice. It is very common in Slovakia to see one's stance on refugees, like Sára, not as a political opinion like any other but as a question of principle. Politics boosts this framing by tying the refugee issue tightly to essential needs such as national security and sovereignty.

Obviously, Sára's position is utterly incompatible with the stance of those who demand tolerance and empathy with refugees. Accordingly, the question of whether or not Slovakia should accept refugees defines political camps that are often seen as indicative of a 'rift' that runs through Slovak society. People either categorically approve of or abhor the presence of refugees in their country, a middle ground is virtually absent. Being a 'deeply divided country' is an often-voiced diagnosis Slovakia shares with Brazil, the United Kingdom, Hungary, Poland, the United States of America, and others—usually in the context of the electoral success of politicians (or projects, like Brexit) at the right margin of the political spectrum. 'Deep rifts' are said to run between different political affiliations but may also split families into irreconcilable halves. The image of the fast and hard line of division that is almost impossible to overcome is powerful. Throughout this chapter, the question that guides me is what to make of the 'divide' that apparently shapes the discourse and practice of refugee support. What is highlighted and what is sidelined in a political epistemology that relies on a binary distinction? And how does this imaginary develop a political life of its own, creating long-lasting realities in which refugee care takes place?

The Coffeehouse and the Extremists

On the other side, opposite my landlady Sára and big parts of the country's political stakeholders, the rift imaginary places the *Bratislavská kaviareň*. Bratislava coffeehouse is the derogatory denomination used by politicians and angry critics to ridicule the intellectuals, artists, journalists, and NGO workers sitting in the capital, sipping their freshly brewed coffee, applying themselves to their aesthetic musings, and caring woefully little about the standard, working-class Slovak from the countryside. Another derogatory term is *slniečkári*, which roughly translates as sun people. It denotes

---

boost; considerable proportions of the population welcomed the Ottoman rulers or at least preferred them over the despised Habsburgs; Protestant life flourished under the more religiously tolerant rule of the Ottomans; Christian forces even constituted a sizable segment of the Ottoman army during the fateful second siege on Vienna in 1683 (Horváth/Kopčan 1971; Perényi 1972; Pirický 2013).

Arguably, the portrayal of Muslims in Slovak collective memory today does not date back to the Ottoman period but rather to the much more recent period of 'National Revival' in the nineteenth century, in which the juxtaposition of virtuous, brave Slovaks and brute, uncivilized Muslims was a common nationalist trope in song and literature, not least as a way to covertly criticize Habsburg supremacy.

approximately the same group and reached new levels of popularity in the context of the refugee crisis in 2015. It is supposed to label those who support marginalized people of all kinds, particularly refugees and immigrants, as ideologically blinded, phony, or just inexcusably naïve. Persons who identify themselves with this milieu of the country's educated elite sometimes appropriate these terms, half-jokingly, half self-critically.

During the first few weeks of fieldwork, as I was waiting for my entry into the first field site and had some spare time, I explored the Bratislava NGO landscape focusing on anti-extremism, antidiscrimination, and anti-racist groups. I went to discussions, film screenings, network meetings, and other events, approaching people out of the blue and with shaking knees, trying to get a grasp of the world of civic participation in the capital.

It was easier than anticipated. Soon, I realized that every new contact I added to my network on a big social media site was already connected to everyone else I knew on the same platform. NGO workers themselves called their ideational and social home the Bratislava *bublina* (bubble), and it really is a life-size filter bubble. The world of NGOs is small, people know one another, and many have collaborated on past projects. Also, the capital Bratislava is more affluent and more cosmopolitan than the rest of the country, with a growing number of EU foreigners finding work in the capital's booming tech and IT sector.[3]

Despite the density of the network, however, the non-profit sector is not an isolated social habitat. Many of its members grew up in small towns and villages across the country; they have strong family bonds and return home regularly. It seems like everyone has a story to tell about that one uncle or that one neighbor who sincerely disavows of the causes they fight for in their professional or voluntary work. At a conference for professionals working with marginalized groups that I attended, Alexandra, a human-rights lawyer who supports refugees in their asylum applications, admitted that her father did not approve of her activities. He told her about a dream he had, in which some miserably looking figures knocked on his door and told him that his daughter had sent them here and that he had to accommodate them now. The daughter's life mission is the father's nightmare. It hurt her that the causes she so eloquently defended across different media platforms did not convince her own family, and like many others, she had resolved to prioritize family peace over steadfastness and not talk politics at home.

After the international populist landslide of the Brexit vote and Trump's election, and the entry of the extreme right party ĽSNS (*Ľudová strana Naše Slovensko*, People's

---

3. According to the 2021 Population and Housing Census of the Statistical Office of the Slovak Republic, 2.72 percent of Bratislava's inhabitants were foreigners with a residence permit. They account for roughly one-third of all foreigners in the country. The proportion of foreigners in the total population is 1.07 percent. Overall, the amount has more than doubled in the previous decade. Aktuality.sk: "Cudzincov s trvalým pobytom na Slovensku stále pribúda." 14.10.2023. Accessed 07.01.2024. https://www.aktuality.sk/clanok/iPnlxUy/cudzincov-s-trvalym-pobytom-na-slovensku-stale-pribuda/.

Party Our Slovakia) into Slovak parliament just over a year before, intellectuals in Bratislava as well as everywhere in Europe were painfully reminded of the fact that they were living in a social bubble. Not everyone shared their leftist-liberal, cosmopolitan, and tolerant worldview. Not everyone spoke several languages, had studied abroad, and perceived foreign cultures as something to approach with respect and curiosity. Not everyone shared their conviction that the EU was a blessing. Not everyone was a feminist, believed in the effectiveness of civic participation, or considered environmental protection a priority. There was a shared sense of urgency to promote all these matters more inclusively, but there was a lot of insecurity about how to approach people on the other side of the political spectrum.

David, a student and NGO employee I met during these first weeks of fieldwork, found a succinct way of describing this collective self-doubt by saying, "I have no language to speak to them." He had just helped organize a conference on radicalization and violence as an intern in a Bratislava-based NGO and had to admit that their programs, however elaborate and ambitious, tended to reach the ever-same people who shared the same values and intentions already. Not only did his association with a George Soros-backed NGO, and his socioeconomic standing more generally, make him an unacceptable partner in conversation for many; but he really lacked the life experience and insights that would make people assume standpoints so fiercely opposed to his own. Despite his efforts to use the weapons of a sociology student and analyze the determining socioeconomic factors through social theory, he was out of his wits when he witnessed his classmates in his hometown Banská Bystrica vote for the anti-tsiganist and anti-Semite Marián Kotleba, leader of ĽSNS, as city mayor. Similarly to David, many active members of Slovakia's civil society realized that they had occupied themselves with issues far removed from a majority of Slovak citizens' everyday concerns and had advanced their progressive and liberal projects without communicating them sufficiently. Some even contended that a certain snobbish attitude, a tendency to ridicule or discredit anyone who did not share their views, had deepened the rifts that ran through Slovak society and made constructive debate almost impossible.

For the ĽSNS, fueling the image of the fundamental opposition of "coffeehouse" and "normal people" was a core political goal. Before and after each election on the local or national level, a lot of attention would go to the 'extremist threat' emanating from Kotleba and his supporters—this framing boosting the party's popularity within its electorate (Kluknavská 2015). The party is commonly labeled as ultranationalist or fascist/neo-Nazi extreme right (Mesežnikov and Gyárfášová 2017; Kluknavská and Smolík 2016; Kluknavská and Huška 2019; Žúborová and Borárosová 2017b) but attributes like "intrinsically populist" (Kazharski 2019, 1), "populist and nativist frames" (Kluknavská and Huška 2019, 60), or "anti-system" (Gyárfášová 2018) also feature prominently in such characterizations.

The party was the second attempt of Marián Kotleba, an industrial engineer by training and PE teacher by profession, to enter politics, after his first party *Slovenská pospolitosť—Národná strana* (Slovak community—National Party) was banned for violating the constitution (Gyárfášová 2018). The ĽSNS, founded in 2010, has been more persistent, although only mildly more moderate. The party systematically radicalized its profile by constructing a broad range of frontiers: "between 'traditional values' and the 'liberal culture of death,' 'perverts' and 'normality,' 'Gypsies' and 'decent people,' 'multiculturalism' and the 'nation state' and between 'Slovakia' and the rest of the world which is ruled by 'financiers,' 'Zionists' and other global elites" (Kazharski 2019, 9). All these single antagonisms are fused into one overarching people-system juxtaposition, responding to popular frustration with mainstream politics (Kazharski 2019, 5). The connections between these disparate enemies are drawn, if necessary, with the help of conspiracy myths.

However, none of these polarizations or enmities is exclusive to the ĽSNS. *Slovenská národná strana (SNS)*, the Slovak National Party, is the established nationalist force in the country which has promoted Slovakia as a nation of ethnic Slovaks since the early 1990s. It was an essential player in Czechoslovakia's dissolution in 1993 and has capitalized on vilifying and othering the Hungarian and Roma minorities since its beginnings (Kluknavská and Smolík 2016). *Smer—socialná demokrácia* (SMER-SD), Direction—Social Democracy, the dominant party in Slovak politics, which has been part of almost all governments since 2006, stands for "combining law-and-order policies with anti-establishment and redistributive populism" (Pytlas 2013, 169). Since 2001, Smer-SD has been the only large party with a declared political orientation to the left and a commitment to social democracy of the Western type. It did pursue some popular social reforms like free train rides for pensioners and free lunches for school kids but has also adopted the same hostile attitudes as the nationalist parties promote (Rydza 2020): whether Roma or Hungarian minorities, migrants, LGBTQ and feminism, the public stance of Smer-SD is always rather restrictive and hostile than open and accommodating (see below).

All these parties deploy strategies of hostility that are common features in a particularly Central Eastern European right-wing populism. Across different understandings of populism in current scholarship (as an approach to statecraft, political ideology, discourse, logic, or as political communication and style, s. Moffitt and Tormey 2014), the construction and passionate propagation of simple antagonisms is a key characteristic. Ernesto Laclau has described populism as a binary political logic, its defining characteristics being the construction of two mutually exclusive, irreconcilable camps, one of which is the 'people' and the other is its enemy. The 'people' are imagined as united in their 'righteous wrath' over unmet demands, which a prevalent structure or authority denies them (Laclau 2005).[4] Most visibly, 'the people' react against a detached 'elite' (Mudde 2007) that pushes an (in this context, liberalizing) agenda against the people's will. Populist ideology often revolts against granting tolerance and entitlements

---

4. Laclau has been criticized for equating populism's paradigm of 'the people' with the logic of the political within, making it difficult to use the term to diagnose or analyze specific historical and politico-geographical situations.

to anyone outside the in-group of 'the people'—be it minorities, refugees, people with LGBTQ identities, and feminists.

Ivan Krastev and Seth Holmes (2018) argue that the feeling of patronage and disenfranchisement in the postsocialist context is caused by what they call the "imitation paradigm" (117). The authors see the illiberal backlash as the outcome of a futile catch-up race with Western Europe post-1989. Hence, an arrogant and presumptuous Western Europe emerges as the enemy, against whom countries in the East assert their more primordially European identity. Recently, empirical social science has rather downplayed the significance of real-life disadvantage and precarity as a precondition for populist preferences (Žúborová and Borárosová 2017b; Mudde and Rovira Kaltwasser 2017; Gusterson 2017), pointing at ideological illiberalism's strong presence among middle classes. Note, however, that a look at the demographics of populist parties' electorate in Slovakia prevents us from discarding socioeconomic explanations entirely.[5]

These antagonisms come hand in hand with a language and performance that consciously breach conventions regarding politeness and political correctness in favor of brashness, vulgarity, and unmediated emotionality (Moffitt 2016; Ostiguy 2017). William Mazzarella notes that the efficacy of populism hinges upon "intensified affect" and access to the "collective flesh," the embodied existence of the people who are disenchanted or disillusioned with the cool, bureaucratic, depersonalized political jargon (Mazzarella 2019, 49f.).

While these attributes of populism, in global comparison, are not exclusive to right-wing political formations, in Slovakia (and analogously in the other Visegrád states) they certainly originate there. As political scientist Bartek Pytlas (2014) argues concerning the radical right in Central and Eastern Europe, issue adoption from the far-right is a tested strategy mainstream parties use to contain the success of extremists and broaden their own voter base. I agree with Nitzan Shoshan that we should, with the help of ethnographic methods, "develop concepts that, rather than entailing a separation between the extreme and the mainstream, will help us find the former as already in the latter, as emerging from it and rooted in it" (Bangstad, Bertelsen and Henkel 2019, 103). The rift does not simply run between voters of extremist parties and the rest. My landlady Sára, for instance, had only contempt for Kotleba and would never vote for ĽSNS, given that her predecessors were murdered by the Nazis.[6] The feeling of being

---

5. In the 2016 parliamentary election, the right-wing populist party ĽSNS and the social and national populist Smer-SD had the lowest shares of voters with university-level education (20.5 percent and 19.8 percent), and the biggest shares of voters with basic education (6.8 percent and 7.6 percent). ĽSNS also had the highest rate of unemployed voters (4.8 percent) (Gyárfášová and Slosiarik 2016, 3). The districts where ĽSNS had its best results—Banská Bystrica (10.45 percent), Žilina (9.76 percent), Prešov (9.44 percent) Tenčín (8.73 percent), and Košice (7.81 percent) (Sme.sk: "Výsledky parlamentných volieb 2016." 30.09.2016. Accessed 21.11.2020. https://volby.sme.sk/parlamentne-volby/2016/vysledky.)—are also the five districts with the lowest GDPs per person in Slovakia (Štatistický úrad Slovenskej republiky 2018: 214–215).

6. Between 1942 and 1945, around 70,000 Jewish Slovaks were deported from Slovakia, most of whom were killed or died in concentration camps. The fascist regime under Tiso paid Germany 500 Reichsmarks for every deported Jewish person (Vrzgulová 2016).

part of the disenfranchised or patronized people precedes and exceeds the ultranationalist's momentum; and so does the perception that the people one identifies with are morally superior to those who threaten them.

As a consequence of an "intensified affect," confrontations between both sides often play out not as competition over the better argument but about who has the moral higher ground. A telling example of the significance of such sentiments of moral superiority is the ownership over 'decency' as a political leitmotif. *Slušnosť* (decency) has traditionally been the trademark buzzword of Marián Kotleba and his supporters. Social media postings, party newspapers, and public speeches never fail to point out the 'decency' of the party and its leaders. *Za slušných ľudí* (for the decent people) became their most prolific campaign slogan. The 'decent people' who want a 'normal life' are not only pitted against the 'indecent' elite but also anyone outside the norms for a traditional, ethnically Slovak family.

However, the word 'decency' was later picked up by the protest movement *Za slušné Slovensko* (for a decent Slovakia) that emerged after the murder of journalist Jan Kuciak and his fiancée Martina Kušnírová in February 2018, a traumatizing and formative event for large segments of the Slovak population. Kuciak's investigative work had exposed the far-reaching influence of the Italian Mafia organization 'Ndrangheta involving actors on the highest levels of the Slovak administration. The horrible crime and the entanglements it brought to light upset many Slovaks and left them with the impression that parts of their elite were indeed so power-hungry and corrupt that they literally walked over dead bodies to maintain their status. Tens of thousands took to the streets in the following weeks to demand not only a quick and comprehensive investigation of the murder, but also a fundamental change in the country's political culture, highlighting transparency, responsibility, and honesty (Lang and Walther 2020). I participated in rallies in Bratislava and Nitra, both of which achieved the status of the largest political gatherings since the Velvet Revolution. They were extraordinarily quiet and respectful gatherings. People lit candles and jiggled key rings, a tribute to the protesters in 1989 who used keys as a symbol for freedom and political self-determination. There was an emphasis on mourning and remembering the two victims before moving to the utterance of political grievances. Rather than aggressive blaming and shaming, many speakers were remarkably self-critical, maintaining that the construction of a truly 'decent' society needs to start with each and every one of those present.

Nicolette Makovicky, Jonathan Larson, and Juraj Buzalka (2020) take the emergence of 'decency' as a keyword as an example of the "inherent instability of political signs" and claim that during the protests, the "two meanings appeared to merge"—meaning the ideals ĽSNS, respectively the protesters in 2018 saw encapsulated in the term. To me, it appeared that on the scale of public conversation, rather the opposite was true. Choosing Za slušné Slovensko as a name was also an attempt to reclaim the vocabulary from the extremists and endow it with a different meaning: the 'decent Slovakia,' in the imagination of this movement, was not only conditioned upon the abdication of a corrupt elite but also an enhanced sense of alertness and commitment to exposing power abuse throughout the whole population.[7] The people who marched with Za slušné Slovensko encompassed all demographics (although members of the Bratislava coffeehouse were undeniably especially visible), *with the exception of* the ultranationalists. As time went by, the initiators also directly spoke out against extremism and ultranationalism.[8] The far-right received the message that they were not included in Za slušné Slovensko's rendering of decency, and they reacted accordingly—dismissive or suspicious of the movement. In Kotleba's opinion, it was "cynical" to instrumentalize the death of two young people politically.[9] Media outlets with close ties to, or ideological identification with, the right fringe (*Hlavné Správy, Infovojna,* and *Zem a Vek*) reported negatively on Za slušné Slovensko (Petriska 2019), doubting the initiators' moral integrity and claim of apolitical decency, and spreading the conspiracy myth of protesters being coordinated by George Soros or other 'foreign powers' (a suspicion also shared by Smer-SD's prime minister Robert Fico, who was forced to resign over the protests but managed to preserve his party's government and avoid new elections).[10]

Decency is an unstable term open to varied readings but at the same time an inherently normative concept. No matter the specifics of one's understanding, designating something or someone as decent is always an attribution of moral integrity. Here, decency is fashioned as a moral requirement of political legitimacy: the opposite sides measure each other by their respective standards for decency and inevitably arrive at the conclusion that those 'others' do not qualify for it. It becomes a token of competition and demarcation. But are the definitions really that incompatible? Both sides associate decency with a desirable and somehow primordial way of relating to others that vanishes if people are alienated from traditional social contexts and 'corrupted' by egocentrism. Essentially, all users of the term agreed that the current power holders were the epitome of *in*decency. The shared anti-establishment sentiment was not

---

7. In the manifesto on their official webpage, they state: "We support Slovak citizens in taking an active part in public life. Politics should not be a dirty game for one's own benefit. Slovakia is a parliamentary democracy, created by active citizens and responsible politicians." (my translation, Slovak original: "Podporujeme občanov Slovenska v tom, aby sa aktívne zapájali do verejného života. Politika by nemala byť špinavá hra o svoj vlastný prospech. Slovensko je parlamentná demokracia, ktorú tvoria aktívni občania a zodpovední politici. My všetci voláme po tom, aby do politiky išli slušní ľudia, ktorým záleží na Slovensku a sú pripravení zodpovedne vykonávať službu vo verejnom záujme.") Accessed 06.08.2020. https://www.zaslusneslovensko.sk/manifest/).

8. Webnoviny.sk: "Nepodliehajte nenávisti a silným rečiam, varuje Za slušné Slovensko pred mítingmi kotlebovcov." 16.12.2019. Accessed 21.11.2020. https://www.webnoviny.sk/nepodliehajte-nenavisti-a-silnym-reciam-varuje-za-slusne-slovensko-pred-mitingami-kotlebovcov/.

9. Aktuality.sk: "Marian Kotleba: Slovensko by malo rovnomerne spolupracovať so všetkými štátmi sveta. Anketa." 13.03.2019. Accessed 21.11.2020. https://www.aktuality.sk/clanok/674842/prezidentske-volby-marian-kotleba/?fbclid=IwAR2Vr95dp3Y5EIQBMV1dlTzD6ju82PoKR_SIqIARe5D5DPkP8YQnO27Jxf8.

10. Euractiv: "Fico blames Soros for provoking instability in Slovakia." 06.03.2018, updated 07.03.2018. Accessed 21.11.2020. https://www.euractiv.com/section/elections/news/fico-blames-soros-for-provoking-instability-in-slovakia/.

enough, however, to make nationalists overcome their reservations toward more liberal civic activists, or for the initiators to lift the cordon sanitaire between them and the far-right. I believe this is an example of the persuasive performative force of the trope of a deep rift that runs parallel to the refugee debate: the imaginary of the divide is self-perpetuating. It becomes an end in itself, thus sidelining the specifics and ambiguities of antagonisms on different subject matters.

As an ethnographer, I am neither impartial to nor uninvolved in the self-perpetuating logic of the rift. I hold the normative position that the resurgence of the extreme right and a politics that builds on the vilification of marginalized minorities is very problematic—I would even claim that one legitimately arrives at this conclusion when looking at reality from an anthropological point of view. At the same time, I want to understand divisions not as realities of an almost material quality, but as discursive formations that float and attach themselves to different actors. Although it is not the focus of this book, a necessary part of this analysis is looking at the divide from the side scholars and anthropologists in particular are usually unsympathetic to (Bangstad 2017).

Luckily, I can draw on ethnographic accounts of scholars who immerse themselves in the life-worlds of people with an inclination to support far-right parties or populist politics, allowing a close-up perspective on the emotional dispositions of this side of the rift. I want to mention two ethnographies, Arlie Russell Hochschild's *Strangers in Their Own Land* (2016) about supporters of the Tea Party movement in Louisiana and Hilary Pilkington's *Loud and Proud* (2016) about Britain's English Defense League as particularly empathetic and therefore insightful accounts. Both scholars do not suspend their political opinions but still manage to bracket common evaluative schemes and reflexes of dismissal. They show that the mix of outrage and grievance that has become the trademark of these groups is not (solely) a strategy or a rhetoric device, but an authentic emotion that causes intense suffering. Members share a feeling of being treated unjustly, of staying behind their possibilities not at their own blame. They unequivocally view themselves as victims, perceiving themselves as doing worse than they rightfully should. This constellation is a prototypical breeding ground for "dark emotions" and destructive desires, like vengeance or scapegoating (Duijzings 2020, 270).

Looking to identify the culprits of their unfavorable situation, they turn to groups like migrants, minorities, and women who are de facto and relatively recently competing for the same resources as them, including welfare, housing, education, and jobs, denying or ignoring that "the rise in socioeconomic inequality continues to affect minorities and immigrants to a much greater extent than white working-class people" (Bangstad, Bertelsen and Henkel 2019, 100). This personalized threat is experienced as the most immediate, overshadowing the more abstract adverse effects of neoliberal and austerity politics (which they often also identify as hostile to them).

In the context of the Visegrád states, ethnographic accounts of right-wing extremist movements or parties are rare. Hungary is a noteworthy exception. Catherine Thorleifsson (2017, 2019) has been engaging, among others, with Jobbik supporters in Hungary and has found the same patterns of existential fears and lack of acknowledgment. In *Revolt of the Provinces* (2018) by Kristóf Szombati, the intensification of anti-gypsyism and concomitant rise of Jobbik is described as linked to the struggles of the post-peasantry in the disoriented post-Transition agricultural sector.

It is an omission, Pilkington argues, to place "subjects whose political views we do not agree with as 'out of bounds' for research" (Pilkington 2016, 14–15), and explains:

> This moral overdetermination of power and powerlessness obscures a more complex understanding of social relations in which the oppressed can also perpetuate oppression. Of course not all socioeconomically and educationally disadvantaged people take political paths that oppress the rights of others, but that does not take away their own disadvantage or make it unworthy of social research; if this is a possible outcome of it, indeed, it becomes all the more important to understand. (Pilkington 2016, 33–34)

But dealing with (for us) objectionable political views and their proponents is exhausting (not only) for researchers. One easily runs into discrepancies that evoke emotional responses and trigger premature judgments. Hochschild talks about "empathy walls" (Hochschild 2016, 5) in this context: those hurdles or barriers that seem impossible to overcome without letting go of one's treasured values and positions. They prevent understanding the other's "deep story" (ibid.), tracing where these individuals come from and what motivates their opinions. Hochschild's own sociocultural dispositions, and the fact that they differ so strongly from her subjects', brings inconsistencies in the latter's conceptualizations into sharp relief, while she is, as she confesses, inclined to overlook those in her own convictions.

Her description of her moral and emotional tornness and the image of the empathy wall resonated with me while reading news coverage and social media discussions on the subject of refugees, and also through encounters like the one with Sára. Although my reflex reaction was disgust and a feeling of moral superiority, a certain openness to her proud Slovak and European identity, and where it came from, helped attenuate this 'intense affect.' On the other side, regarding refugee supporters, my positionality resembled theirs in many ways, and hence their struggles to overcome the divide were intuitively understandable to me.

Overcoming the Divide?

My participants experienced the discomfort of empathy walls acutely. For them, being part of the liberal-left-wing bublina my research was largely situated in, the huge support for Kotleba's party in 2016 was a wake-up call. Suddenly, there was a whole segment of Slovak society that made it very clear that they disapproved of everything the NGO bubble stands for, as well as of the democratic state and its institutions. The openly propagated despise of foreigners and minorities, and the revisionist rehabilitation of National Socialism outraged members of the bublina the most.

The unanimous intuitive reaction to this shocking discovery was to reach out, bridge the rift, and enter into a conversation. In David's words, they were trying to find a language, maybe invent a new one, to enable these kinds of encounters. Most of the Bratislava coffeehouse held the benevolent view that although extremism should be condemned, it did not come without its reasons. Michal, a Bratislava-based architect, decided he did not want to remain passive and reached out to journalist Andrej, asking if he wanted to found a civic association together with him. This is how *Zabudnuté Slovensko* (Forgotten Slovakia) came into being, a group of individuals organizing discussions on the topic of extremism and radicalization all over the country. Michal was born and raised in Brezno, a small town with one of the largest followings of Kotleba in Slovakia. Time and time again, Michal was shocked and saddened by the fact that yet another old friend or neighbor joined 'the other side.' But he insists on a differentiated view of this phenomenon, arguing that there are many reasons why people are attracted to extremist positions:

> Whether it's their social surrounding, or they don't prosper at work, or they are disenchanted with politics, or they pursue personal aims like getting into politics themselves, or they hope to get advantages. [...] The party members built strong networks, and friends of ĽSNS may get preferential treatment in tenders and such.

When he discusses politics with his family from Brezno, conversations often revolve around the stagnating development of the *regiony* (regions, a shortcut used basically for anything except Bratislava). Seeing that support for ĽSNS came predominantly from the rural areas in the center and the east of the country, facing slower economic development and higher rates of unemployment, he understood that feelings of being ignored, ridiculed, and left behind might be a great catalyst for radicalization. The real culprits were corrupt politicians who filled their own pockets instead of addressing inequalities and supporting underdeveloped regions. This is how they came up with the name Zabudnuté Slovensko. But he believes in the reconciling power of talking to one another, and he sees the fact that the discussions, however loud, usually remain decent, as a confirmation of his belief.

In a similar vein, several NGOs launched programs in which they had foreigners and refugees visit schools in more or less remote areas and introduce themselves to the students, believing that interpersonal encounters were the most suitable tool to counter prejudice and dispel fears. Some of these projects were initiated by migrants themselves like the *Center for Migration and Integration*, headed by an Afghan refugee who regularly packed some of his friends into a truck and toured schools and community centers—all at his own expense. Peter, a successful marketing specialist, who accompanied the electoral campaign of the former president Andrej Kiska, the liberal center-right candidate in 2015, made his own crowd-funded newspaper which he distributed for free in those districts with the biggest support for ĽSNS. The whole project had started as a joke when Peter was mocking Kotleba for not having secured legal protection for the name of their party bulletin, *Naše Slovensko* (Our Slovakia), and he simply adopted the name for his own publication. With the subtitle *Magazine about the country that we love*, Peter applied a soft pedagogical approach aimed at making people think about patriotism differently.

Most of these projects target the spatial or geographical dimension of the divide—the fact that extremists and those who challenge their views are rarely in the same place at the same time—and create moments of personal encounter. They do not overcome the empathy wall just enough to notice that 'Forgotten Slovakia' is a project name that somehow stigmatizes its target group, or that the people on 'the other side' might find the missionary approach of the *Magazine about the country that we love* infantilizing. However, that does not mean they missed their mark entirely. The following vignette describes one of these encounters and shows not only how they are sabotaged by the depth of the divide but also how they can give rise to a fragile hunch of connection and exchange.

I accompanied Zabudnuté Slovensko to one of their events in 2017. The destination was Čadca, a small town in the structurally weak north-western region of Žilina. At the time of our trip, it was early December, and the archaic landscape of Kysuce remained soaked in murky, milky light throughout the day. The panel discussion was scheduled to begin at 7 p.m. at the local cultural center, a gray socialist-functionalist gem. At 6:55 p.m., there were only four people present in the auditorium, and Andrej joked that they might have to relocate the meeting to the local pub and discuss there instead. Suddenly, the door swung open and a group of 15 young men in green shirts entered and took their seats in the middle of the auditorium. The members of Zabudnuté Slovensko are accustomed to this kind of audience; a busload full of Kotleba supporters comes to their discussions from time to time. They decided to tolerate them; after all, it is their own declared aim to talk to everyone, and it is not a secret that the men in green shirts are the reason the whole project exists.

After 40 minutes of discussion between the host, journalist Andrej, and four panelists, the audience is always invited to enter the conversation with their own thoughts and questions. On that evening, the spokesperson of the ĽSNS delegation, a middle-aged man with a bald head and a training jacket, was the first one to rise and speak. He stated (I am paraphrasing here) that all the talk about extremism was nice and well, but: see, without us, your "most loyal fans," you would be almost alone here. You are clearly alienated from peoples' actual problems and worries. He continued, stating that extremism is not the problem, it's that people can't find a job and if they do, they might not even make a living, so they need to abandon their families and go abroad to work.

Andrej tried to mediate and find common ground, replying that they were equally affected by all these problems, "We are all sitting in the same boat." The real culprits were corrupt politicians who abused their power instead of serving their people, the morally reprehensive elite which Marián Kotleba was a part of, by the way—it is well-known that he indulged in clientelism during his time as mayor of the city of Banská Bystrica. He would be glad to discuss these issues constructively, but not as long as they, Kotleba's fan club, adhere to their fascist repertoire of symbols and vocabulary. The bald man in the green shirt complained about Andrej's evocation of the Nazi label. What followed was an exchange of verbal blows between the panel and the green shirts. Kotleba's men complained that they did not find their views (including 'alternative' accounts of Slovak history) represented in the mainstream media, that their opinions were marginalized, silenced or ignored, and that they were never talked to on eye level. The panel fired back, arguing that it was difficult to enter a decent and dignified discussion as long as their counterparts negated some of the most violent events during World War II, and even had the guts to lie about it. After two hours of what was mostly a painstaking meta-discussion on who was allowed to talk about whom with whom, Andrej finally called it off: "Thank you for coming and for the fact that, despite everything, a discussion was possible until the end." But even after his closing words, men in green shirts assembled around Andrej and the other team members and tried to hold them accountable for all the evil things they associate them with: and what about the EU's liquidation of nation-states? What about Georg Soros? What about the migrants who came to eradicate our Christian culture?

Everyone was exhausted when we finally fell into the seats of the car. I was deeply irritated: "Why are they so eager to discuss with you when they know they can't change your mind and you won't change theirs?", I asked them. Monika, a historical ethnologist who participated in the panel, replied with a shrug: "At least we talk to them."

The evening in Čadca was rife with animosities and bitter reproaches, making a productive exchange of arguments, let alone a minimal consensus, impossible. The discussants were very invested in making their adversaries correspond to their image of them, thus reaffirming the unbridgeable difference. At the same time, both sides insisted on being wholly different from what the others imagined, accusing the others of believing a caricaturesque stereotype. Either way, there was an urge to be acknowledged, heard, and understood as what one *actually* was. Andrej and his team were careful to empathize with the situation of the deprived rural population and recognize and validate their dissatisfaction. And the men in green shirts seemed to seize the opportunity to finally present their views to those who disagree—it is hard to tell whether this was for the joy of provocation or whether there was a wish for sincere reactions. The divide provides both comfort and irritation. The existence of a different world behind the empathy wall is a source of discomfort that can only be attenuated by reaffirming the division after peeking over it.

I said that the division manifests most evidently in public opinion on refugees and asylum. In the historical overview that follows, we can see that this has not always been the case but developed simultaneously with the image of Slovakia as a 'deeply divided country' in the mid-2010s. The events around the *utečenecká kríza* (refugee crisis) had a catalyzing effect on this development, bringing the issues of asylum and migration to the center of public attention with unprecedented force. It had a lasting impact on how refugee integration is perceived and handled in Slovakia today, and it shaped my participants' life worlds profoundly.

The Refugee 'Crisis' in Slovakia and Beyond

I examine the Slovak government's response to the 'crisis' in the context of its Visegrád neighbors. Similar arguments, fears, and objections appeared in all four countries, and their maneuvers were performed in close coordination. This paratactic comparison will show that the Slovak experience is exemplary for Central and Eastern Europe in many ways.

Asylum policy in the Visegrád states

The Visegrád countries' stances toward the 'refugee crisis' intersected not least because they all share a similar historical trajectory regarding the development of migration and asylum policies. Most members of the former Eastern bloc have always been countries of emigration rather than immigration. Even before the era of socialism, tens of thousands left the Czech and Slovak lands to flee Habsburg domination. Later, about 500,000 people fled the communist regime in the Slovak part of the country alone, especially after the failed reform project of the Prague Spring (1968) and toward the end of the socialist era (Borárosová and Filipec 2017). But there was immigration as well, mostly in the framework of guest worker treaties with other communist states— neighboring ones, but also Vietnam, Angola, or North Korea (Divinský 2007). The country also accepted refugees, mainly persecuted members of socialist parties in non-socialist countries, notably 13,000 individuals from Greece (Szczepanikova 2011). After the Velvet Revolution of 1989, the newly constituted democratic Czechoslovak state rapidly established a rather liberal immigration policy. This was to demonstrate their newly attained openness to the world and to symbolically recompensate for the many Czechs and Slovaks who had made their way through the Iron Curtain and had been welcomed by other states (Szczepanikova 2011). Czechoslovakia rapidly became a significant transit country, sheltering 150,000–200,000 refugees from countries of the dissolving Soviet Union, most of whom moved on or returned within three years (Borárosová and Filipec 2017).

At that time, the Western European states, meaning the early members of the European Union usually referred to as the EU-10, were already pursuing quite a different agenda with regard to refugees and migration: they were securing borders and minimizing the numbers of arrivals, and were enticed by the possibilities to shift responsibility for refugees, especially those arriving by land from the former Soviet republics, Afghanistan and even the Middle East, to the states in the eastern parts of what was now an undivided continent. They made the new members of the Western world sign the Geneva Convention while introducing the secure third-state principle which obliged refugees to file for asylum in the first safe state they set foot in. By measure of signing the Geneva Convention, states were declared safe countries. Almost immediately, this led to increasing or even exploding numbers of asylum cases in the region (Miciukiewicz 2011).

In the following years, all Visegrád states succinctly adopted new asylum and migration policies as part of the process of accessing the European Union. New legislation meeting the requirements of the Acquis of the EU was an important factor in accession talks; nevertheless, most states went through several attempts to introduce legislation that covered the minimum requirements. Financial aid was made available for laying the groundwork of an asylum infrastructure, but progress was slow. Current evaluations suggest that the structures for accommodating asylum seekers, as well as the policies and mechanisms for their integration, remain underdeveloped in all V4 states. Financial support is scarce, and necessary infrastructure, such as language courses, education programs, and training courses for NGO employees, and so on, are missing (Borárosová and Filipec 2017, 62; Divinský 2007, 302–304; Miciukiewicz 2011, 189).

The developments of Slovak asylum policy strongly resemble those of its V4-neighboring states. In 1993, the Slovak *Migračný úrad* (Migration Office) was established which took over responsibility for most matters related to flight and asylum, except for regime and visa questions, for which the Foreigners' Police was created within the Police Presidium. In the same year, the *Principles of the Slovak Migration Policy* were adopted, mainly corresponding to the need to implement the Geneva Convention and approach EU standards, since Slovakia was already an accession candidate at that time (Borárosová and Filipec 2017, 59–60).

Interestingly, refugees and asylum never became a topic of intense public or political debate, even in the period between 2002 and 2004 when, according to the Migration Office's statistics, as many as 9,000–11,000 people applied for asylum in Slovakia (Divinský 2007). The number of actual asylums granted was extremely small in comparison, amounting to only 11, 20, and 15 cases in the three respective years. However, many of the applicants did not await the decision of their trial but left the country shortly upon arrival. After 2004, the number of asylum seekers declined steadily—a development that affected the whole of Europe and was partly caused by improved stability and security in some conflict zones like the Balkans and Afghanistan, but also the tightening of restrictions and border security (UNHCR Slovensko 2006). The Slovak asylum apparatus continued to work largely outside the purview of public interest.

It all changed with the 'refugee crisis' which for months in a row put asylum and migration into the spotlight of international public attention. The 'crisis' arrived at a convenient time for several of the Visegrád countries. Hungary's Victor Orbán was faced with declining approval rates due to his party Fidesz's unpopular internet bill (effectively taxing internet usage); he used the emerging 'refugee wave' to shift public attention to security and identity politics. Poland had a change of regime in 2015, allowing the now ruling PiS party to sharpen its profile and stake out a clear position against its predecessors' (the Civic Platform's) liberal approach. The Czech Republic's president Miloš Zeman owed his electoral success two years earlier to a large extent to his blunt anti-German and anti-migration rhetoric, and he lived up to his electorate's expectations when sharpening his tone toward the EU in reaction to the unfolding situation. In Slovakia, Prime Minister Robert Fico took advantage of the tension building up between the 'Brussel bureaucrats,' and the Visegrád governments, to demonstrate his assertiveness and fighting spirit. He quickly turned the refugee topic into the decisive electoral topic for the parliamentary elections in the spring of 2016 (Beger 2018).

It is important to highlight the strategic political potential of the refugee topic to understand the turbulent dynamic that emerged in the following months. The escalation of intra-EU relations and the prominence the topic gained and maintained in the press and public discourse was more than welcome to the political leaders of the region, and many of them were keen to fuel the flames. It is difficult to distinguish between politically engineered scaremongering and an already existing, deeply seated fear and resentment of strangers among the populace (Chudžíková 2016; Žúborová and Borárosová 2017a). Opinion polls indicate that xenophobic, Islamophobic, and anti-migration attitudes were already widespread in the Visegrád countries for years but grew even more in the course of the 'refugee crisis.' For example, in a 2017 survey of the Slovak Academy of Science in the framework of the European Value Study survey, 54.4 percent assigned 'Muslims' as 'undesired neighbors,' ranking them as the second least favored group before the Roma. In 2008, only 23.1 percent had responded like that

(Kusá et al. 2017). In a 2011 Eurobarometer poll, 70.1 percent of Slovak respondents were in favor of protecting and helping refugees in their country (European Commission 2014). In a corresponding survey from 2015, only 34 percent responded affirmatively to the question as to whether Slovakia should accept refugees from conflict zones, and only 26 percent were willing to accept refugees from Africa and the Middle East. Overall, only 31 percent of Slovaks approved of the redistribution of refugees among EU member states, placing them at the bottom of the ranking of EU countries (average 78 percent) and alongside their V4 neighbors (European Commission 2018a).

Indeed, it was the mandatory quotas that the EU suggested for a redistribution of refugees with good prospects for asylum that sparked the outrage and resistance of political leaders in the region. The rise in numbers of refugees in and of itself was hardly felt by these countries, with the notable exception of Hungary, which received over 42,000 requests for asylum in the first six months of 2015. The quota system was designed to support Italy and Greece, which had a far bigger challenge to face, not least due to the secure state directive and the Dublin II Regulation. The initial plan for the quota regulation foresaw Hungary to be one of the beneficiaries of the program, but the government refused to be part of such a mechanism (Beger 2018).

On September 22, 2015, the European Council adopted a decision to establish "provisional measures in the area of international protection for the benefit of Italy and Greece." As part of this, the relocation of 66,000 asylum seekers was proposed, out of which 190 from Italy and 612 from Greece were assigned to Slovakia (European Council 2015). The plan stirred controversy long before it was implemented. Especially the Visegrád countries were alarmed and used their joint semi-official platform, which they had founded in 1991, as a mouthpiece for expressing shared political interests. The political leaders issued a common statement on June 19, 2015, stating, "We do not deny the spirit of solidarity but we firmly argue the contradictory effects and pull factors of a possible mandatory redistribution scheme for asylum seekers."[11] They successfully averted the proposal the first time it was put to vote, on June 25th. As the situation deteriorated in Europe's Southeast, the council finally approved the decision against the dissenting votes of Hungary, Slovakia, the Czech Republic, and Romania—Poland voted in favor (Beger 2018).

Many commentators in the countries concerned used the phrase "about us, without us" to criticize the outrageousness of this measure. The quote is mainly associated with the Munich Agreement of 1938, a Czechoslovak national trauma when France, Italy, and the UK agreed to leave the Sudetenland with its majority German population to Germany.[12] The irony of this situation in which the predominantly wealthy EU-10

---

11. Visegrád group: "Joint Statement of the Heads of Government of the Visegrad Group Countries" 19.06.2015. Accessed 30.12.2023. https://www.visegradgroup.eu/calendar/2015/joint-statement-of-the.
12. For example: Idnes.cz: "O nás bez nás. Kvóty připomínají Čechům Mnichov, říká Bělobrádek." 05.05.2016. Accessed 30.04.2019. https://www.idnes.cz/zpravy/domaci/belobradek-rozhovor-kvoty-mnichov.A160505_112808_domaci_hro, or Lidovky.cz: "Arogantní Západ nesmí rozhodovat o nás bez nás, komentuje Klaus migrační kvóty." 24.06.2017.

states, having pursued a restrictive refugee policy for decades, were now condemning their allegedly xenophobic eastern neighbors from a position of moral superiority, was not lost on the V4 leaders. Slovak prime minister Robert Fico, for instance, labeled the quotas as "irrational" since refugees did not want to stay in Slovakia anyway, and accused his western neighbors of "moralizing and preaching."[13] In early December, Slovakia filed a lawsuit at the European Court of Justice, while Hungary followed suit the next day. The (ultimately unsuccessful) plea for annulment referred to procedural reasons and alleged that by adopting the scheme through a majority vote, the Council violated the principles of institutional balance, legal certainty, representative democracy, and proportionality.[14]

The parliamentary election campaigns

The confrontation began as a contestation of the EU's decision-making with the term 'sovereignty' remaining at the center of the debate all along. Political elites were mainly concerned with delegitimizing the EU, especially its most influential member states, Germany and France. A few weeks into the debate in Slovakia, politicians, especially those of the ruling party Smer, started introducing alternative lines of reasoning against accepting refugees. In August, Fico began to delegitimize the refugees as well, claiming that they were mainly "economic migrants." The implications of this terminological shift are clear: while refugees were trying to save their lives and had to be protected, economic migrants were 'only' looking for economic advantage and preyed on Europe's hard-earned wealth. In his official statements, Robert Fico conveyed the impression that the whole 'crisis' was based on dishonest interests:

> The question is, how to position ourselves towards a mass of maybe one million people. Whether we open our arms and promise to take everyone in, or whether we behave rationally and in solidarity. That means we need to identify who is actually a threatened refugee. Is someone who can spare 5,000 € for a smuggler starving? Just look how many young men are among those who come to look for a job, they make up about 90 percent.[15]

Accessed 30.04.2019. https://www.lidovky.cz/domov/evropska-unie-nesmi-rozhodovat-o-nas-bez-nas-komentuje-klaus-migracni-kvoty.A170624_153820_ln_domov_ELE.

13. Slovak Spectator: "V4 united against quotas." 08.09.2015. Accessed 30.04.2019. https://spectator.sme.sk/c/20060186/v4-united-against-quotas.html.

14. Slovak spectator: "Refugee crisis affects Slovak politics." 28.12.2015. Accessed 30.04.2019. https://spectator.sme.sk/c/20068371/refugee-crisis-affects-slovak-politics.html.

15. "Otázka je, ako sa postaviť k mase možno viac ako jedného milióna ľudí. Či otvoríme náruč a povieme, že všetkých berieme, alebo sa budeme správať racionálne a solidárne. To znamená, že musíme identifikovať, kto je ohrozený utečenec. Trpí hladom ten, kto nájde 5,000 eur na pašeráka? Pozrite, koľko je tam mladých mužov, ktorí prichádzajú hľadať si prácu, je ich medzi nimi 90 percent." Sme.sk: "Fico: Je otázne, či trpí hladom ten, kto má päťtisíc eur na pašeráka." 05. 09. 2015. Accessed 01.12.2020. http://domov.sme.sk/c/7992429/fico-je-otazne-ci-trpi-hladom-ten-kto-ma-pattisic-eurna-paseraka.html as in Chudžíková 2016, p. 106, my translation.

At the same time, the problem, as manifested in political discourse, took on an additional cultural dimension, namely that migrants from outside the EU are too "culturally other" to adapt to Slovak society (Žúborová and Borárosová 2017a, 5). This otherness that was cast as undesirable, even dangerous, was largely defined in religious terms. The refugees that were discursively dispelled were imagined exclusively as 'Muslim' (Kissová 2018). There was an implicit consensus that somewhat different standards applied to non-Muslim refugees, for example, for Ukrainians from the Donbas region who were seeking shelter in Slovakia but were largely absent from the public debate. The othering worked in two directions: it was claimed that refugees would be inevitably unhappy in Slovakia. Smer-SD's Minister of the Interior Robert Kaliňák, for instance, explained:

> Refugees are not like sand, rice, or some commodity that we have to apportion. They are real people with relations to their relatives, their own culture and religion. At the end of the day, those who will be the most dissatisfied with the quotas are the refugees themselves, and it is all about them.[16]

In its more taunting form, the argument contained the view that the "Muslim migrants" are neither willing nor able to accommodate to Western culture. In a press conference, Robert Fico said that his government had always been opposed to the EU "forcing the member states to accept refugees with diametrically opposed values and ways of life" and a "different relationship to women." He then added that Muslim refugees were "impossible to integrate."[17] A very common argument was likening migrants to other 'cultural others' Slovaks are more familiar with, and who pose a major challenge to society: the Roma minority. Fico stated, "We are unable to integrate the Roma, so let's not pretend that we can integrate someone who comes here with an entirely different religion and tradition."[18] Similarly to the 'economic migrant,' Roma are often stigmatized in Slovakia (and other V4 societies) as 'freeloaders' who rely on social benefits and have little contribution to make (see Stewart 2012).

September marked another turning point in the debate: on November 13, Islamists carried out terrorist attacks in Paris, killing 130 people and leaving over 400 injured. In

---

16. "(U)tečenci nie sú zrnká piesku, ryža alebo nejaká komodita, ktorú musíme prerozdeliť. Sú to živí ľudia s väzbami na príbuzných, náboženstvo, kultúru. [...] Na konci dňa s kvótami budú najviac nespokojní utečenci, a predsa o nich ide." Sme.sk: "KDH s kvótami nesúhlasí, Bugár nevidí aktívnu pomoc vlády." 09.09.2015. Accessed 01.12.2020. http://domov.sme.sk/c/7996803/kdh-s-kvotami-nesuhlasi-bugar-nevidi-aktivnu-pomoc-vlady.html, as in Chudžíková 2016, p. 106., my translation.

17. Euractiv: "Slovak PM: It's impossible to integrate Muslims." 08.01.2016, updated 11.01.2016. Accessed 21.11.2020. https://www.euractiv.com/section/central-europe/news/slovak-pm-it-s-impossible-to-integrate-muslims/.

18. "My nie sme schopní integrovať Rómov, tak sa netvárme, že sme schopní integrovať niekoho, kto sem príde s úplne iným náboženstvom a tradíciami." Sme.sk: "Fico hovorí aj o vojenskom zásahu (utečenecká kríza – víkendové fakty)" Sme.sk: 06.09.2015. Accessed 01.12.2020. https://domov.sme.sk/c/7993540/fico-hovori-aj-o-vojenskom-zasahu-utecenecka-kriza-vikendove-fakty.html., as in Chudžíková 2016, p. 102., my own translation.

Slovakia, these events led to a shift from stigmatizing refugees culturally, to declaring them a security risk. In mid-October, Smer-SD changed their main campaign slogan from "We are working for Slovakia" to "We are protecting Slovakia" (Žúborová and Borárosová 2017a, 6). Fico declared that every Muslim in the country was being monitored, sparking outrage among the local Muslim communities.[19] In early December, the government launched a set of "anti-terrorism" measures, including more powers for police and secret services, longer detention time for terrorist suspects, and better protection of witnesses. Fico made it explicit that the measures were connected to the heightened risk due to "migration."[20]

This multitrack strategy of the government to amplify the discourse on refugees and present itself as assertive manager of the 'crisis' was barely met with any resistance. In an analysis of print and online media reporting on the 'refugee crisis' in 2015, Alena Chudžíková (2016) found that news outlets did not necessarily promote a negative, biased view of refugees. However, articles that would contextualize the debate or provide the bigger picture were scarce; they were by far outweighed by unchanged agency reports which again consisted mainly of summaries of politician's utterances, especially those of the ruling party Smer-SD. Oppositional politicians were rarely consulted, although this did not matter much in terms of discursive diversity: in fact, all relevant parties for the parliamentary race unanimously opposed refugees (Borárosová and Filipec 2017, 66). The only exception was President Andrej Kiska who actively combated the trope of the 'economic migrant.' According to Kiska, the question of how Slovakia would treat these strangers would be decisive for the future of the country:

> We will lose the battle for the heart and soul of our country if we, both as citizens and as politicians, are not able to make a distinction between fearing the unknown and unconcealed hatred, contempt for human life, extremism, xenophobia and fascism [...]. And also if we fail to refuse such expressions of intolerance clearly and categorically.[21]

The very least attention was paid to the voices of refugees themselves; in the dominant rhetoric of protection and prevention, the fact that refugees continued to arrive in Slovakia outside of existing relocation programs, simply by entering Slovak national territory, was sidelined (Chudžíková 2016).

In the parliamentary elections of March 2016, Smer-SD became the strongest party, once again able to dominate the government as a leading partner in a three-party

19. Slovak Spectator. 2015c. "Security more important than migrants' rights." 16.11.2015. Accessed 30.04.2019. https://spectator.sme.sk/c/20063953/fico-security-more-important -than-migrants-rights.html.
20. The Slovak Spectator: "Cabinet passed special anti-terrorism legislation." 30.11.2015. Accessed 30.12.2023. https://spectator.sme.sk/c/20065078/cabinet-passed-special-anti-ter -rorism-legislation-parliament-to-okay-it.html.
21. Slovak Spectator: "Kiska: Attitude to migration crisis to define the character of Slovakia." 07.09.2015. Accessed 29. 04.2019. https://spectator.sme.sk/c/20060149/kiska-attitude-to -migration-crisis-to-define-the-character-of-slovakia.html.

coalition. Despite having lost over 12 percent of voters since the last parliamentary election in 2012, Fico was confirmed as the prime minister. Experts assume that their strategy to shift the debate to migration turned out to their benefit.

Aftermath of 2015

After the elections, the topic of refugees disappeared from the newspapers quite rapidly, but it nevertheless flared up immediately at every public event remotely related to migration. At the turn from 2016 to 2017, the government passed a law that made it harder for religious minorities to be officially recognized, receive state funds, and construct their own places of worship. Although not mentioned explicitly, it was clear to anyone that this was meant to bar Muslims from practicing their religion more freely (Lenč and Zaviš 2018). The Global Pact for Migration of 2018 also caused a major public uproar,[22] with many suspecting this to be another covert move to deregulate migration and force Slovakia into accepting refugees.[23] During the next parliamentary elections in 2020, the refugee topic played only a marginal role, partly because it was overshadowed by more acute concerns over the aftermath of Jan Kuciak's murder, but also because it seemed that Slovakia's stance on the issue was already firmly established. Most party leaders simply declared that they would continue to defend the country's current restrictive policy. Only the newly established liberal, center-left parties *Spolu* (Together) and *Progresívné Slovensko* (Progressive Slovakia) developed a more pragmatic and compassionate approach toward migrants, but they refrained from placing this issue high on the agenda of their public campaign.

The European Court of Justice ultimately dismissed the lawsuits Slovakia and Hungary had filed against the European Council in the summer of 2017, which meant that Slovakia was formally obligated to accept their quota of 802 relocated refugees. By that time, it transpired that the implementation of the quota system was going to be harder than anticipated (Zaun 2018). Most Western states had only fulfilled a fraction of their obligation, reducing the expectations toward Visegrád countries. Poland had initially diverged from the V4's line and voted pro, but after winning the elections in October 2015, the PiS government canceled its commitment. Yet it accepted a substantial number of Ukrainian refugees, which served Poland's leadership as a token to demonstrate goodwill. The Czech Republic finally accepted 12 resettled refugees, Slovakia

---

22. The UN's Global Compact for Migration is framed as a 'lesson learned' from nation-states' struggle to respond to the challenges of the events in 2015–2016. Its main intention is to improve collaboration among sending, transit and receiving countries and agree on guidelines to make migratory movements safe, regulated, and legal. It is not a legally binding international contract but a memorandum to commit to mutual support and an institutionalized exchange of expertise. It was endorsed by the United Nations General Assembly in December 2018 (Angenendt and Gnesa 2018).

23. HNonline.sk: "Fico vo videu kritizuje globálny pakt OSN: Migranti prinášajú so sebou obrovské riziká." 18.11.2018. Accessed 21.11.2020. https://slovensko.hnonline.sk/1844585 -fico-vo-videu-kritizuje-globalny-pakt-osn-migranti-prinasaju-so-sebou-obrovske-rizika.

16—to demonstrate that their refusal of quotas was neither caused by a lack of solidarity nor xenophobia but that it was solely the quotas' coercive character that had antagonized them. However, the attempts to find suitable candidates and organize their transfer were soon stalled altogether; the numbers were too far below the quota to even have symbolic validity (Beger 2018). Hungary had the most sustained controversy on the refugee issue: Orbán implemented several measures to prolong this for him useful 'crisis.' A national consultation in 2015 should provide large democratic legitimation for the crackdown on migration, like increased border patrols, the construction of a fence at the borders with Croatia and Serbia, and changes to the asylum procedure which made it more difficult to contest a negative decision. In October 2016, a controversial referendum was held on the question whether citizens agreed that the EU could oblige Hungary to resettle non-Hungarian citizens without the consent of the Hungarian parliament. With a turnout of only 41 percent, the referendum was invalid, but since most participants voted in Orbán's favor, he declared it a success anyway (Priebus and Beger 2017).

Many of the antagonisms associated with the rift I described above fit seamlessly into the anti-refugee narrative as it unfolded in Slovakia and beyond, showing disdain for the disaffected Western European elites and slniečkári in the capital, proclaiming the primacy of ethnic Slovaks over non-Slovaks, voicing racist and xenophobic prejudice and the perceived disenfranchisement of the Slovak people to be remedied with urgency. This explains, to a large degree, its appeal to politicians: it was a topic political leaders could trust to cause intense emotional investment and little controversy—and "[n]othing is as threatening to populist conviction as waning affect" (Mazzarella 2019, 52).

Refugee Supporters' Motivations and Beliefs

On the side of the rift I focus on in this book, the Bratislava coffeehouse and the slniečkári, mainstream politics in 2015 and after certainly instigated intense affect. Among the refugee supporters I met in the field, many began their engagement out of their personal dismay about political reactions to the 'refugee crisis,' and those that had been active before reported that this period profoundly changed their work. NGO workers and volunteers, and even employees of the Migration Office, were equally appalled by the undifferentiated accounts of politicians and the openly racist utterances of their co-citizens, although they, as mentioned above, leaned toward giving opportunistic, power-hungry politicians the lion's share of blame for the derailment of public discourse. In interviews, mostly conducted in the early stages of my fieldwork, I asked my counterparts why the refugee topic had become so polarized, and why they had chosen to challenge the predominant scheme with their words and deeds. I will devote some space to their insights, which will also serve as an introduction to the protagonists of this book.

A central incentive for getting active was an outrage over the politicians' incompetent reaction and the alarmist nature of the whole debate: Helena, manager of the volunteer program at Obývačka, said, "We didn't have a refugee crisis here, we had a refugee hysteria without refugees." Magdalena, volunteer for Obývačka, recalled:

My main motivation was the negative approach of our state representatives. Politicians said, we won't help refugees, we won't accept anyone. And I was ashamed. I thought I had to show that there are also other people here who do want to help.[24]

Katka, who used to manage an integration project of the Catholic Charita, explained:

Those in power are populists. They "hear the voice of the people," and that voice is fuelled by the fear of the unknown. Of course, they won't get involved with refugee policies when all the people are against accepting anyone. But people are not sufficiently informed, they don't communicate that there is nothing to be afraid of. The media also plays an important role in this because they cover only scandals, terrorist attacks, only the negative aspects. And, let's say, not all Slovaks have developed the capacity to think critically. They only hear *one* radio station, watch *one* TV channel, read *one* daily newspaper. They don't compare information. I think it's primarily the politicians and the media that failed in not talking about refugees truthfully.

My respondents attempted to approach refugee opponents empathetically by understanding their fear as a normal, comprehensible reaction. People who were socialized under state socialism, they claimed, grew up in a relatively isolated country. They were never encouraged to develop the capability to 'think critically,'[25] and were hence incapable of withstanding politicians' fearmongering. Nevertheless, the primary reason for their fear 'of the unknown' was connected to Slovaks'—perceived or actual—lack of experience with foreigners. "Everyone is prejudiced, even me," argued Zuzana, a manager of antidiscrimination education projects, and explained:

I think it's natural that people are afraid of the unknown. They say Bratislava is one of the least diverse capitals, compared to Vienna or even Budapest. The people just don't encounter diversity when they walk through the streets, like people with different skin colors and a different faith. It's a conservative country, most people confess to the Catholic faith (even if many are not religious), they know almost nothing about Islam, and it immediately triggers their fear, that someone might go against us.

Many interviewees expressed the hope that the lack of experience and resulting reservation of Slovaks can be undone—through personal encounters. Marcela, manager of ASPR's refugee integration projects, coordinates school visits to enter into such conversations:

Paradoxically, it's a problem that so few foreigners live here because people don't get to meet them. Slovaks are actually quite friendly and accepting once they meet one in person. That's the level at which prejudices can be defeated.

---

24. All quotations are my translations of interview recordings or field notes in Slovak language.
25. For a comprehensive dissection of this assessment which plays a pivotal role in contemporary debates on political education and civil society, see Larson (2013) on *Critical Thinking in Slovakia after Socialism*.

However, many refugee supporters mentioned the historical experience Slovaks could and should draw on to develop empathy with refugees: the past and present of Slovak emigration.[26] Helena from Obývačka, who worked and studied in several Northern European countries, cynically criticized her compatriots who are against refugees but move to Britain "for 200–300€ more." She added, "Sometimes we tend to be quite indifferent when it comes to making a change for our country, and very judgmental towards refugees for not fighting for theirs, in horrible circumstances." Many supporters explicitly referred to their own experiences abroad to contextualize their empathy with refugees. Jana, the volunteer manager of Obývačka's branch in Košice, drew on her years of living in the Netherlands, where her husband worked in the diplomatic service:

> I was very lonely. I know what it's like without social networks or help. One day I was sick with the flu and my husband too, but our three-year-old was up and clambering about, and we just didn't have the energy [...] We didn't have anyone around whom we could just call and ask "Hey, can you come over?" It affects every area of life.

Like in all Visegrád countries, there is an influential narrative of historical oppression and brave self-assertion of the Slovak people. Memories of the rocky road to Slovak statehood and independence resonate with the refugee issue in complicated ways.[27] National independence is seen as a hard-won, precious good that needs special protection, and there is a heightened sensitivity to any signs of tutelage that might constrain national sovereignty. The moral claim and imperative made on Slovakia to accept refugees is interpreted as an attempt to dominate Slovakia from abroad. Alena and Elena from the Institute for the Research of Ethnicity and Culture, which engages in research and policy consultation on migrant integration, interpreted this as a lack of orientation that comes with being a young state. Alena explained:

> We as a country never had a phase of self-realization, of finding out who we want to be. We just rolled along with the transition which was mainly an economic process. We were

---

26. Around 500,000 people left Czechoslovakia between 1948 and 1989 (Szczepankova 2011). In 2016, 160,000 Slovak citizens were working abroad. Most of them were living in the UK, the Netherlands, Austria, and Germany (Grenčíková, Skačkauskienė, and Španková 2018).
27. Apart from the short intermezzo as an independent fascist state under Tiso, Slovakia had never been self-governed; despite a 'National Revival' in the eighteenth century which coincided with the codification of the Slovak language, and constant pushes of Slovak officials in democratic and later in socialist Czechoslovakia for more autonomy (Schulze Wessel 2018), the creation of a positive collective identity was seen as major challenge when Slovakia finally gained independence after the so-called Velvet Divorce from Czechia in 1992. Shari Cohen (1999) argues that although the state socialist ideology was little persuasive, the regime still succeeded at repressing alternative systems of moral orientation. Accordingly, the elites that seized power of the state in 1993 developed a style of "politics without a past" (ibid.), marked by the absence of ideological commitments or meaningful references to a shared history. Instead, they exploited the disorientation of the public by crafting a superficial nationalism easily subjectable to their self-interest. The persona of Vladimír Mečiar stands paradigmatically for this style of governing (Leško 1996).

happy that we joined the EU and the economy was growing. There is no public discussion on values.

Her colleague Elena added:

> This is the main challenge for the next years: Finding out where we belong. Do we belong to the EU? If not where else? I think we do, but there needs to be a discussion about it.

Refugee supporters are also often avid supporters of the European Union, and the question of solidarity is not unimportant to them. Slovakia benefited tremendously from accessing the Eurozone and receiving EU funds, and they do not want to seem ungrateful or arrogant to their European neighbors. Ivana from the Human Rights League commented on Slovakia's lack of will to cooperate on the refugee issue in the pragmatic terms of a lawyer:

> Sure, it is quite sad that we have three refugee facilities here which are almost empty and there are more employees than refugees; when you go to other parts of Europe you see overcrowded camps. The burden is divided unequally. We have much more capacities and could help other states and people that are there but it's just not happening. We have the capacities, and they are not used; there's a lot of space to help more. In the framework of international law, it is an obligation to help each other in a community of states, so responsibilities are clearly defined in this respect.

Most importantly, and opposed to the anti-refugee discourse, refugee supporters foregrounded solidarity with the refugees themselves. Katka from the Charita said, "I bow to these people. If a person tells me their story, I feel honored to be able to do this kind of work." Refugees did not want to leave their home country but had no other choice—that is what all my respondents agreed on. For them, it was uncontested that people who apply for asylum have gone through horrible ordeals. Volunteer Magdalena explained:

> I think protecting life is the first obligation of each human. It doesn't matter if they are war refugees or economic migrants, who flee from starvation. I only see that they need help.

This standpoint also reveals that refugee supporters usually have a far more positive outlook on their own country than their antagonists. Rather than a poor and stagnant place with too many problems and marginalized people of its own to take responsibility for strangers, they see it as a member of the first world, of the prosperous West. When I asked her how she feels about Slovakia, Elena replied:

> I realized that I must like this country very much [laughs], and that's why I'm doing this job. That was a recent observation of mine. Because I would like to make this country a better place for all people. That's pathetic maybe [laughs]. When I came from Buenos Aires back to Bratislava, I thought: wow, it is such a nice, quiet, clean place to live. It is home. And Bratislava was wonderful. It is hard to explain my feelings. [...] But I think Slovakia has great potential and we should work on that.

Veronika, the PR manager of Obývačka, also stressed Slovakia's "huge potential" and explained why she decided to move back after having studied abroad and traveled a lot:

> When I was young, I really wanted to go anywhere except Slovakia. But the more I travel, the more I want to come back. My values have shifted. You see, people easily forget what happened in the past and how well-off we actually are today. Slovaks tend to be dissatisfied with what they have, but they made great progress. I'm proud to be a Slovak. We have an amazing country, a great landscape, and innovative people, more and more of them. Right now, my outlook on Slovakia is sunny, maybe not too *slniečkársky*, but definitely positive. We have the financial means and capacity, so why wouldn't we help people in need if they helped us 60–70 years ago when we were in need?

Some people refer to their Christian ethics as commanding them to help refugees. *Karma nie je zdarma* (karma doesn't come for free), said Boris, a social worker of the Migration Office. He added that loving your neighbor was the foundation of Christianity, and not differentiating in terms of the religion he or she belongs to was an essential part of it. Some also expressed disappointment with the churches remaining silent on the refugee topic. Even Veronika, the Protestant pastor in Bratislava, whose parish offers accommodation to refugees, was disenchanted with her church:

> What our parish does is not representative of the Protestant Church in Slovakia. It is very sad but it is like that. [...] And if the Ministry of the Interior doesn't want to accept these people, because they are afraid, the churches should be the ones who tell politics that it is ethical, and it is necessary. Who else should it be, if not we as a church?

Others claimed that their religious affiliation, although important to them personally, did not feature in their decision to help refugees, that they considered it "human and normal" to help people in need. "I don't care whom I help!"—was the bewildered response of Marina, a volunteer for Obývačka, to my question about why she had decided to engage in voluntary work with refugees. She explained that charity was firmly integrated into her life and sense of self. Excitedly, she told me about the two African children she sponsored and even got to visit two times. Obývačka's volunteer program was just another opportunity to help others which she had come across accidentally.

Many see working with refugees as an opportunity to further enhance their personal development. They benefit from these encounters because they enjoy meeting people and learning about other cultures. Ivana from the Human Rights League claimed that by helping refugees, "we are egoistic, actually. The right to asylum is a human right. We would also want our rights protected if we ever were in the same position."

The Deserving Refugee

Somewhere in her monologue on refugees and Muslims, almost as a side note, my landlady Sára made the following remark: "Of course, it's different if someone *really* had no other option. If a single mother with children knocked on my door, I would let them in immediately." Does this reasoning not resemble the one of the slniečkári above? Extending a helping hand to the less fortunate, treating others the way one would like to be treated?

It is a misconception that political and public opinion categorically rejects the idea of asylum. If refugee supporters maintain that it is a human obligation to help those whose only option to preserve their life and bodily integrity is to flee, most of their opponents would agree. Upon closer inspection, the interpretation of asylum that is widely approved of is a rather narrow one. The politicians in power were very careful to stress that Slovakia was ready to help particularly needy individuals. They insisted that the refugees whom they had to accept as part of the EU's quota distribution be all women and children.[28] Single mothers who were imagined as desperate to offer their fatherless children a better future were apparently deemed to be received favorably by the population. The acceptance of 160 Christian Iraqis persecuted by Daesh followed a similar reasoning. In 2018, Prime Minister Peter Pellegrini even demonstrated willingness to accept 60 Syrian orphans—arguably the most indisputably innocent recipients of help.[29]

Behind this perhaps surprising convergence, there is a particular understanding of what or who a refugee is that has emerged over the past decades and as a direct consequence of efforts to restrict the availability of asylum and exempt people from its scope of application. In the last segment of the chapter, I retrace the rise of this nowadays largely uncontested, commonsense understanding and explain why refugee supporters have little other choice but to adopt it in their communication, as well.

The origins of the label 'refugee' as a globally acknowledged legal category lie in the period after World War II, when millions of people were on the move in Europe, requiring a standardized way to deal with these masses of displaced persons. The devastating experience of the Holocaust and the brutality of the war still fresh in mind, the Declaration of Human Rights was adopted in 1948, and refugee rights played an important role in it. The Geneva Convention regulating the status of refugees followed only three years later. Inscribed in international law and monitored by humanitarian organizations, failure to adhere to it may perhaps not lead to sanctions but it will damage a state's reputation. A modern state cannot (at least not openly and sweepingly) reject those who look for shelter *and* maintain an image of humanity and progressivity.

Hannah Arendt observed how in the postwar era, nation-states were consolidated as the only authority to grant rights—even 'universal' ones that were designed to function independently of origin and citizenship (Arendt 1996 [1955]). The universal right to asylum forced states to grant refugees some rights usually reserved for their citizens. This turned them into a potential threat to the authority and legitimacy of modern sovereign states. Peter Nyers states that "refugees are included in the discourse of 'normality' and

28. Pravda.sk: "Prijmeme ďalších utečencov, hlavne matky s deťmi." 02.06.2016. Accessed 02.05.2019. https://spravy.pravda.sk/domace/clanok/394999-prijmeme-dalsich-utecencov -hlavne-matky-s-detmi/.

29. HNonline.sk: "Slovensko by mohlo prijať sýrske siroty, pripúšťa Pellegrini." 29.09.2018. Accessed 21.11.2020. https://slovensko.hnonline.sk/1816922-slovensko-by-mohlo-prijat-syr- ske-siroty-pripusta-pellegrini.

'order' only by virtue of their exclusion from the normal identities and ordered spaces of the sovereign state" (2006, xiii). Hence, efforts to restrict or annul the rights granted through asylum began to emerge as soon as the Geneva Convention was implemented.

Since the 1980s, as outlined in the Introduction, efforts to reduce refugee numbers and prevent people from staying (Malkki 1995) have multiplied. Recently, scholars have analyzed the way states twist and tweak the label 'refugee' and change the mechanics of labeling to their benefit. The process can be subsumed under the heading "From right to favor" (Fassin 2016). Ticktin (2012) and Fassin (2005), for example, have analyzed the development of asylum policies in France over the past decades, reporting a sharp decline in cases in which political asylum, that is, a life-long right to residency, was granted. At the same time, politicians have been promising the population a much more restrictive immigration policy. The standards for being given 'political' asylum were drastically raised and doubtful cases were dropped. People's chances of being granted asylum are hence largely restricted to the 'humanitarian' track which is dedicated to vaguely defined individual emergencies. The characteristics the recipients of humanitarian asylum are expected to display are, according to the parameters determined by Fassin and Ticktin, helplessness and humble gratitude. They need to perform innocence and passivity, but also authenticity, because distrust arises when similar stories are being told by a large number of applicants. These requirements have come to define not only the prototype refugee but the nature of asylum too: rather than returning people their basic human rights after them having been violated by another state, it now appears as an act of charity, a generous humanitarian gesture. Ticktin summarizes this situation by arguing that the only worthy recipients of asylum are thus "morally legitimate suffering bodies" (Ticktin 2012, 4).

The paradigm shift I recapitulated according to Ticktin's case study applies far beyond France. Similar developments can be observed all over Europe: granting asylum is depoliticized, it becomes an act of morality, and an expression of empathy or compassion. The Visegrád states have fully adopted this ideal of humanitarian morality. They realized that something can be gained by framing the acceptance of refugees as a generous gesture: the semblance of moral integrity in the eyes of the population, and leverage toward the EU's demanding institutions (see Ticktin 2017). This sets a high threshold for asylum applicants. It is easy to spot 'flaws' in the stories of nearly every asylum seeker. Their bodies might be suffering, albeit not morally legitimate: the term 'economic migrant' insinuates, for example, that economic hardships are not severe enough to be deserving of foreign help. Or the migrants are accused of having forfeited their moral capital by fleeing instead of fighting, which would have been their 'duty.' In some cases, their body is assumed not to be suffering at all, but vital and instrumental in a conspiracy to harm their hosting society.

Slovak politics has obviously enacted the "morally legitimate suffering"—threshold for asylum since 2015. A crucial effect of showcasing impeccable victimhood is that it becomes easier to delegitimize asylum seekers who do not indisputably fit into that category. These individuals are not only denied asylum, but they are also morally reprimanded or even criminalized for trying to claim refugee status 'illegitimately,' thus polluting the label. Sinister stereotypes for asylum applicants are established and consolidated; they are imagined as "preemptive suspects" (Stephen 2017) or "crimmigrants" (Haggerty et al. 2011).

Refugee supporters' priority, in this heated climate, is to enhance the legitimacy of 'their' refugees and protect them from hostilities and even violence. In their endeavor to rebut common fears and prejudices, refugee supporters too focus on the refugee's vulnerability and misery—thus making them correspond to the same label. Refugee support organizations are often gatekeepers for the media, connecting journalists and refugees who are willing to tell their stories. They often select and present those refugees with particularly grim fates in their countries of origin: the couple whose children were kidnapped, the boy who lost both his parents, the female TV producer who lost her job and prestige because she was too successful "for a woman," as she reported. They do so for a good reason: media outlets that do make the effort and talk to refugees are eager to present them as 'legitimate,' to convey to the reader the feeling that they deserve to be in Slovakia and are immensely grateful for it. They never fail to inquire about abuse, violence, persecution, and feelings of fear and gratitude; and if respondents provide such statements, they usually make the headline of the article (E.g., "It is possible to forget the attacks, but life without a husband is hard,"[30] "A Burundian in Slovakia: Europe is like paradise for us,"[31] "Refugees experience Christmas without war and fear"[32]). NGO employees themselves also highlight their clients' pain and suffering; they often give a poignant and dramatic account of their fate whenever they are in contact with external service providers such as doctors or state officials. When social worker Uršuľa tried to enroll the child of a client in a kindergarten, she presented the family as follows:

> I really admire them. They lost the life standard they were used to, and it takes all of their energy to build an existence in Slovakia. But they have more freedom here. The children enjoy cycling around town in the evening, especially the girls. They would never be able to do that in Iraq because it's too dangerous.

This short empathetic appeal alludes to an easily recognizable and universally acknowledged spectrum of suffering, innocence, and legitimacy: a despotic regime, a guiltless child, an oppressed female, resilient victims. Every social worker has a repertoire of these miniature testimonials of impeccable victimhood to negotiate their clients' access

---

30. Apríl Magazín: "Na útoky sa zabudnúť dá, no život bez manžela je ťažký. Takto sa v Bratislave žije Somálčanke Khadre a jej synčekovi." 26.09.2017. Accessed 21.11.2020. https://aprilmagazin.curaprox.com/na-utoky-sa-zabudnut-da-no-zivot-bez-manzela-je-tazky-takto-sa-v-bratislave-zije-somalcanke-khadre-a-jej-syncekovi/.

31. Aktuality.sk: "Burunďan na Slovensku: Európa je pre nás raj." 28.11.2017, updated 11.01.2018. Accessed 21.11.2020. https://www.aktuality.sk/clanok/536917/burundan-na-slovensku-europa-je-pre-nas-raj/?fbclid=IwAR3mPOf5WSbardJWs-_80THo_BDujvLBhbF3sAbuR29ekCxqNT2sAwlctxI .

32. Katolícke noviny: "Utečenci prežijú Vianoce v mieri a bez strachu." 30.12.2016. Accessed 30.04.2019. https://old.katolickenoviny.sk/5152-2016-utecenci-preziju-vianoce-v-mieri-a-bez-strachu/.

to just and equal treatment and shed the suspicions that 'their' refugees exploit the social system, pursue economic interests, or concoct criminal plans.

In short, refugee supporters have to adopt the 'moral legitimacy' paradigm to counter their opponent's accusations effectively. In doing so, they perpetuate and legitimize a much more exclusive understanding of asylum than they perhaps could: sentimentally charged favor rather than immutable right. The comprehensive imperative to see the lines of division between political opponents as hard and fast and discard ideas from one's opponents perpetuates the impression that there is a categorical clash of opinions. In reality, supporters and opponents largely recur to the same definition of legitimate asylum claimants, the first using it primarily to argue that particular individuals correspond to it and the second to argue that they do not.

We have seen that the idea of a rift running through Slovak society is based on actual differences and disagreements, but the demarcations are much blurrier than this image suggests, and efforts to bridge it are part of the political agenda of both 'sides.' It is upheld mainly to protect and repeatedly reaffirm one's own deep moral convictions and value system. Hence, like-minded people gather in communities that are separated from each other through imagined, but impactful empathy walls toward those with fundamentally different views. The distribution of refugee supporters and refugee opponents into irreconcilable camps forms an indelible part of this image which shapes the political realities in which refugee care takes place.

Throughout the rift imaginary, individuals' understandings of themselves as moral persons play a very important role in where people place themselves politically and how they come to think about refugees. These moral dispositions are closely tied to their emotional commitments and bonds with other people. This is the focus of the next chapter—in which I describe the theoretical framework of individual morality and emotionality and conceptualize the capability to act within emotional and moral 'messiness.'

Chapter 3

MORALITIES AND EMOTIONS

Who Is Jakub?

A few weeks into fieldwork in Nitra, I met up with Jakub in a local park to discuss my impressions from my research up to that point. I had known Jakub longer than other interlocutors since we had met at a three-day workshop on "Fighting radicalization with art," an event organized by a Bratislava NGO, aimed at activists and pedagogues right at the beginning of my fieldwork. Now, a few weeks after I started doing participant observation at Pomoc a Nádej, I felt it was the right time, and Jakub was the right person, to go beyond discussion of everyday matters and the little crises of refugee work and address some of the questions I had been brooding over: about refugee supporters' biographies, their negotiation of values and political pressures, their attitudes toward their clients—and how their actions and decisions emerged from the messy situation surrounding them. It was a warm day in mid-April, enticing dozens of families to recover bikes and roller skates from their garages and take them outside to the sunlight for the first time this year. Amid this jolly and noisy crowd, sitting on an ale bench, with a fragrant beer in front of him, Jakub looked like a man quite content with his life. Jakub was my gatekeeper at the organization in Nitra. Less than two years earlier, he had assumed the project manager's position for a refugee help organization, leading a small team of three social workers, an administrative worker, and a standby interpreter. Jakub was known for getting along with anyone and his extrovert approach and tireless effort to liven up every situation with his witty, mocking, but never harmful jokes.

On the sunny bench near the Nitra park kiosk, Jakub reflected on the recent changes in his life. They were quite substantial. Jakub had abandoned his job as a researcher and pedagogue at the University of Prešov's Faculty of Engineering. It was the kind of work he loved and considered himself to be good at, but the quickly eroding state of the Slovak education system and the meager financial prospects pushed him out of university. Now, about three years later, he did not regret his decision. His new life in Nitra suited him—not only because he liked his current job as a project manager and it paid him more but also because Jakub felt that this surrounding made it easier for him to be the person he wanted to be—in short, to be good. In Prešov, he had a circle of close friends, he often went out drinking with colleagues and students, returning home early in the morning. However much he enjoyed that lifestyle, it led him to neglect his health as much as his spiritual development.

The boredom of the little mountain town brought Jakub a new focus. This also concerned his religiosity. He saw his work as an important output of his faith: working evenings and weekends to help others certainly meant putting his strength to a good end.

When he was younger, the collection bag in church always made him feel uncomfortable. He did not like the competition it introduced among community members, the fact that it was mandatory, and that you did not know what the money was used for. He felt that with his charitable work, he found a way to make a much more direct and meaningful "sacrifice." In addition, he advances in his development as a Christian. Working with a disadvantaged group like refugees is an exercise in optimism, not letting yourself get pulled down by setbacks and difficulties. It was hard but ultimately necessary to acknowledge that humans cannot do everything on their own: they need to be humble, patient, and ultimately trusting in divine guidance. Whenever Jakub catches himself getting angry or grumpy with a client, he is consoled by the certainty that each day is a new chance to start over and be better. "If you want to do it alone, it's going to come out bad," Jakub said with confidence and a smile. This is why, despite all the flaws and deficits he has discovered in himself, he is still sure that he is where God wants him to be.

On a different occasion, a few days before, when we were driving back to the office after visiting a client, Jakub told me how he got his job as a project manager. The match was so random and accidental that it can easily pass as fateful. One day, Jakub visited the woman who would soon become his girlfriend. This happened to be in the office of the refugee organization in Nitra. As luck would have it, the project leader at that time was about to step back from his post and was desperately looking for a replacement for him. The jolly stranger who was dropping by the office to chat with one of his employees seemed like a perfect fit. He asked her for information on her suitor, and called Jakub soon thereafter, offering him the part-time position of a project manager. Jakub accepted the offer.

Holding the steering wheel casually with one hand, Jakub went on to say that the best thing about this job was that it was not "classic management" at all. It does not mean sitting in an office and looking at numbers, no—it is a very hands-on job. It includes several hours a day of engagement with people, partly difficult ones, and tons of practical assignments like helping people move, putting together furniture, and the like. He has to bear so much in mind about the families and each member individually, with their respective problems, educational issues, health conditions, and plans for the future. It is a huge responsibility. Although, as he adds, pensively, after a little pause, he did not want to make too many decisions but rather empower others to make the right decision for themselves.

Know Thy Neighbor as Yourself

Introspection as a heuristic device

I wanted to know what kind of person Jakub was, and Jakub was eager to explain what kind of person he was. However elusive, partial, and biased this account may be, I feel that I have conveyed to the reader what moral principles drive Jakub and how he feels about being a project manager in refugee support. These statements may seem plausible, but they draw on several presumptions that deserve closer scrutiny. I want to show in my ethnography of refugee supporters how aspects as intimate and individual as personal morality and emotion are indicative of their nestedness in their social world, featuring in their practice of refugee care. To argue that this narrow and individualizing perspective has epistemic validity, we first have to assume that we can understand what our counterpart wants to communicate, and we also have to suppose that the other person has the capacity to know him- or herself well enough to talk somewhat truthfully about their own emotions and moral guidelines. We have only limited access to how other people work. Can we assume that pieces of information gained from introspection and external investigation are compatible, and can thus come close to something like assured knowledge? And what do we as ethnographers do with the contradictions, inconsistencies, and incoherences in such fundamental matters as emotion and morality? Which theoretical tools can be used not only to acknowledge but to analyze these ambiguities? These are the questions I will focus on in the upcoming introduction of the theoretical deliberations and concepts that inform my ethnography. I will use glimpses of my ethnography to point out the theory's links to empirical facts already while unfolding it.

Aware of the urgency and difficulty of these issues, Nigel Rapport (2007) suggests conceptualizing anthropology as a cosmopolitan endeavor, with 'everyone' being its subject, and introspection as the prime methodological approach. This runs counter to the dominant narrative anthropology has established over decades of existence as a scholarly discipline, as Rapport's genealogy reveals. Anthropology has always been proud of its accomplishment of putting the power of culture in the spotlight and demonstrating through thick ethnographic description how thoroughly individuals are shaped by their social surroundings. Anthropologists challenged the Enlightenment idea of the reasonable individual, equipped with the intellectual resources to make sense of her or his life, and unearthed an abundance of cultural constraints, expectations, gendered norms, unwritten rules, social roles, and other conventions imposed by a collective structure. With this perspective in mind, anthropology contributed to dividing humanity up into holistic (usually national or ethnic) communities that homogenized people's behaviors, reducing individual personality to an actualization of a shared collective consciousness. Of course, this worldview easily lends itself to ideological endeavors, which Rapport summarizes as a "romantic conditionalism" (Rapport 2007, 261).

At the same time, anthropological methods have always assumed a basic commensurability of human experience. Ethnography only works if you assume that 'outlandish' behaviors and customs become palpable upon closer inspection, and that unfamiliar norms and feelings lose some of their opacity after prolonged exposure.

Rapport calls for a new awareness and appreciation for this general familiarity of the human condition, an acknowledgment of individualism and universalism at the same time. Humans are congruent in many ways: we have a body and a psyche; we are aware of our mortality; and we are situated in a social or cultural context in which we need to fashion ourselves and maintain relationships. Rapport lists the ways the experience of being human might help us to understand other humans:

> I know myself to be a complex, even conflicted whole, comprising rationality and passion, will and self-defeat, desire and nostalgia. It is this recognition that I advocate translating into anthropological method. It is not a "stepping into another's shoes," not to be

metaphorized quite like empathy. It is more like recognizing a radical otherness, a gratuitous individuality. [...] While not claiming to put one in another's place, introspection gives
onto a recognition of Everyone's practising an individuality commensurately. Everyone is
capacitated alike amid the diverse embodiments of individual lives. (Rapport 2007, 26)

Resorting to introspection as a yardstick for proper understanding and action is, of
course, not an anthropological prerogative but a very common everyday technique. For
example, refugee supporters revisit feelings of loneliness and vulnerability they experienced when they studied or worked abroad to develop an understanding of their clients'
situation.

The ubiquity of inconsistency

Let's assume that we can know about others because we know about ourselves. But what
exactly is this self of ours and others we aspire to know about? How definite and reliable
can this knowledge be if the 'selves' that we meet keep eluding our grasp?

One day, I was sitting down for lunch in a canteen with Jakub, the interpreter, and
one more employee. Milan, the interpreter, only works for the NGO upon demand.
Otherwise, he is a journalist and a well-traveled man. While we were waiting for our
food, Milan was getting worked up. The conversation had started out by complaining
about the tendencies of the NGO's clients to ignore well-meant advice. He backed up
his portrayal of them as being stubborn and unteachable with stories of other so-called
primitive communities that came to his mind. Among others, he told the story of a
missionary who could only convince some African residents to introduce a disinfection
habit at their local hospital after making it look like it was their idea—it was the only
way to get it into their "slow little brains." The succession of anecdotes was random but
the derogatory undertone was clear.

What caught me off guard was Jakub's and his colleague's silent approval of this
inflammatory narrative. Not only did they sit motionlessly through the racist slurs—
Jakub even picked up the thread and continued to explain that counseling his clients
and repeating the same advice, again and again, is the best he can do. His job is to
integrate "these people," so he has to continue doing what he does, even if the chances
for some individuals to succeed are highly unrealistic. He did not correct Milan's gener-
alizations and did not disapprove of the insinuation that the failure of refugees in Slovak
society could be explained by a lack of cognitive capacities.

If Jakub suddenly appears to be a different person than on the park bench, if how he
acts is not in tune with what he said or did in that setting—how do I know who among
the two persons I seem to have met is actually Jakub? This did not seem to be the Jakub
I spent most of my time in the field with, one who saw his manager position as a blessing, and as his sacrifice to God, one who thought he was right where he belonged and
insisted that his clients had the same right as anybody else to take a loan, buy a car, or
have another child. I was struggling to integrate that lunch scene into the image I had
acquired of Jakub as a person and as a professional. Introspection reminds me of how
hard it may be for me as well to interfere with people who speak in a frenzy, especially

if that person is a friend or someone I need to get along with. I also know the satisfying feeling of being told that the job you do is crazy hard. In Rapports' words,

> [l]ooking inside oneself one knows the complex connections among one's thoughts, emotions, and actions. One knows one's habits of doubt, hope, and desire. One knows the seamless continuity (and variety) of consciousness which overrides differences in external context and relationship in significant ways. One knows one's centerdness in one's own life. One knows the tensions arising from being with or for oneself as against being with or for others: the issues of self-presentation. (Rapport 2007, 268)

If we recognize, from our own experience, the irresolvable conflicts the consciousness is constantly struggling with, it is only proper to question the stability of the self more generally and to do so without moralizing. This does not mean sacrificing conceptualizations of the autonomous self completely in favor of biological and structuralist or culturalist angles.[1] I will elaborate further on how practice theory addresses the simultaneous autonomy and inconsistency of the individual by pointing to the multiplicity of fields people engage in, and the slippages and transferals that occur between those. We shall also see shortly that morality and emotions have both been particularly contentious issues in this debate, oscillating between expressions of utmost innerness or as realizations of genetic information or cultural templates (and everything in between).

Along with most contemporary theorists, I believe it is reasonable to envision the self as being caught in between multifarious constraining factors and a space on its own. One of the biggest challenges of taking the individual seriously and putting it at the heart of an analytical inquiry is that people are indeed messy. How can one

---

1. There is a tendency in social theory to shift back and forth between problematizing and asserting the individual subject as an identifiable entity. Especially within poststructuralism, the idea of any form of 'I' or 'self' is challenged, at least one that has the capacity to reflect, critique, and exercise agency. This has even led theorists to announce the 'death of the subject.' As a consequence, 'morality' is seen mostly as a farce, actors are deceived into believing they have deliberative freedom when all they do is enact preconceived structures (Mattingly 2014). In her now classic review of anthropological theory in the decades before 1980, Sherry Ortner (1984) identifies the turn from structure and determination toward practice and agency as one of the most consequential changes of direction the discipline ever experienced. In the late 1970s, scholars came to realize that they might have neglected the capacities of the individual to know him- or herself and act autonomously. When seeing 'culture' or 'structure' behind everything, two problems arise: Firstly, these approaches struggle to deliver a satisfying account for social change (while we observe that cultures are highly dynamic and can change at a considerable pace!). Secondly, the fact that every articulation of culture still emerges from an individual mind and not some detached collective transcendental entity is strangely blurred. Ortner observes that most scholars do not take the study of structure and individual practice and agency to be mutually exclusive; rather, one can be a valuable amendment to the other. The problem of change and the problem of the knowledgeable subject need to be thought together. By highlighting agency, both problems can be linked persuasively: people have needs, desires, and plans that do not agree with conventions. Through the tensions and frictions that arise in such situations, changes occur. They may have minimal impact at first but also potentially shake entire systems.

assume fully self-aware individuals who can acknowledge the ways in which they are influenced, perform a cognitive evaluation of themselves, and make value judgments on particular aspects of their existence, if what people say and do at any given time remains so obscure and unpredictable? David Berliner (2016) addressed this issue in a programmatic discussion piece in *hau,* calling for an "anthropology of contradictions." He observes the frequency, one might even say the ubiquity of contradictive behavior, in a doctor who smokes, an environmentalist who is also a frequent flyer, a feminist student singing along with a sexist but catchy tune (or a well-traveled interpreter who is racist?). These apparent clashes, says Berliner, should urge us to revisit notions of the unified and consistent agent. He is particularly intrigued by how easily people ignore these inconsistencies, accepting them into their lifeworlds without tangible distress. "For anthropologists, I believe, it is time to bring back ambivalent statements, contradictory attitudes, incompatible values, and emotional-internal clashes as research objects" (Berliner et al. 2016, 6).

I am particularly interested in how emotions and value judgments, and adjunct decisions on how to practice refugee care, oscillate in daily practice. I want to unpack how they reflect but never reproduce the polarized public debate at large. When I followed Jakub and the others doing their daily work and listened to their explanations of what they were doing, they enacted ideals simultaneously that actually seemed to be on opposite sides of a spectrum: paternalism and empowerment, friendship and professional detachment, appreciation for or problematization of cultural difference. Actors were often aware of these incoherencies and discussed the respective opposing arguments at length—without arriving at a unitary frame. Thus, these issues stayed within the realm of everyday decision-making. I, therefore, apply an anthropology of morality approach which acknowledges the fundamental contingency, maybe even fragmentation, of the self, and assumes a degree of awareness and command. In the following paragraphs, I will give a short overview of anthropological approaches to morality and emotion. Only if we conceive of emotional reactions and moral guidelines not as predefined and lasting, but volatile structures can we gain a deeper understanding of how moral persons in refugee care encounter, engender, and process contradictions.

Morality and Emotions as Evaluations

Morality and emotion have been studied in parallel fashion, and sometimes in explicit connection, insofar as they are situated somewhere at the border between cognition and intuition or the mind and the body. The question of whether to attribute these motions to the cognitive or unconscious realm is particularly complex, regarding the fact that they are evaluative. Both concepts of emotion and morality circumscribe dimensions of being-in-the-world that are not indifferent—they entail an enmeshment in the world around us that activates normative value judgments. While being moral, we ask ourselves what is 'right' and what is 'wrong,' and while being emotional, we determine the importance of a particular event or circumstance for our personal well-being (Laidlaw 2014; Nussbaum 2001). More often than not, these two evaluations come to bear on each other (Solomon 1988; Prinz 2003): doing the right thing feels good (or bad), and feeling a certain thing is regarded morally wrong (or right). It is only through their evaluative function that morality and emotion together inform action. How do these evaluations come about, are they more akin to conscious reflections, or automated impulses? In this muddled borderland between cognition and intuition, it becomes difficult to neatly circumscribe the realms of morality and emotion respectively: several components of doing morality, like having a bad conscience, empathy, pity, or an 'impulse to help' stem from the semantic field of affect and emotion. One way of thinking about morality is that it is an engagement with the impression of what *feels* wrong or right. (The question of how far this preemptive feeling is already a product of cognitive activity will be addressed below.)

During my fieldwork, I witnessed refugee supporters debating excessively about what is 'right,' weighing intuition and rationality, reflecting on their spontaneous reactions and juxtaposed alternative approaches while continuing to act in conflicting and incoherent ways. These evaluative judgments are intrinsically but inconclusively linked to action, and therefore I want to examine morality and emotion in tandem, building and expanding on existing attempts to conceptualize the intersection between both concepts.

The anthropology of morality

I will first introduce the anthropology of morality framework that I am employing here. This I will use as a contrasting foil to point out parallels and convergences with the study of emotions. The anthropological engagement with morality is as old as the discipline itself, but over the past 20 years, a broad effort to reconceptualize morality as a core theme of anthropological inquiry has led to the emergence of a comprehensive and, despite some contested issues, incremental and cohesive body of literature that, taken together, allows a sound analytical grasp of the issue. Contributors to this so-called moral turn include Joel Robbins, Jarrett Zigon, Michael Lambek, James Laidlaw, James Faubion, and Cheryl Mattingly. Although their approaches and contextual frameworks vary, their agenda remains essentially this: to raise awareness for ethics and morality as a key subject of anthropological research, long hijacked by an overwhelming reliance on the Durkheimian paradigm, which assumed that the ethical is basically congruent with the social and not worthy of particular attention. Their move against this still prominent conceptualization starts from the acceptance of the subject as free and ethical, and morality as practice, and as ordinary.

What the scholars of the moral turn aim for is not to understand ethics and morality as a distinct domain, but to use it as an epistemological tool to refine the understanding of social life (Lambek 2010). That means their premise is neither a normative one, like assuming that people generally are or strive to be 'good'; nor do they want to abstract rules for what is universally considered good and just behavior. Their project starts from the rather simple observation which I already mentioned above, namely that people are evaluative. Refugee supporters, for example, critically engage with the Migration Office's, their colleagues' and their opponents' take on refugee care, they compare approaches in terms of their overall goodness, they review their own past behavior, and all these judgments have tangible impacts on the way they act (Laidlaw 2014). This approach stands opposed to that commonly referred to as Durkheimian, namely that any form of human action is an actualization of a given set of dominant social norms. This perspective suggests that the constraints of the social structure determine individuals' behavior as long as they are successful in promoting the common good, inspiring each community member through institutional socialization (Lambek 2010; Faubion 2001; Laidlaw 2014; Mattingly 2013, 2014; Zigon 2011). In this model, there can be no dilemma about what the right course of action is, because obligations are tightly woven into the tissue of any given society and automatically felt to be 'good' (the fact that it might be challenging or exhausting to *implement* the right course of actions being a different issue altogether).

Critics have maintained that the aforementioned authors do not do justice to French sociologist Émile Durkheim, who had a more sophisticated view of morality than these abridged versions suggest. Durkheim acknowledged very well that the "tendency of the moral conscience to link the morality of the act with the autonomy of the actor is a fact one cannot deny and which must be accounted for" (1973 [1925], 112, as in Dyring 2018, 228). However, what contemporary scholars of morality attack is not so much Durkheim himself but the social scientists following him, heralding the persuasiveness of the social as their primary concern, thus equating the moral with what is socially desired and the immoral with that which is socially sanctioned. These critics discard this view as unrealistic: it is quite simply inconceivable to create a moral codex so extensive and convincing that any possible situation is covered. They fill the vacuum between moral philosophy and anthropology and regret that an account for ethical freedom is missing or denied in the discipline. Cheryl Mattingly (2014) claims that the followers of Durkheim commit an epistemological fallacy: people do not think of themselves as duplicates of a universal model, as occupants of a third-person category; even if their perception may be influenced by their previous engagements with the social world, they still maintain first-person access to their own experiences, then attune it to the outside world. Given the contingency of the social world and the existence of subjects who are aware of themselves at least to a certain degree, it becomes possible to envision a space for freedom in the moral domain. Laidlaw, Robbins, and Zigon discern 'ethics' as an everyday activity that presupposes thought, reflection, and voluntariness. They assign this activity a different quality than mere rule-following, automated and embodied behavior that is instilled with certain ideas about the good and just without the reflective elements, which they contrastingly call 'morality.'[2]

The ethical subject which is created through such an intellectual move is still elusive, however. Different circumstances allow varying resources for reflective practice,

---

2. The distinction between the two denotations 'morality' and 'ethics' is made a little bit differently by each author. I find it hard to identify a decisive advantage of any one of these sophisticated distinctions for my project that would provide an epistemological surplus to the commonsense uses of these words. I thus stick with the conventions of everyday language (like Mattingly and Lambek) which do not provide a neat delineation but associate 'morality' rather with the primordial, unconscious, embodied, ordinary, malleable end of the spectrum, while 'ethics' invokes thought, reflection, ideals, and commitment.

institutions can be more or less repressive, and relations of power can be more or less asymmetrical (Laidlaw 2014, 109). What exactly ethical freedom entails in any concrete situation is thus historically and culturally specific.

Acknowledging freedom in individual ethics and morality does not mean ignoring patterns and codes provided by society; indeed, the declared mission of the theorists of the moral turn is to scrutinize the interface of free ethical choice and the "reference to ideals, values, models, practices, relationships, and institutions that are amenable to ethnographic study" (Laidlaw 2002, 327). Just note, as we have seen in the previous chapter, how deeply embedded people are in their respective filter bubbles concerning refugee care and acceptance. Despite all ambiguities, it is reasonable to assume that their identification with the respective side of the rift is of paramount importance for moral and emotional evaluations and consequently for action. Laidlaw suggests seeing culture as circumscribing a domain for choice—this way one must not discard the valuable insights from the literature on social determination but can focus on the complicated ways in which individual freedom and 'structure' work together.

Nevertheless, theorists reject the idea that freedom in moral questions simply means deciding which of the various moral codes at one's disposal in a given situation is applicable. Robbins affirms that individual choice is located at the points of friction between different value spheres. Ethical subjects may break with the reproduction imperative and assume freedom of choice (Robbins 2007, 299). But moral decisions are not always experienced or framed as meaningful symbolic acts, nor preceded by lengthy considerations. A lot of it happens on the fly. This is why the concept of "ordinary ethics" presented in an anthology of the same name, edited by Michael Lambek (2010), yielded a lot of agreement. For Lambek, ethics is 'ordinary' firstly in that actors can never evade the ethical condition. Ethics is intrinsic to human character formation; it is deeply embedded in language and needs not be singled out as a separate category of human thought or action. Secondly, it usually flies below the radar. Morality, in most cases, is simply *done* inconspicuously rather than stimulating excessive deliberation. Lambek decidedly pledges to searching morality in continual practices rather than singular acts and understanding it as a property of action rather than a product of reason. "In this sense, the ordinary is intrinsically ethical and ethics intrinsically ordinary. Insofar as ordinary ethics refers to the actual and circumstantial—specific instances of conduct, insight, action or dilemma—anthropology, in its ethnographic refraction, can usefully respond to Austin's request for 'fieldwork in philosophy'" (Lambek 2010, 3–4).

To recapitulate, the authors of the moral turn develop an anthropological theory of morality that sees it as an evaluative response to a complex and equivocal world, being constituted by divergent social norms, shaped through practice, and manifested in action. They thus assign it a never precisely localizable position between those realms of the human condition that are amenable to agentive manipulation and those that are not.

The anthropology of emotion

In the literature on emotions, human nature and 'structure' have been juxtaposed similarly, while the existence or scope of the conscious or the autonomous within the self has been contested. Similar to morality, the nature-structure dichotomy can be projected onto a body-mind dichotomy. The preferred approach is to assume an inner and an outer world, weighing their respective importance and impact on the unfolding of individual emotionality against each other. The proponents of 'nature' assume the source of emotionality to be located in the physical structures of the body, while those of 'culture' prioritize the norms, patterns, and so on, that play out in intersubjective space and are absorbed by individual minds (Rosaldo 1984; Svašek 2005; Josephides 2005; Throop 2012; Scheer 2012).

This debate has been fought in close connection to discussions around ethical questions. In the philosophical canon, we usually read about 'passions' as an element of the human physical existence, having a role in either obstructing or fueling virtuousness. One tradition, exemplified by the Stoics, Descartes, Montesquieu and, more recently, Alasdair MacIntyre (2003), speaks of the necessity to 'tame' desire to cultivate a virtuous and socially compatible person.[3] This has been denoted, among others by historian Barbara Rosenwein, as a "hydraulic model," ascribing emotion as a destructive force if insufficiently contained (Plamper 2010, 53–54). The other tradition, proposed by Scottish moral sense theorists like David Hume and Adam Smith, and also by Jacques Rousseau, is to locate the source of goodness exactly in the emotional realm and demand it be freed from the 'unnatural' constraints and distortions of civilization (Throop 2012; Svašek 2005; Lutz 1986; Solomon 1988). In the positivist age, emotion appeared to be first and foremost an evolutionary necessary biological response to stimuli (Damasio 2005 [1994]). If we see a snake, we feel fear; the processing of the visual information directly translates into a bodily and life-sustaining reaction, like rising adrenaline levels and a heartbeat that prepares for flight or fight. Neurobiological findings challenge the humanities to take the material/bodily side of emotionality seriously (Prinz 2003; Svašek 2005; Scheer 2012).

Early moral philosophy and neurobiology remains influential, but most theorists nowadays imagine emotion in a broader, more flexible sense. There is a consensus among social scientists and philosophers that emotion, like morality, entails both cognitive and more primordial elements, and that both its expression and its contents are socioculturally constructed and thus historically and culturally specific (Hitzer 2011, 6). Another parallel to theories of morality is the volatility and indeterminacy that characterize emotionality when it is not regulated by comprehensive norms or rules.[4] William

---

3. The idea that emotional states are associated with lower levels of intelligence, intentionality, and consciousness is, of course, a deeply gendered understanding and was used throughout (at least Western European) history to legitimize the inferiority of female assumed 'sentimentality' compared to male 'restraint' (Lutz 1986, 291). It does not only concern 'dark' emotions that pose a threat to the social fabric of a given community, like anger or jealousy. Even the expression of affectionate and caring movements is, under certain circumstances, decried as weak or sentimental.

4. Again, there are many sophisticated terminological distinctions between the more physical, immediate and the more pronounced, culturally codified manifestations of feeling, referring to words such as mood and affect for the first and emotion for the latter. They often take the fundamental contrast Brian Massumi develops in *Parables for the Virtual* (2002) as a starting point and add their own refinements and restrictions. Again, I refrain from adopting any of

Reddy, who combined approaches from anthropology and cognitive psychology for his pathbreaking *The Navigation of Feeling* (2001), juxtaposed just that, individuals' efforts to navigate feeling, to learned and internalized "emotional regimes" (ibid., 129). Emotion emerges from an ongoing conversation between individuals and the world that surrounds them. To get hold of an emotion, the individual has to translate back and forth between 'inner' experience and the ever-deficient frameworks and vocabulary society provides to make sense of these sentiments—a process that he characterizes as imprecise, although not completely arbitrary (ibid., 80).

As I mentioned above, morality and emotion are similar (and often intersect temporally) because they represent evaluations. In my view, Jesse Prinz's formulation "evaluative judgments plus responses to bodily states" (2003, 73) applies to most contemporary theories of emotion. The idea of identifying the cognitive component of emotion as a form of judgment goes back to Aristotle. He used the example of anger, which is essentially the processing of a real or perceived offense, the recognition of an unjust treatment directly followed by a desire for remedial action, for instance in the shape of revenge (Solomon 1988, 79). Robert Solomon calls emotions "self-interested, desire-defined judgments" (1988, 80) and Martha Nussbaum notes that they are "cognitive appraisals or evaluations, they focus on my goals, and they incorporate external objects in the scheme of my goals" (2001, 4). Being emotional, then, means that something with an immediate effect on my well-being has happened. Jesse Prinz explains that "[i]n assenting, one evaluates a judgment about well-being as appropriate. If I feel sad, it is not just that I recognize a loss; I also judge that my sense of loss is warranted" (2003, 72).

These judgments which set the object and the subject into a meaningful relation, then, share some specific characteristics. Jesse Prinz calls them "embodied appraisals" (2003, 69)—they are embodied insofar as they are closely coupled with bodily states that respond to the way the external factors bear on a subject's well-being. Solomon develops a theory of emotional judgments which he characterizes as "prereflectively constitutive of experience" (1988, 81). They are spontaneous rather than deliberative, usually remain unarticulated, and have the action potential already built into them. He also maintains that moral judgments are often included as already "essential ingredients" (ibid., 85) of emotion. If anger entails the judgment that one has been wronged, there must be some existing, underlying method of telling right from wrong. A particular emotion, then, results from a system of judgments which are importantly informed

---

the suggested distinctions or developing my own. This is, firstly, because I believe that the wealth of related but slightly different definitions hampers rather than stimulates a productive scientific discourse on fundamental issues like the ones that are being negotiated here. Secondly, I find these kinds of categorizations a bit arbitrary. Like in the case of morality and ethics, it is certainly possible to identify different manifestations of feeling with diverging emphases, but it is very difficult to determine where one category should end and the other should begin. If claiming that even vague, emergent feelings are socially and culturally informed, and (with Reddy) that even identified and publicly proclaimed emotions are subject to change and re-evaluation, a binary distinction does not seem to sufficiently account for these differentiations.

by memory. Thus, the judgment, however embodied, is culturally informed by past experiences, education, socialization, and so on.

Emotion and morality are thus not only simultaneous judgments, but they also oscillate between being quite intuitive, pre-reflective, bodily mediated responses and processes more akin to what is commonly understood as 'decisions' in which the mediating role of an autonomous self becomes conceivable. To understand how morality and emotion congeal in the self to form judgments, it is essential to note that the question of "Who do others/who does society want me to be?" is closely connected to the question "Who do I want to be?" It feels good to be good to others; being a good person is a source of purpose and validation. The persons we interact with, are dependent on, or responsible for (in the jargon of the anthropology or morality usually referred to as 'ethical others'), are inseparable from our own existence (Faubion 2011, 120). Mattingly maintains that we make commitments about social practices not, or not only because they have a constraining force, but also because "they matter to us" (Mattingly 2014, 12). We regard them as part of a life that we consider happy and worthwhile. Tragically, as Martha Nussbaum notes, it is exactly the relationships with other people, especially those involving liable emotions like love, friendship, and responsibility, that bring the greatest joy and are at the same time the biggest risk factors for pain and suffering. There is no beauty without vulnerability (Nussbaum 2011 [1986], 2). Nussbaum advocates an Aristotelian approach to this dilemma which, instead of eliminating the risk that is connected to these emotions, the "incursions of luck" (Nussbaum 2011, 3) from one's life, promotes embracing life's vagaries and developing and "excellence" in managing difficult emotional situations safely.

This is why morality is often examined in the private domains of life in which we invest emotionally, like family life or faith. Many theories of morality focus on these domains. Bernard Williams (Smart and Williams 1973) coined for this purpose the term "ground projects," those fundamental goals or tasks in life that are most intricately linked with a person's identity. Failing at these projects is easily equated with having a failed biography altogether; it has disastrous outcomes on a person's relationship with him- or herself. Raising a child, sustaining a family, or striving for eternal salvation are the most obvious examples of such all-encompassing life missions.

In line with this, I claim that the depth of identification of refugee supporters with their work makes the workplace an equally important outlet for moral becoming. Throughout my ethnography, I show how refugee supporters are emotionally invested in their professional projects. They develop affectionate and caring attitudes toward refugees, rejoice in their successes, and empathetically share their pain and suffering. They experience intense disappointment, anger, impatience, frustration, anxiety, and exhaustion in their work every day; their well-being is crucially linked to the refugees' behavior and performance. For Jakub, helping Iraqis means having a sense of purpose, *and* it helps him develop into the kind of person, the kind of Christian he wants to be. He is so absorbed by his emotional attachment to his protégées that he blurs the boundaries between work and the private sphere: being available beyond office hours, sacrificing weekends to provide his friends even greater help and orientation, is a sign for Jakub that he is doing his job the way he should!

At this point, I have to make a concession: the altruist ground project was just one of several into which Jakub fit his job. On many occasions, Jakub told me quite the opposite, that his aim was, essentially, to make himself superfluous. His job description told him to aim at integrating and emancipating his clients as soon as possible, and that meant minimizing rather than maximizing his effort and interference. "Having a good relationship is nice, but I prefer a professional relationship. Sympathies can change in a day, and then it's good to have a sound professional basis to fall back on," he told me. It was clear that he was also addressing himself, knowing well that he had already spent many evenings and weekends on friendly turns that were not part of his job description. He was fully aware that his actions were sometimes at odds with one another, perceiving this as the outcome of a struggle of mind against heart.

All the anthropologists of morality observe that "[a]ctually living a life requires doing so with reference to values that make conflicting demands and managing the inherently irresolvable tensions between them" (Laidlaw 2014, 169). They denote this quandary as "multiple moralities" (Zigon 2011), as "moral pluralism" (Mattingly 2014, 8), various "value spheres"[5] (Robbins 2007, 298), or as "ethical complexity" (Faubion 2011, 14). Some communities might even be suffering from a lasting "moral torment," which comes, as the term suggests, with considerable emotional repercussions. This is the case with the Urapmin in Papua New Guinea Joel Robbins describes in his influential work *Becoming Sinners: Christianity and Moral Torment in a Papua New Guinea Society* (2004). This tribe was Christianized only recently, trying to live up to the requirements of their new faith system as well as to their traditional Urapmin culture, which differ from each other in significant ways. Most notably, the Pentecostal Christian ethics demand them to disregard their innermost wishes, needs and desires and generally condemns the 'will' as sinful, whereas the traditional culture regards the will as something very positive if used to deepen and expand social relations. Robbins observes that they are constantly aware of this moral divide, and as a result, they experience their moral life to be extraordinarily difficult.

This observation can easily be replicated for emotions: evaluations, as contained in emotional responses, can be equally confusing and heteroglossic. The equivalent to "value spheres" in the study of emotions are "emotional communities" as developed by historian Barbara Rosenwein. "Emotional communities" are "social groups whose members adhere to the same valuations of emotions and their expression" (Rosenwein 2010, 1). At any time in history, each individual belongs to several emotional communities at once and commonly switches between diverging codes without giving it much thought, except if one is confronted with a markedly different set of beliefs and standards about emotionality, which can lead to confusion and turmoil (Rosenwein 2010, 24). But not just the cognitive dimension of emotional judgment is complex and enigmatic,

---

5. He borrows this terminology from Max Weber. The spheres taken for themselves are "rationally consistent," but they want to subsume all others, which, when spheres come in contact with one another, leads to clashes. In a famous metaphor, he likens these irreconcilable conflicts to "warring Gods between whom people must choose" (Robbins 2007, 297 and 299).

its outward expression can also produce puzzlement. Usually being intersubjective, the expression and reception of emotions are prone to false or partial understanding (Scheer 2012, 227).

With insights into morality, emotions and their intersections in mind, let us turn our attention back to the specific contradictions that pervade refugee supporters' care practices. As I indicated in the Introduction, there are two types of conflicts in which refugee supporters are enmeshed: the meta-level clash of a humanitarian versus nationalist, resp. liberal versus non-liberal policy approach to acknowledged refugees, and micro-level struggles that appear in the everyday confrontations with different institutions and actors. I already outlined the clash of polarized opinions on refugee policy—the suspicious and restrictive approach of official policies and large parts of the public, versus the empathetic, charitable, relativist view expressed in the language of social work and international humanitarianism. Those are the official frontlines refugee supporters are well aware of, and which they have to navigate tactically and considerately. They subscribe to an NGO's set of values, but they are also dependent on state sponsorship and the legal framework of official policies. As we shall see, they develop quite elaborate routines for making this constant confrontation manageable, and they spend a lot of time discussing things with their colleagues and trusted friends. One could say that they are permanently suspended between two different "value spheres," and corresponding "emotional communities," arresting them in a feeling of "moral torment" that never quite fades to the back of the mind.

But then again, reality is infinitely more complex than this simple juxtaposition between state and NGO approaches. Ethical demands emerge everywhere and are extended to the refugee supporters from a plenitude of collective or single actors, constituting a veritable "ethical complexity." Firstly, 'the state' and 'the humanitarian community' are large compounds whose messages and ethical demands toward refugee supporters are not as plain as the above portrayal of the debate suggests. Then, there is a variety of other actors and institutions with their own sets of values and expectations, which are in themselves contingent: schools, municipalities, healthcare facilities, job centers, religious communities, and so on, also form 'ethical others' who articulate varying demands. Not always do the expectations refugee supporters have toward these authorities overlap with their actual goals and motivations. Finally, the individual human beings who are the target of all these demands are as conflicted and unpredictable as the refugee supporters themselves: refugees do not form a homogeneous group, they have highly specific plans and expectations, and their dispositions change over time or are subject to spontaneous modifications in particular situations. Navigating the vagaries of every day costs refugee supporters immense efforts. There are too many voices to hear, too many imperatives to tend to, and too many interests to negotiate, as to design a clear moral roadmap to cover all eventualities.

As noted above, I am interested in what happens at the intersection of contradictory demands and actions, how actors attune their emotions and moral orientation to a complicated, contradictory world, and how its messiness is reflected in the things they say or do. Before turning our attention to the coping techniques they develop in the face of constant tensions and unresolved conflicts, I want to provide a more thorough account of the threshold between judgment and action. There are two major competing ways in which theorists have envisioned the translation of individual morality into action or into patterns of behavior, one of which can be summarized under the heading of self-fashioning and the other under virtue ethics. As we shall see, these two schools also have different ideas of how actors negotiate diverging ethical demands, which in my view are not mutually exclusive but complementary. Again, I will first introduce these approaches to moral practice, and then show that similar considerations apply to the anthropology of emotions as well.

Moral and Emotional Practice

Self-fashioning

Foucault's thoughts on "self-fashioning" inspired many empirical accounts of individuals' ethical behavior.[6] The term refers to all those activities aimed at shaping, forming, and adjusting the self as a result of reflective evaluation to attain a certain "subject position" (Faubion 2011, 14); to correspond to a given ideal or template in the most flawless way or perfectly fulfill certain obligations. Acts of self-fashioning

> permit individuals to affect, by their own means, a certain number of operations on—their own bodies, their own souls, their own thoughts, their own conduct—and in this manner so as to—transform themselves, modify themselves, and to attain a certain state—of perfection, happiness, purity, supernatural power. (Martin 1988, 18)

Of course, these techniques are modeled along templates that a given culture provides, suggests, or coerces with varying degrees of force. But even though this process is very much based on following certain rules and conventions, it is a highly conscious, reflective labor. Mattingly uses the image of the artisan workshop, the ethical subject being craftsmen who are aware of their imperfections but nonetheless tirelessly strive for artistic perfection (Mattingly 2013, 303). Foucault himself talks about the ambition of turning oneself into a piece of art (Foucault and Rabinow 1984, 351); an activity that requires a large amount of skill, patience, and sense of aesthetics—all highly cognitive capacities.

However, freedom in self-fashioning pertains less to the execution and more to the "selection," "the condition of the assignation of the subject or the subject's self-assignation to a subject position of a qualitatively distinguishable sort" (Faubion 2011, 115). Self-fashioning complicates our understanding of ethical freedom because it can well have complete and utter submission as a goal, for example, the ascetic lifestyles that

---

6. It is a widely shared belief that Foucault, with his focus on power, governmentality, and subjugation, denied the importance of the individual for most of his live and only hesitantly turned to a subjectivist position in his later work. Faubion gathers that this is a misconception, that Foucault never denied the self and that the individual as a location of potential resistance forms an essential part, even a presupposition for his definition of governmentality (Faubion 2001, 86).

the followers of certain religious communities or monastic orders choose to observe (Mahmood 2005; Hirschkind 2006).

Navigating feeling forms a central element of most self-fashioning projects. Many cultural schemes around the world sanction the free expression of feeling as a display of egocentrism or lack of manners, and most religions prohibit not only the following of destructive impulses, but also the emotions that may precede them. In other contexts, the absence of emotional self-expression is interpreted as unnatural or a form of "estrangement" from the social world (Lutz 1986, 290). In short, inhabiting as well as avoiding emotional states is important in terms of disciplining the self and fashioning a moral person, and oftentimes tensions arise precisely between the two motions.

With a self-fashioning framework in mind, one could envisage Jakub as striving to assume a new subject position after moving to Nitra. Naturally, he had no functional peer group as a newcomer in Nitra. Thinking about how to approach this new episode of his life, he decided that he did not need it anymore, at least not in the sense he was used to, a bunch of peers to go out and grab drinks with. He entered an ongoing commitment to avoid socializing occasions outside work and focus on himself instead. His personal re-leveling also included targets for his emotional makeup, like becoming more balanced and maintaining control of his moods so as not to cause any harm or offense. This social restraint is by no means a self-evident step for a natural extrovert like Jakub who is readily liked by everyone around him. In a way, he subjected himself to a regime of his own making, inspired by Catholic ascetic practices like a monastic lifestyle.

Virtue ethics

Foucault belongs to those thinkers who define 'ethics' as a reflective process. The notion of 'thought' as a vehicle for knowledge of the self and planning action is of prime importance in his treatment of ethics:

> Thought is not what inhabits a certain conduct and gives it its meaning; rather, it is what allows one to step back from this way of acting or reacting, to present it to oneself as an object of thought and to question it as to its meaning, its conditions, and its goals. (Foucault and Rabinow 1984, 388)

Herein lies the key difference to the second school of thought anthropologists turn to for analyzing ethical behavior: virtue ethics. Although reflective thought plays a role in this school, ethics is seen as a result of motivation and desire rather than sheer abstract reasoning and is best described as the outcome of practice, repetition, and mastery. A virtue ethics approach relies on classical Greek and Kantian ethics and has been made popular by several British scholars of moral philosophy, such as Anscombe, Foot, MacIntyre, Taylor, Wiggins, Williams, Nussbaum, Arendt, Murdoch, and Cavell, starting from the 1970s. They combine both Kant's deontological project which aims to deduce normative rules from sheer reason, and a consequentialist (utilitarian) stance which normatively defines 'good' courses of action from the perspective of the most favorable and happiness-procuring outcome. The classic reference for this school is, however, Aristotle. The Greek philosopher thinks of human life as a form of 'becoming.' He was convinced that ethical excellence resides less in the internalization and reproduction of rules but in developing an ability to reflect, judge, and arrive at the best possible course of action autonomously. This skill can only be acquired by living a life and confronting oneself with ethically challenging situations, emulating role models or 'masters.' This sets as given, of course, that life is abundantly complex, and conventions can only provide limited guidance.

As mentioned above, in this approach, emotion is closely coupled with morality, as moral virtuosity in action can only succeed when it is matched by corresponding internal desires and motivations. The vocabulary of practice, repetition, and mastery brings practice theory to the table. Reckwitz's definition of a practice as "a routinized type of behavior which consists of several elements, interconnected to one other: forms of bodily activities, forms of mental activities, 'things' and their use, a background knowledge in the form of understanding, know-how, states of emotion and motivational knowledge" (2002, 249) resonates with all those theories which conceptualize emotions as dispositions that are experienced as well as done, respectively "evaluative judgments plus responses to bodily states" (Prinz 2003, 73). Indeed, an approach building on Bourdieusian practice theory is being developed and promoted by a steadily growing number of anthropologists and historians of emotion, key among them cultural and historical anthropologist Monique Scheer's with her treatise "Are emotions a kind of practice (and is that what makes them have a history?)" (2012).

Scheer puts a particular emphasis on the embodied dimension of emotion, as the "action of the mindful body" (2012, 220). In this, she seems to stray away from virtue ethics which attempts to derive moral action from reason. But the body in her approach is conceptualized as quite permeable, as inner and outer experiences flow seamlessly into one another: emotional practices "encompass a learned, culturally specific, and habitual distribution of attention to 'inner' processes of thought, feeling, and perception" (ibid., 200).

Practice theory is particularly suitable to analyze contradiction and inconsistency in action because it offers a perspective on individual emotional subjectivities that remains elusive and contingent: according to Bourdieu, a person's habitus is a unique integration of different practices, which include embodied learned behaviors and past coping strategies, and which can be in friction with each other or with one's current surroundings.

> It leaves space for behaviors not entirely and always predictable, which can also instantiate change and resistance rather than preprogrammed reproduction. [...] The plurality of practices suffices to explain historical changes and shifts, because they collide with one another, causing misunderstandings, conflicts, and crossovers between fields. (Scheer 2012, 204)

Looking at Jakub from the angle of virtue ethics and practice theory, some other aspects come into view, like the processual, adaptive, inventive character of his ethical decision-making. He took the conditions he was faced with and that were beyond his control (the state of the higher education system, the new job offer), evaluated them individually and came up with his own self-optimizing plan. He knows that this plan is provisional at best, it can fall victim to the vagaries of the world again. He didn't have a clear roadmap in mind, just an overall attitude: whatever happens to him is part of God's larger plan which he can neither know nor influence; he tried to do the best he can within the given circumstances. Although subscribing to an entirely different set of routines and ideals than before, Jakub did not experience his relocation to Nitra as a crisis, nor did he dissociate from his former self. He did not condemn his previous gregarious lifestyle, he simply contended that this phase of his life was over, and the new phase, demarcated by external changes, challenged him to a corresponding internal change. Neither the aim nor method is fixed but is derived from each situation specifically, adapted and applied flexibly.

Moral breakdowns and moral laboratories

I now show how scholars have used the two schools to make sense of people's contradiction management in their everyday life—two theoretical tools used to analyze the responses and patterns of action that emerge in the face of constant tensions. Zigon's "moral breakdowns" and Mattingly's "moral laboratories" are terms that explain the decision-making or judgment of individual actors in challenging surroundings in an evocative manner. Despite diametrically opposed assumptions, both not only draw up prototype scenarios that are rife with precarity, insecurity, and emotional strain but also pragmatism and ingenuity.

Jarrett Zigon defines morality as a largely unconscious process: as long as there is 'business as usual,' individuals repeat trained conduct and unquestioned moral norms. Zigon even claims that "it is this ability to be non-consciously moral that allows humans to be social beings" (Zigon 2008, 164). Only at special moments, the comfortable ordinariness is disturbed. He calls these moments moral breakdowns. Drawing on Foucault's notion of "problematization," Zigon describes a state of being which was formerly taken for granted but becomes the object of conscious scrutiny. In other words, in the case of a moral breakdown, morality is retrieved from the unconscious and undergoes a process of legitimization or re-evaluation (Zigon 2007). "Thus, this moment of ethics is a creative moment, for by performing ethics, people create, even if ever so slightly, new moral personhoods and enact new moral worlds" (Zigon 2011, 11).

Moral breakdowns usually result from moral dilemmas, instances in which rehearsed behaviors fail because competing moral schemes crash. For Zigon, there are three sources of morality: institutions, the public discourse around morality, and embodied (unconscious) dispositions. On the occasion of a moral breakdown, aspects from all these spheres come together to "inform" the decision which the individual makes to return to the "nonconscious" mode (Zigon 2008, 165). A sort of inner dialogue with institutions and public discourse, elements of introspection as well as "freedom, creativity, and emergence" thus come together to create an ethical moment (ibid.). The purpose of a moral breakdown is, simply put, to return to the security and comfort of unreflected, embodied morality and carry on with one's daily business.

Moral breakdowns can be grasped empirically through ethnographic fieldwork: only through lasting engagement with particular persons and a prolonged presence in the field can the significance of such moments be fully captured (Zigon 2007). In Nitra, the employees of the NGO kept referring to an event that had, quite obviously, stirred their concept of the group they had been working with lastingly: even before the 149 refugees arrived, some people of the local community had thought about ways to support the newcomers in their first months in Slovakia and make them feel at home. They started a call for donations and collected a dozen bikes which would, so they thought, offer the children a fun way to mingle and discover their new surroundings. Months later, they found out that some families had sold the bikes. Their impulse had been to support needy and helpless families, and they had put a lot of thought into what the most beneficial gift might be. By claiming their own agency and arriving at a different conclusion of what was best for them, the clients had disrupted the predominant perception of them as helpless and thankful beneficiaries.

This breakdown propelled supporters to reflect on their status as social workers, question their assumptions, and reevaluate suggested modes of interaction with clients, albeit in different ways. Some recalibrated their image of refugees, as they understood for the first time how seriously the families were affected by financial hardship, and they acknowledged them as independent individuals capable of acting in their best interest without outside guidance. Others interpreted the move to 'sell a gift' as a lack of gratitude and good manners. This experience harshly confronted them with the state's dominant reading: that refugees were seeking their own advantage, possibly at the cost of the local population. Maybe, some NGO employees concluded, this cynical government perspective had not been so inadequate all along, and they made it their task to put attempts of 'profit-seeking' on close watch.

In Laidlaw's opinion, Zigon's approach is flawed in that it restricts ethics to fleeting moments of clarity in which the constraints and conflicts of underlying moral tendencies come to the surface. "The result is that Zigon returns to exactly that kind of negative concept for freedom Foucault sought to overcome, as the space for choice created by a temporary absence or ineffectiveness of the habitus and structured discourse" (Laidlaw 2014, 125). Zigon disregards the possibility that people are permanently uncomfortable and constantly aware of their discomfort.

Cheryl Mattingly (2013, 2014), on the other hand, developed a conceptualization of human engagement with moral dilemmas that encompasses this option: the moral laboratory. As the image suggests, two dimensions are essential for decision-making in the moral laboratory: experience and experiment. As noted above, Mattingly subscribes to a strand of first-person virtue ethics that positions an individual's perception at the heart of their sense of self and provides him or her with the capacity to navigate an extremely complex moral world. Trying to live up to expectations and realizing ground projects can be torpedoed from several sides at once and lead to outright moral drama. Mattingly claims that people pace through these risky moral worlds experimentally; they take one step at a time, monitoring and evaluating outcomes. They develop, at the same time, several future scenarios of hope and possibility. Moral laboratories are not exclusive moments but are realized amid everyday life, in an ongoing process of testing, reiterating, and appropriating moral behavior. Experiments are transformative events: moments in which something old is pitted against something unlikely or new. "Each experiment holds its perils. Each provokes moments of critique, especially self-critique, but also sometimes challenge of the social and moral categories in which it is placed" (Mattingly 2014, 27).

Mattingly also observed that narrative access to one's biography is particularly compelling, to preserve a sense of coherence as a person, and to interpret a life course as a constant progression rather than being at the mercy of random "incursions of luck" (Nussbaum 2011, 1). As such, people's imaginations of futures and pasts are fluid and adaptable; they may even have different parallel narratives of the self to choose from (Mattingly 2014, 18). Andrea Smith aptly appropriated Bakhtin's term "heteroglossia" to describe this plurality of incompatible remembered pasts and identity constructs, each providing a distinct viewpoint on the world, which can all be encompassed in the same person (2004, 251).

The example Mattingly uses to illustrate her concept is a tragic one: Andrena, a black, technically single mother from an underprivileged neighborhood in Los Angeles, whose daughter Belinda is diagnosed with an aggressive form of brain cancer. She decides to hold on to hope, to continue planning the near and further future for Belinda, and to spread positivity. At the same time, she actively engages with mothers who do lose their children, hence, in a way, grappling with the loss of her own child even before the event. Andrena needs to hold the difficult balance between feeding into both storylines carefully but consistently, and not letting the brutal incompatibility of both options overwhelm her.

I repeatedly saw this tentative development of two alternate identities in my research, although of less dramatic proportions as in Andrena's case. That early spring day, when we were sitting in the park, Jakub also confessed that he had not really cared about refugees prior to his professional encounter with the topic. He neither hated nor supported them; he had just never bothered to develop an opinion. When he was offered the job as a project manager, Jakub worked as a medical equipment salesman, a job he had accepted immediately after quitting academia. Upon receiving the surprising suggestion, Jakub made the following considerations: his current job did little more than pay the bills. There was no room to develop new skills, and no prospect for promotion. This new job had more in store for him to evolve professionally and as a person. He also strategized that if he ever wanted to return to the field of his original training, technical engineering, it would be good to have experience with project management which had not occurred during his university career.

While understanding his work as a humbling spiritual practice, he also sees it as a career springboard. This is not to say his altruistic motivation and his concern for his clients aren't sincere, they certainly are. But the pragmatic, goal-oriented considerations Jakub introduced to his decision-making process are just as real. His life episode at the NGO in Nitra fits into two separate life projects which, although they seem to have rather different ends, are not entirely disconnected: him becoming a better person and a better Christian, and his progression and personal development as a professional.

Everyday Vagaries

With this chapter, I hope to have shown that linking emotional and moral acts together as interconnected practices offers a suitable frame to analyze refugee supporters' engagement with messiness and contradiction. This is because morality and emotion analogously translate evaluations into action, uniting bodily or instinctive and cognitive reactions.

The technologies of the self and the virtue ethics approaches develop divergent trajectories of moral and emotional evaluation, but they both propose compelling images that helped me grasp and understand particular aspects of my participants' professional life. One provides the framework to understand the conversations I witnessed on which moral paradigm to follow in refugee care—and the other helped me identify the trial-and-error approach in 'ordinary' everyday activity which does not always align with the outcome of these discussions. So I find myself caught up in an uncomfortable duality of views on my actor's moral practice, unable to tell with certainty my final call on whether I identify with the virtue ethics or the Foucauldian school. Thus, I will remain in a state of suspension between both perspectives throughout the book, taking into account the contingency of life which not only my participants experience, but we as theorists, or anthropologists. After all, adherence to incommensurable frameworks is a property of 'everyone'—the universal predicament of the human experience, as resounded from the work of Rapport and Berliner at the beginning of this chapter.

The same complimentary approach I apply to moral breakdowns and moral laboratories. Although the two concepts emerge from the engagement with two different schools of moral philosophy which are contradictory in some ways, I think both have great analytical traction if applied to empirical situations. Both include elements of reflection and creativity and are thus suitable to account for how people react to conflicting moral demands originally and flexibly. But while Zigon describes exceptional moments of insight and conscious change, Mattingly talks about the ongoing everyday labor of maintaining an ethical identity. Additionally, Zigon's breakdown is a means to end incoherence, while Mattingly's laboratory decidedly allows for ambiguities and inconsistencies to be perpetuated. Interacting with people in Slovak refugee care, I observed both: moral dilemmas occur which stimulate a lot of thought and debate among colleagues, they evoke negative emotions and urge people to redesign their activities with new and binding rules for interaction with clients and other counterparts. Such moral breakdowns are very visible and invariably make it onto the ethnographer's notepad. They produce the most tangible shifts in the organization's templates for 'good' and 'bad' practice. But there is also the explorative approach to moral vagaries in the field in the shape of a daily balancing act, one that pushes refugee supporters to nourish several professional personas at once. Comprehending these experiments requires looking and listening closely over extended periods, and even so, they remain elusive.

As previously stated, the following chapters will all be roughly composed around a major dilemma refugee supporters grapple with. They are the instances in which the clash of value spheres is most pronounced, resp. in which ethical complexity is at its densest. Each of the ideals pitted against one another in these dilemmas does not only carry the aura of moral superiority, but also intense emotional implications, especially about the feelings refugee supporters have for the people they work with. These, as we shall see, can grow quite intense: When finding informal solutions instead of enacting formal rules, refugee supporters often act on empathetic impulses to provide quick help instead of working toward more sustainable structures (Chapter 4). When deliberating whether to accept cultural differences or push refugees toward cultural adaptation, they also negotiate the level of interference their relationship with individual refugees warrants them (Chapter 5). Swaying back and forth between trusting and mistrusting refugees, refugee supporters weigh their pity for their clients against their other liabilities—toward their communities, their country, and themselves (Chapter 6). And while navigating paternalizing and emancipating behaviors toward their protégées, refugee supporters acutely feel that the very human desire to 'do good' can end up doing harm (Chapter 7).

These are particularly striking sets of contradictory demands as identified and discussed by my participants. Of course, with a moral anthropology framework in mind, it is to be expected (and will be confirmed again and again) that ethical complexity usually does not just mean reconciling two but rather a plenitude of contradictory demands—all with varying degrees of urgency and persuasion. Hence, the dilemmas really contain various versions or gradings of the same demand, and they intersect and clash with other dilemmas. Ultimately, the intense 'messiness' that refugee supporters felt stuck in was an effect of these diverging moral requirements *and* from their *emotional commitment* to continuously bettering themselves, finding an even more adequate balance between care and caution and doing justice to their clients', politics', and society's demands.

Chapter 4

FORMALITY AND IMPROVISATION

Individuals in Charge

Whenever I was addressing the state of the Slovak refugee care system with my inter-locutors, the workers at the NGOs, schools, and even the state institutions opened up really quickly and did not hold back with their frustrations and complaints. Often, they delivered a crushing critique of the formal procedures, only to express their discomfort about the informal means (involving rule-breaking and their own over-engagement) they applied to make up for these deficits.

Katka, the manager of the state-led integration project, which had been imple-mented by Charita and had already ended by the time of my fieldwork, elaborated:

> It was difficult to riešiť (solve) anything with the officials. Often, the bureaucrats didn't even know what subsidiary protection is, or how it differs from asylum. What authorities they have, which competencies [...] they were totally lost in that. [...] Often, I received only minimal information from officials as long as they [the refugees, author's note] were in the retention or accommodation [camp, author's note] [...] We knew their name, first name, birth date, and that was basically all, maybe their country of origin. So, it was difficult for the social workers right from the beginning. Oftentimes, we didn't even know if a particular person could communicate in any foreign language, or if we should organize an interpreter. Often it happened that they came into the office and we ended up just sitting there, laugh-ing, because we didn't understand each other. Then we had to organize an interpreter as quickly as possible, but it's not so easy, it's not like they are just readily available at any time. [...] Those were some of the real-life problems, from the terén (field), which we needed to solve. Ad hoc. Immediately as they appeared.

Renata, the vice president of a school that accepted two Syrian refugee girls, explained:

> We, the teachers, are not prepared; we don't know how to správať sa (behave), how to work with kids who come here from different countries, especially kids who had to flee from countries affected by war. [...] In many of the things we do, we emanate from the experi-ence of colleagues who worked abroad, [...] what proved successful there, and, na kolene (on a shoestring), we try to implement it here as well. We mastered some things, others we didn't manage, sometimes we were successful, and sometimes we said we would certainly do it differently next time. Our mantra is: we try.

Miriama, a representative of the migration and integration department of the Ministry of the Interior's Migračný úrad, had the following opinion:

The NGOs are naïve! Sometimes they have no idea what they are doing there. They can do what they want, but ultimately, they don't have responsibility. For example, they threw somebody out of their program because he didn't stick to the rules which they set up for their clients. Great, but that person is still here and now the Migration Office still has responsibility for him, and the responsibility is particularly high because he is frustrated and might radicalize. We always need to bolster everything. [...] During the refugee crisis, many new NGOs were founded, well, that's nice. But they are not coordinated, and refugees are confused, they don't know to whom to turn for what. They need to cooperate a lot more and split the workload in a way that makes sense.

In these accounts, 'messiness' is a recurring theme. Slow communication, unclear mandates, missing networks or go-to partners, and a lack of legal norms and schemes for action make work within this field of refugee integration exhausting. Alongside all expressions of frustration and anger, there is always also a certain sense of achievement for beating the odds and providing sensible and comprehensive solutions for clients. Refugee supporters are proud of their capability to cope—or *riešit*. The lack of clear-cut schemes and patterns necessitates—but also allows for—creativity and customized approaches.

"Getting things done," compensating for or circumventing dysfunctional 'official' approaches is also the minimal definition of informality Alena Ledeneva offers in the preface to *The Global Encyclopaedia of Informality* (2018, vii). Another important feature of informality is the centrality of personal connections in the enactment of informal practices: in a summary of sociological approaches to the concept, Barbara Misztal writes they "describe either more intimate, face-to-face social relationships or more personal modes of social control or types of social organizations and pressures, while formality is thought to enable the preservation of social distance and structures of power" (Misztal 2000, 18).

In the scholarly literature on informality, especially in a postsocialist context, state legislation and informal approaches are often envisioned as antagonistic, with the flourishing of informal practices pointing at loopholes or deficits in the formal procedures. Abel Polese and Jeremy Morris (2015), for instance, define the applicability of informality as "beyond, or in spite of, the state" and maintain that "its reality shows the failure of certain measures and perforce prompts a change in attitude or policy-making itself" (Polese and Morris 2015, 2). In Slovak refugee care, informality is indeed an expression of a certain insubordination of non-state actors in the field toward migration authorities, and it does fill gaps and loopholes in state structures. At the same time, rules and disobedience are not as antagonistic as it might seem, but very much entwined. It is an informality within and below the state: informality does not pose a threat to the official order but undergirds it. A close look at the government agencies' minimalistic infrastructure of refugee support suggests that they are implicitly counting on non-state actors, and tacitly endorsing their unconventional methods.

Hence, the moral dilemma I explore in this chapter lies not so much between the moral implications of rule-following and rule-breaking. There is a broad consensus that the rules are flawed and inherently immoral. Providing quick solutions in situations of dire need always takes precedence. But refugee supporters are very aware that in doing so, they scaffold a deficient formal order, keep up appearances of a functioning refugee care system and possibly prevent the introduction of fairer and better structures. When I introduce both the legislations and regulations, and the informal strategies to circumvent them, in more detail below, I also show how refugee supporters imagine a third, ideal order while at the same time perpetuating and cherishing their very own improvised solutions.

The Formal and Informal Order of Refugee Care

Slovak refugee care is composed of state and non-state organizations as well as various individuals without organizational connection. The state is represented by the Migration Office of the Ministry of the Interior.[1] Established shortly after Slovak independence in 1993, it is the primary decision-making body that grants asylum and subsidiary protection and coordinates the 'integration' of successful applicants into Slovak society. The Migration Office employs roughly two dozen people, plus a few more permanent employees in the three Slovak refugee facilities that accommodate pretrial asylum seekers. The visiting address is a bungalow tract located in the wasteland between the city center and the residential districts of Bratislava and was formerly used as a kindergarten. The remote and substandard localities that the state provides for these institutions "symbolically express the stance of other political resorts towards migration" (Tužinská 2020, 48, my translation). All issues concerning integration on a practical level are routinely delegated to NGOs or civic associations which are, in the jargon of the Migration Office, referred to as *služobné organizácie* (service organizations)[2] or *realizátori* (implementers). At the time of my research, Refúgium, ASPR, and Pomoc a Nádej occupied this position; Refúgium was in charge of the East, ASPR of the West of the country, and Pomoc a Nádej for the Iraqi community in Nitra. Before that, Refúgium had run the project country-wide alone for four years, and before that, the *Katolícka Charita* (Catholic Caritas) and *Slovenská humanitná rada* (Slovak humanitarian council) had had their consecutive turns.

Cooperation between the state-run Migration Office and the 'implementers' is unsurprisingly tricky, as organizations with vastly different missions and backgrounds are bound up in a complex and constantly changing web of mutual dependencies,

1. The integration of foreigners with other forms of residence in Slovakia is managed by the Ministry of Labour, Social Affairs and Family (Ministerstvo práce, sociálnych vecí a rodiny SR) (for other state organs involved in the integration of foreigners in Slovakia s. Bagerová, Fajnorová and Chudžíková 2011).
2. The term 'service organization' is used in scholarly literature and occasionally as a self-designation to underline the eye-level and trusting character of the relationship between providers and clients and avoid the term 'help' which implies hierarchy by default (Hlinčíková and Sekulová 2015, 66). I adopt this terminology also because I believe it to be the most poignant description of their broad spectrum of activities, ranging from support with everyday issues such as shopping and public transport to complex administrative tasks.

chains of decision-making, and resource distribution. The legal documents which are supposed to conduct and regulate this interplay rarely go beyond a declaration of intent.

As I mentioned earlier, the legal groundwork for refugee and migrant integration was laid at a time when Slovakia was an EU candidate country, and the requirements of this process were still present in the legal paperwork at the time of my research: at first sight, Slovak legislation on migration and asylum, in particular, corresponds to EU legal guidelines for migration policy, which emphasize the positive effects of migration on host societies, the moral imperative to assist persecuted and threatened individuals, and the maintenance of human rights and equality. It promotes a process of integration which is locally rooted and relies on close cooperation between the national government, local administrative bodies, civil society as well as media and science (Gallová Kriglerová 2016, 65).

The *Koncepcia integrácie cudzincov v Slovenskej republike* (Conceptualization of Integration of Foreigners in the Slovak Republic), the first legal document of this kind which was passed in 2009 after long and controversial negotiations,[3] begins with giving definitions of assimilation, multiculturalism and integration, and commits itself entirely to the latter model while rejecting the first two:

> [The conceptualization] tends to the integrative model, which is built on a mutual adaptation in the integration process, in which foreigners contribute to the forming of a shared culture while the majority respects them and supports their diversity/heterogeneity.[4] (Ministerstvo práce, sociálnych vecí a rodiny Slovenskej Republiky 2009)

The follow-up document, *Integračná politika* (Integration policy), which was passed in January 2014, is written in the same spirit, understanding migration as a valuable asset and creating conditions for the development of migrant's full potential. It supports

> a bottom-up creation of policy. The subsequent implementation of integration policy into action plans shall reflect the actual needs of the target group as indicated by the respective responsible actors in the field of integration policies. (Ministerstvo práce, sociálnych vecí a rodiny Slovenskej Republiky 2014)[5]

---

3. Refugees count among the foreigners this legislation is addressed to. They are granted the same rights and privileges. The rules and guidelines for the particular case of people with asylum and subsidiary protection, pertaining, for instance, to the allowance of benefits and insurance, are specified in the national implementation plans for the EU funds which finance large parts of refugee integration in Slovakia, AMIF, and ERF; see footnote 9 in this chapter.

4. "[Koncepcia] prikláňa [sa] k integračnému modelu, ktorý je založený na obojstrannej adaptácii v integračnom procese, v ktorého rámci cudzinci prispievajú k formovaniu spoločnej kultúry a zároveň ich väčšinová spoločnosť rešpektuje a *podporuje* ich rôznorodosť." Koncepcia integrácie cudzincov v Slovenskej republike. Ministerstvo práce, sociálnych vecí a rodiny Slovenskej republiky, 2009. Accessed 22.05.2018. https://www.employment.gov.sk/files/slovensky/ministerstvo/integracia-cudzincov/dokumenty/koncepcia-integracie-cudzincov-v-slovenskej-republike.pdf, my translation, emphasis added.

5. "Integračná politika podporuje vytváranie politík 'zdola', pričom následné rozpracovanie Integračnej politiky do akčných plánov má odrážať aktuálne potreby cieľovej skupiny, tak ako sú indikované príslušnými, zodpovednými aktérmi v oblasti integračných politík." Integračná

The thrust of this policy seems to be informed by common critiques of integration policies elsewhere (see Chapter 6), adhering to moral standards most refugee supporters would subscribe to. The text reads like a letter of intent or blueprint for future action; indeed, specifications were promised to follow, in close cooperation with migrants and organizations that represent them. However, during my fieldwork period four years later, in 2018, no further legislation had been passed. People who worked in refugee care for years recounted hearing announcements of an overall integration plan "about to be implemented" since 2005, and it had become a running gag among colleagues to express some faint hope in its imminent arrival. The lack of progress regarding refugee integration policies from 2008 until the time of my research consistently received bad marks from scholars of migration in Slovakia. Their assessments were negative during the previous 10 years (Kriglerová 2016, 65; Hlinčíková and Sekulová 2015; Bargerová and Divinský 2008, 41; Tužinská 2020).[6]

The points of criticism are manifold. It starts with the observation that the initial encounters between refugees and the Slovak state are usually all but appreciative and equitable, resulting in one of the highest quotas of rejected asylum requests in the EU. Helena Tužinská has studied asylum cases in court since 2005, accumulating comprehensive evidence to support her interpretation of the asylum process as a communicative act, shaped by the "persistence of structural inequalities" (Tužinská 2020, 27). She shows how the "applicants' structurally complex and emotionally charged narratives stand in sharp contrast to bureaucratical formats which suppress contextualization [...] and, indeed, also the right of all who participate in the communication to dignity" (Tužinská 2020, 23). When the Slovak police arrest people for illegal border crossing, they are placed in detention centers until they file an asylum request, in which case they are transferred to a *záchytný tábor* (reception respectively retention camp) in some very remote areas, undergoing several weeks of quarantine. During their first encounters with the police, they receive scant information about the process and the meaning of the required administrative steps, and it is not uncommon for them to sign declarations and protocols without fully comprehending their content (Tužinská 2020, 139–151). NGO workers who visit the camps, notably from the Human Rights League, are usually the only ones providing information and guidance during this phase.

The *rozhodovači* (decision makers) of the Migration Office are the first to issue an acceptance or rejection, based on interviews with the applicants. Asylum seekers can appeal the decision at a *Krajský súd* (regional court) and subsequently at the *Najvyšší súd* (Supreme Court). However, the courts cannot grant asylum on the Migration Office's

---

politika. Ministerstvo práce, sociálnych vecí a rodiny Slovenskej republiky, 2014. Accessed 22.05.2018. https://www.employment.gov.sk/files/slovensky/ministerstvo/integracia-cudz-incov/dokumenty/vlastny-material-integracna-politika-januar-2014.pdf, my translation.

6. The most comprehensive analysis of the practice of refugee integration in Slovakia has been carried out by ethnologists Miroslava Hlinčíková and Martina Sekulová and was published in 2015 by the independent Slovak Institute for Public Affairs. This extensive empirical study backs many of my own observations, so I therefore reference it wherever my findings converge with Hlinčíková's and Sekulová's assessment a few years earlier.

behalf, they can only invalidate the primary decision and send it back to the Migration Office to process the case again, which may but usually does not lead to a different outcome. The whole 'cycle' through the institutions takes one year or more and can be repeated indefinitely (Tužinská 2020, 46). Tužinská observes a problematic style of interrogation and investigation at all levels: the use of suggestive or closed-ended questions, repeated inquiries to provoke inconsistencies, insufficient provision of legal background information, ignorance of cultural and paralinguistic cues (silence, gratuitous concurrence, avoidance of eye contact), the constant pressure to speed up the process, and so on (Tužinská 2019). Not having had the intention to come to Slovakia is seen as a justification to decline asylum pleas, the authorities seeking corresponding evidence diligently, for example, failure to answer geographical questions about Slovakia (Tužinská 2019, 84).

Another major problem is the acute lack of interpreters, especially in non-European languages. Courts regularly must resort to interpretation 'under oath': people without relevant education can act as interpreters if attesting under oath that they are capable of interpreting and are familiar with the laws and the professional ethics code. Many of them have insufficient proficiency in Slovak, and most are unaware that they need not only to provide literal translations but also explain the cultural context for the deciders, and legal and administrative jargon for the applicant (Tužinská 2020, 54). Information about countries of origin is collated by the Migration Office and, in the eyes of applicants and legal representations, is often superficial, if not biased. Many asylum seekers experience the procedure as a farce, suggesting that deciders' and judges' decisions are not exclusively informed by the hearings or interviews but rather compliant with instructions 'from above' which have been issued beforehand (Tužinská 2020, 42 and 109). Most of those who have successfully undergone the procedure after several appeals and renewed decisions experience deep insecurity and humiliation and are disenchanted with the Slovak state authorities and disappointed by the European Union, which does not manage to implement equitable legal standards everywhere. For the general public, however, the conveyed impression is that the Slovak asylum process is particularly strict and thorough, underpinning the handful of recognized refugees' legitimacy.

The administrative efforts put into denying international protection suggest that the intention is to keep numbers low and resources spent on integration at a minimum. For instance, the "Integration Policy" explicitly counts on the local administration's cooperation in refugee care without offering any financial support or advice (Hlinčíková et al. 2014). The way in which this document is interpreted by actors in refugee care, foremost the Migration Office, omits the concessions to identity preservation and cultural diversity, following instead a paradigm of assimilation. For instance, the integration contract refugees sign after they receive a positive notification from the asylum court requires them to visit language courses and accept job offers; if they fail to meet these requirements, their meager social benefits are cut and finally suspended (Hlinčíková and Sekulová 2015, 113). Also, despite announcing support for the preservation of their cultural and linguistic heritage, supplementary lessons for school kids in their native language are not considered a conceivable option (Gažovičová 2011, 36).

No mention is made of increasing public awareness, in order to create an accepting and friendly social surrounding for foreigners, which would form part of a truly integrative effort (Hlinčíková and Sekulová 2015, 153). Whatever organizations do to this effect, be it education programs at schools or public campaigns, they do it on their own initiative, having to find the financial resources within their small budgets. Indeed, some employees of the Migration Office were among the first to invest effort into raising public awareness by producing a series of video profiles of their clients' stories, but they soon faced such a severe backlash in the form of hate speech emails and comments on social media that Slovakia's National Criminal Agency had to investigate these offenses (Tužinská 2020, 51).

If we subsume the legal framework, and the Migration Office's interpretation of it, under the formal heading of asylum policies, we can see two major incompatibilities which pave the road to informal, improvised solutions: Firstly, it is clear that they are inherently contradictory, providing diverging paradigms between which actors must choose in a concrete situation: the human-rights centered, integrative approach that follows the European guidelines, or the stricter, assimilationist line that shines through some of the more specific prescriptions. Secondly, the policies are simply not as developed, realistic, or differentiated as practitioners would wish (Hlinčíková and Sekulová 2015, 55–56), and therefore they need to be constantly adapted to the 'unruly' life worlds of refugees in Slovakia, circumventing or supplementing the protocol.

In her preface to the *The Global Encyclopaedia of Informality*, Ledeneva (2018) describes practices of informality as categorically ambivalent. Informal practices are characterized by several irreconcilable contradictions: they evoke a certain sense of secrecy while simultaneously being known to all; they mean liberation from imposed rules while creating new constraints, undermining and perpetuating 'official' power.

These considerations point to the complexity of the relationship between (state) power and individual action in the context of informal activity. As I observed above, informality cannot be equated with subversion or resistance, but neither is it always (knowingly) complicit with state power. In accounts of their work, refugee helpers often take a critical stance toward the state's unhelpful approaches. This pertains particularly to the dearth of resources and the pressure for refugees to become financially independent while financial means to enable important tasks, like socializing, language acquisition, and recovery from traumatic experiences, are missing. And yet, every time they engage in "making do" (Certeau 1984, 34), with every access they negotiate to schools, jobs, or language courses despite the scant resources, they contribute to the impression that the system as a whole is functional, justifying the passivity of the state.

Actual accountabilities

The imbalanced relationship between state resource allocation and informal distribution is frequently seen as a legacy of state socialism. Some scholars have claimed that strong informal networks and practices are an almost inevitable result of the communist system (Henig and Makovicky 2017; Ledeneva 1998), forged not only by the notorious shortage of resources and rigid state control, but also by the camaraderie and collective values propagated by the state ideology. In this vein, many social scientists expected informality to disappear once these societies internalized 'Western' principles like transparency and impartiality, and capitalist modes of distribution. When informality persisted, they argued that economic uncertainties following the political transformation necessitate this kind of flexibility (Burawoy and Verdery 1999; Hann 2006; Humphrey 2002; Kalb 2001). The reliance on informality (mostly through personal networks and bribing) is often interpreted as a consequence of the lasting disenchantment with politics and loss of trust in institutions during socialist times. Supposedly, these led to a withdrawal into the private realm and an engagement with institutions that was merely opportunistic (Howard 2003).

Recently scholars have dismissed these "systemic" path dependencies as dated and "benevolent" (Brković 2017, 2) as casting informality as the long shadow of past experiences only partly explains the persistence of dependency on social ties. Instead, informal practices should be acknowledged as essentially contemporary phenomena which are purposefully promoted and consciously perpetuated (Brković 2017; Stan 2012). The withdrawal of the state from welfare and the resulting lack of trust is certainly one reason why many Slovaks, including those working in refugee care, try to minimize interaction with the state, striving for autonomy. The (over)reliance on civil society which increasingly substitutes state functions also fits into a twenty-first-century model of neoliberal statecraft:[7] Nikolas Rose has described the concept of "ethical citizenship," denoting the modern state's inclination to foster "a new politics of conduct that seeks to reconstruct citizens as moral subjects of responsible communities" (2000, 1395). Similarly, Andrea Muehlebach (2012) has examined volunteers working in Italy's welfare system, who make up for the shrinking supply of state resources to support the poor and marginalized. The neoliberal order posits itself as ethical because it incorporates existing moral configurations of exchange, like Catholic notions of charity, and communist concepts of solidarity.

> As the state shifts the burden of the reproduction of solidarity onto a citizenry conceptualized as active and dutiful, solidarity is outsourced [...] onto citizens, every one of which is now co-responsible for the public good. The ethical labor of citizens is thus much more than merely cheap. It has, precisely because it is unwaged, become the pathos-laden vehicle through which collective transcendence and meaning and value get conjured. (Muehlebach 2012, 12)

It is well documented that postsocialist states in Central and Eastern Europe have taken up neoliberal forms of governance with particular zest (Dzenovska 2018; van Baar 2012; Ther 2014). In Slovakia as well, the state has increasingly abandoned its

---

7. I understand neoliberalization as a compound of economic policy developments which is forwarded globally, including an emphasis on free market economy, a politics of austerity and a withdrawal of the state from social welfare, and a promotion of the entrepreneurial self-sufficient individual (s. Harvey 2005).

former role as a provider of social services and welfare. Apart from religious forms of charity, people maintain, or reinvent, behaviors from socialist times to substitute the absent state.

The Ministry of the Interior's nearly complete abstention from the implementation of its refugee integration policy is part of this development. Its role is rather inhibiting than enabling, supervising and rigidly controlling the financial framework, while most of the work that requires direct contact with clients is done by NGOs and volunteers.[8] The state accepts only marginal financial responsibility for the integration programs: only 25 percent of the service organizations' budget is state-funded. The remaining 75 percent is covered by EU funds, specifically ERF (2008–2014) and AMIF (since 2014) (Hlinčíková and Sekulová 2015).[9] The state remains indifferent to current needs or bottlenecks: in 2015, an EU funding scheme ended in March while the next one started in the winter of the same year (Hlinčíková and Sekulová 2015, 148). For several months, the NGOs had to reduce their activities to an absolute minimum, since no additional government funding was available.

The *Národný program AMIF* (National Program for AMIF) specifies which tasks need to be fulfilled using the available funding between 2014 and 2020. It provides the following list of services nongovernmental stakeholders are expected to provide:

> legal and administration counseling, language training, employment consultancy, guidance aimed at the administrative system, etc. [...] Moreover, the services will emphasize the integration of the TCNs [third-country national, author's note] in the socio-cultural, political and economic life. (National Program AMIF, p. 16)[10]

---

8. The growing reliance on NGOs in all areas of social and nonprofit service provision is not a distinctive feature of the postsocialist space, let alone Slovakia. The buzzword 'NGO-ization' is used to denote that welfare and social movements have become battlegrounds on which a globally connected but locally rooted NGO sector contests state power (Fisher 1997; Ferguson and Gupta 2005). Some states react to the threat NGOs pose to their sovereignty by sabotaging them, others by trying to co-opt project resources (Sampson 2003b, 308). They do so by nurturing their own state-affiliated NGOs for their purposes. These have been called QUANGOs, quasi-NGOs, and have spread especially in Britain and Eastern Europe (Sampson 2003b, 318). The service organizations I dissect here are also QUANGOs, strictly speaking, since they receive (limited) government funding as well as grants from donors, thus reducing government spending on asylum policies to a minimum. For a comprehensive survey of NGO-ization in Central and Eastern Europe, see Jacobsson and Saxonberg 2013.

9. AMIF (Asylum, Migration and Integration Fund) was launched in 2014 to "promote the efficient management of migration flows and the implementation, strengthening and development of a common Union approach to asylum and immigration." It merged three separate funds that existed before, the European Return Fund (RF), the European Integration Fund (EIF), and the European Refugee Fund (ERF). Accessed 22.05.2018. https://ec.europa.eu/home-affairs/financing/fundings/migration-asylum-borders/refugee-fund_en.

10. "National Program AMIF." Ministerstvo vnútra Slovenskej Republike, 01.01.2014. Accessed 22.05.2018. https://www.minv.sk/swift_data/source/mvsr_a_eu/simons/nove/Narodny%20program%20AMIF%20v%205.0_ANJ.pdf.

The NGOs have to respond to tenders to receive funding for offering these services. The projects that are advertised for bids in refugee care are limited in time, typically lasting between one and two years.

The rigid time and budgetary constraints create a permanent state of insecurity among NGOs: neither workers nor refugees know whether the services will be continued similarly after the next tender. The "projectization" that dominates NGO work worldwide, as Steven Sampson has observed, imposes its own logic and rhythm on the provision and development of social services: once these services are projectized, their availability depends on the renewal of the project, or ends. Rarely do permanent or state-administered policies emerge out of them (Sampson 2003b, 313; see also Sampson 2003a).

The short-lived character of projects means that no sustainable solutions to the challenges of integration governance emerge. This has far-reaching consequences for the agents and recipients of NGO services alike, leading for example to a constant turnover of organizations involved. Every few years, the responsibility for refugee care in a particular region switches to yet another organization which has received the latest grant. There is also a high fluctuation of workers within organizations, not least due to the stressful and emotionally taxing character of their work. That means frequent exchange of staff and rapid loss of expertise. Refugees have to get used to new mentors regularly, making it much harder to develop a durable, trusting relationship. A systematic redesign of the housing or education infrastructure, which would require additional time and staff, cannot be realized.

Employees who start working for a service organization usually have little or no training for the target group, simply because chances to gather work experience in this field are limited. The topic is only starting to be covered in the social work curricula, and there are no further education courses on the matter, let alone obligatory standards for entering the profession (Hlinčíková and Sekulová 2015, 149). Literature for social work students is available (Brnula 2008; Kováts, Miklušáková and Rangelová 2006), but the fact that most NGO workers do not have a background in social work means it is unlikely that they are familiar with it. Usually, NGO employees have to acquire the necessary skills themselves, which usually happens through hands-on engagement. Legislative matters, especially the intricacies of status differences between asylum and subsidiary protection, is complex and subject to change, keeping oneself up-to-date takes a lot of time and remains a source of confusion (Hlinčíková and Sekulová 2015, 76). Competences that exceed the administrative side of refugee care, such as intercultural communication or third-country language proficiency, are rare. The notorious lack of financial resources results in a shortage of staff. NGO employees shoulder an immense workload, which includes producing extensive case documentation for public audit (Hlinčíková and Sekulová 2015, 71–73). Despite all these professional challenges, there are virtually no options for advancement or promotion. My collocutors recall several cases of burnout among colleagues due to the poor work conditions, and others quit their jobs before it got that far.

In short, in the current constellation, responsibilities are outsourced to the service organizations without sufficient resources, and the well-being of refugees in Slovakia hinges to a large degree upon the extraordinary commitment of individual refugee supporters. These have tried to negotiate better conditions for years, demanding more generous financial means and personnel. The Migration Office functions as a mediator in this matter, relaying the organizations' demands as well as their own pledges for more resources to their superiors at the Ministry of the Interior in countless rounds of negotiations, as they reported to Refúgium during one of their control visits. The bureaucrats see themselves as victims both of the precarious political situation and of unjust vilification by the service organizations and are hence pressing the new integration policy with the same urgency as social workers.

Since the completion of the integration plan, which is supposed to redefine responsibilities, has been delayed time and again, the originally provisional arrangement has been in place for over ten years. These delays keep refugee carers in a state of "permanent temporariness" (akin to the typical refugee experience of dwelling in transit while awaiting final decisions on asylum status, family reunion, citizenship, etc., see Tize 2020). As I mentioned in the "Introduction," creating and artificially prolonging a *State of Exception* (Agamben 2005) is a common occurrence in refugee policy, which migration scholars see as endowing governments with greater sovereignty while disabling control systems. The state benefits from its absence, producing what Eyal Weizman has called "structured chaos" (2009, 11): minimalist and selective government action is just enough to keep the system alive without politicians having to publicly engage with these deeply unpopular matters (see Chapter 2). This leads to the widely shared impression that public officials apply a "fire extinguisher" approach (Gallová Kriglerová and Chudžíková 2016, 63)—they tend to issues only when they 'flame up' and solve them in a quick-fix rather than sustainable manner.

The precarity in terms of time and resources leaves refugee care not only 'ever temporary' but also 'ever emergent': there is a lasting sense of having to deal with new challenges in the refugee care network. People continuously stress how new and unfamiliar the situation is. This narrative has an apologetic dimension, presenting failures merely as teething problems, while progress is always a sign of achievement and learning. Innovation plays an important role in the organizations' self-consciousness: Refúgium's psychologist Linda, for instance, introduced a women's circle and proudly showed me the pictures from a professional photo shoot they did together. Pomoc a Nádej invented the position of the 'community leader,' an Iraqi with good English skills who serves as a gatekeeper between the organization and the Iraqi 'community' for a small honorarium. An employee from the Migration Office organized an 'integration platform' in November 2017, calling for regular meetings of all organizations involved in refugee integration. The meeting was attended by all aforementioned groups and also researchers and language teaching experts. The initiative was warmly welcomed by everyone as a possibility to "finally cooperate more." The idea, however, was not entirely new: according to anthropologists who had studied refugee policies in the 2000s, there had been similar regular gatherings between organizations and scholars involved in refugee care at the time. These had been organized by the United Nations High Commissioner for Refugees (UNHCR) National Office in Slovakia and also encompassed training and trips for teambuilding purposes. The gatherings were stalled when the UNHCR funding ended. The second-generation platform of the Migration Office faced a similar fate less than three years after it was founded when organizations disagreeing with its policies withdrew their support and participation. These examples underline how ad hoc and ephemeral many of these innovations are, but they also show how organizations draw self-esteem from makeshift solutions: the absence of any formal and permanent structures adds value to all NGOs' large and small advancements and offers a possibility to showcase their aptitude and dedication to each other and the public in proud social media postings.

Improvisation as self-fashioning

In the Introduction, I have already shown how the concept of governmentality is used to describe how to *"conduire des conduits"* (Foucault 1999, 273) of particular populations, like refugees, and how scholars of migration have used this terminology to highlight the multidirectional dissemination of power across a wide array of actors with unintended consequences and unforeseeable side effects. The integration projects, their design and implementation could easily be studied with a governance and governmentality approach. There are various diverging ideas on how refugee integration should be governed in the frame of these projects—state regulations mainly aim at reducing state expenses for the whole process and ideally also reducing the number of refugees through rejection or deterrence. There are, of course, also governing efforts to turn refugees into independent and 'productive' members of society as quickly as possible. This entails finding housing, entering the workforce, assessing and furthering formal education, and (to varying degrees) providing social benefits for refugees. Through the lens of this regime- or governance-centered framework, I could continue to study, as I have drafted in the previous subchapters, the discourses and their participants, legal, administrative and bureaucratic prescriptions, the political genesis of informality, and show how the imposed structure and insurgence from below interact in unforeseen ways—in short, how power diffuses and meanders between distinct structural positions.

The focus I have chosen instead, the lens of moral and emotional practice, offers a different perspective on the processes outlined above. It concentrates on the individual's engagement with existing structures as a creative and generative process, which I refer to as improvisation. It is a process that requires resilience, originality, and attunement to other human beings, both as collectives and as individuals. Informality as improvisation, from this point of view, appears not just as resistance or resurgence but as a craft with a logic all its own. This approach *also* visibilizes the frictions and clashes between 'bottom-up' and 'top-down,' and demonstrates that the outcomes of these confrontations may be random and unruly. But it allows us to see formal or informal behavior not merely as compliance or resistance—or any kind of conscious reaction to existing structures—but as largely intuitive everyday practice. It shows that the purpose of engaging in improvised informality is not (only) to manipulate the exertion of power and influence but to create and maintain certain subject positions within moral and emotional communities.

Properties of improvisation

The process I refer to as improvisation is the creation of the less-than-ideal yet working solutions that refugee supporters come up with when they say *riešim* (I solve).

Theoretically, the improvisor is envisioned in between an artist and a scientist; hence improvisation fits both the workshop and the laboratory metaphors for moral and emotional practice. In music, particularly in Jazz, improvisation means, most fundamentally, a succession of notes that are unscripted. Nevertheless, and contrary to what one might think, improvisation is not a mere invention either: Firstly, it is anchored in a given setting, an accompaniment which the piece provides in terms of speed, harmonies, character of the melody, and so on. Secondly, time pressure which typically constitutes the improvising situation does usually not allow for originality and flawless execution at the same time. Rather, musicians use bits and pieces of preconceived material. The artistry consists of the ability to draw from a wide range of these snippets and embellish and combine them in an inventive manner. As Weick puts it, "in Jazz improvisation people act in order to think," which means that "intention is loosely coupled to execution, that creation and interpretation need not be separated in time, and that sensemaking rather than decision-making is embodied in improvisation" (Weick 1998, 547).

Following Prinz's and Solomon's considerations about cognition outlined earlier, one could maybe say that improvisation is an 'embodied appraisal' par excellence: not just deliberation, or intuition, it is mainly the quick and creative usage of resources that are stored in the body. A related notion is Claude Lévi-Strauss' (1966) concept of bricolage. He distinguished the bricoleur from the engineer who has access to the expert tools and materials and is expedient in their use. The bricoleur, by contrast, uses whatever skills and resources are available to him, and 'repurposes' them in an 'inappropriate' manner as it were.

Weick points out that the same principles can be observed in organizational structures that engage in improvisation, and this is certainly true for the institutions in Slovakia involved with refugee care. Since tested pathways are absent, they often have no other option than to think and act simultaneously. They sometimes must reach for the 'fire extinguisher' rather than extrapolate a goal and come up with the best possible path. To do what seems 'good' and 'appropriate,' actors reuse preconceived material. They implement methods translated from a different context and, like a scientist, stick to the aspects that have the desired effects while abandoning those that do not prove successful. This problem-fixing approach prioritizes practical knowledge over theory and is guided by templates or paragons rather than established models (Farías 2014). This description resonates with how Mattingly conceptualizes the evolution of moral decision-making in her moral laboratories: what may seem like random and inconclusive behavior is really a sequence of inventions and borrowings, continuously improving one's ability to cope with tricky circumstances.

The main characteristics of improvisation—the simultaneity of intent and execution, shuffling innovative and tested material, piecemeal trial-and-error progression, and continuous compromising—could provide a good starting point for the anthropology of contradiction Berliner has called for, an anthropology that does not try to read sense into individual's inconsistent behavior but to make sense of contradiction itself. Some scholars argue in a sweeping manner that to live means to improvise, implying that improvisation is the standard mode to manage the implacable contingencies of the world (Bruner 1993, 326). Elizabeth Hallam and Tim Ingold have elaborated that "carrying on" is also always an inventive endeavor because the "reproduction of existing forms leads in practice to variations in their situated enactments" (Hallam and Ingold 2007, 19). Parallel to anthropologists of morality's central claim, one could argue that no plan, constraint, or script is ever so all-encompassing as to make improvisation impossible or unnecessary. Even a perfectly thought-through integration policy that is in tune with grassroots' needs would still require creativity and flexibility in its implementation—a moral laboratory that approaches an intangible ideal of refugee care through experimentation and gradual progression. Nonetheless, I think it is fair to argue that in the inadequate formal political setting described above, improvisation plays a particularly important role. In the following paragraphs, I will discuss the shortcomings emerging from the conscious or coincidental omissions by formal stakeholders in their main fields of activity and show how individuals fill these gaps in their own distinctive style.

Improvisation in Practice

Housing

Finding appropriate housing is a major challenge for refugees. Most settle down in urban hotspots where their chances of finding employment are higher. Projects for collective refugee housing, like the integration center in the city of Zvolen, failed (Hlinčíková and Sekulová 2015, 47 and 83). During the course of their project's timeline, Refúgium started a cooperation with the city of Košice to get access to the municipality's social housing; at the time of my research, they were renting four such flats permanently and were hoping to expand their approach in and beyond the city. Housing in larger cities is scarce and expensive. Even locals with vast insider knowledge struggle to find appropriate accommodation. Refugees find themselves in a particularly challenging position, especially at the beginning, when most are incapable of paying the average urban rent, let alone a deposit which is usually several monthly rates. Most refugees are not eligible for social housing, since they do not fulfill the criteria, for example, uninterrupted residence in a given municipality for a duration of five years. Prevalent stereotypes further obstruct the search for housing: many landlords are reluctant to rent their apartments out to foreigners. If the tenant has only the status of subsidiary protection, the landlord has administrative duties toward the *Oddelenie cudzineckej polície* (Foreigners' Police), which makes many shun away. Differential access is structured along lines of race: at the time of my fieldwork, white Caucasian refugees, for example from Ukraine, consistently faced less rejection than People of Color.[11] Most importantly, refugees lack the social ties

---

11. This differentiation was particularly evident at the outset of Russia's war on Ukraine in 2022, when large numbers of Ukrainian refugees crossed the border with Slovakia. There

and networks to help them get quick access to accommodation offers (Hlinčíková and Sekulová 2015, 82–90).

As a result, NGO employees usually search for housing for each refugee person or family individually. They often resort to dormitories, for instance those in which construction workers live during their work assignments. This is considered an inconvenient solution, since clients have no privacy or space to feel at home there, which obviously hampers the process of settling in for individuals, let alone for families (Hlinčíková and Sekulová 2015, 89). Even though this solution is less time-consuming than finding private rentals, there are no predefined quotas, and social workers need to investigate whether there are free beds available for each client individually. As Marcela, manager of ASPR told me: "I wish we would have at least two or three places to turn to, where we would get beds by default. So that we don't have to start the search from scratch each time."

Social workers react to this situation with guilt, shame, pity, but also defiance—emotions that have strong implications for (moral) behavior. What they routinely do when looking for accommodation is grant their clients access to their own social networks, mobilizing their circle of family and friends to help them. Jaromír, the financial manager of Pomoc a Nádej, has been living in a village at the periphery of Nitra for over ten years; he bought a house where he is living with his wife and kids. He is a respected member of the local community, an eager churchgoer, and has easy access to the village's mouth-to-mouth communication system. He did not only find two houses for sale in the village when two refugee families were looking for accommodation. He also convinced his fellow villagers to sell to these families based on his personal recommendation and trustworthiness. Subsequently, he provided much assistance with the restoration of the respective houses. He also employs four refugees in his own installation firm, which is his second job.

A telling example of the pooling of community efforts and resources on one hand, and extraordinary individual commitment on the other hand, is the story of Reem and her daughters. In 2016, the Slovak government accepted a total of 16 relocated refugees on their own terms, possibly hoping that this voluntary commitment would give them leverage for future negotiations with the EU. As I described above, they insisted on all resettled refugees being single mothers and their children. Three of them were Reem and her daughters, Amal and Yana. Having fled Syria, the three ended up in a Greek refugee camp.

At the same time, Veronika, the pastor of the Protestant congregation in the *Staré Mesto* (Old Town) district of Bratislava, initiated a project in support of refugees in Slovakia. The project took place in the framework of the 300th anniversary

---

was a large mobilization within the civil society, far beyond the moral community of refugee supporters, to welcome and accommodate Ukrainian refugees. As the war dragged on, this initial surge of solidarity faded and the social consensus on helping Ukrainians started to crumble. They were even used as political scapegoats in the 2023 parliamentary elections, with some parties promising to minimize support for Ukrainians for the benefit of the "Slovak people" (Walther and Jobbitt 2022).

of the birth of Slovak national hero Ľudovít Štúr, the renowned linguist who laid the groundwork for the Slovak literary language and initiated the Slovak National Revival. He attended the Lutheran *lyceum*, a school which is still under the patronage of the congregation Staré Mesto today. Veronika told me that they wanted to do something more than just "putting up some posters," something that would demonstrate the agility of their community and the values they hold themselves accountable for.

They found a church-owned flat which was in a bad condition and chose to renovate it to accommodate a refugee family there. The congregation was able to collect 8,000€ through a fundraising campaign, the rest was paid for by the congregation's own financial reserves. The renovation itself was carried out by volunteers. It was finished in June 2016, and that was when Veronika asked a friend of hers, a studied theologian who worked at the Migration Office, to help to find a family. He transferred her to the director of the Department for Migration and Integration, who again introduced her to the social worker of the Bratislava office, Peter. They immediately accepted the offer and even gave the church board the opportunity to choose from three possible beneficiaries: two young male students, a young single mom with a boy from Somalia who had already been in Slovakia for a while and had gone through some very bad experiences, including a physical assault, or said mother of two girls from Syria. The church board decided that the Syrian family needed their help the most, not only because they seemed more vulnerable than the young men but also because they were still caught in limbo at the refugee camp, lacking privacy and perspective. They would potentially benefit the most from the secure and accepting surroundings Veronika was planning to provide for them. The fact that the family was Muslim fitted well into the church board's plans, as Veronika explains:

> To demonstrate that we, the church, don't help only those who have the same faith. That was important to us. In the discussions we lead, we mustn't forget that all people are alike. So we show that we won't categorize people into deserving and undeserving. Instead, we demonstrate our belonging together. (*spolupatričnosť*)

The young family moved into the fully furnished flat in December 2016. The church community had furnished the flat with numerous donations from members as well as secondhand items. Tensions started almost instantly: when Reem saw the bed, she burst into tears. It was the same steel frame that she had slept on in the refugee camp, which she had started to resent. Of course, Veronika saw to it that the bed was exchanged for a costlier wooden model shortly after.

Work

Skilled labor as well as low-paid workforce is scarce in Slovakia, a country which has been undergoing a severe demographic crisis and an economic boom at the same time. At least in the larger cities, there is a significant number of job offers. NGO workers report that although it is tricky and time-consuming, it is possible to find work for all of their clients. Of course, this only applies if concessions are made, especially regarding salary and job appeal. The probability of having degrees and certificates from third countries acknowledged is rather low (Bargerová and Divinský 2008, 82). Just like on the housing market, racism and stereotypes have an exacerbating effect. Employers are obliged by law to give domestic workers priority over foreigners (Gallová Kriglerová 2016, 68). The key problem during the job search is low or missing Slovak language proficiency. Courses usually do not accommodate refugees' needs, they collide with standard working hours, and they start only at certain times of the year, so little differentiation in levels is possible (Bargerová and Divinský 2008, 83).

Most refugees find that their only chance is accepting low-skilled and badly paid jobs as cleaners, kitchen assistants, and workers in manufacturing (Filadelfiová et al. 2011, 47–53). The entry-level salaries for those jobs are barely enough to cover living expenses in the larger cities. Being unfamiliar with the language and the local labor market, refugees are particularly prone to being lured into the informal labor market, where neither insurance and worker protection nor reliable, timely payment of salaries are the norm (Hlinčíková and Sekulová 2015, 107). Again, the lack of a social network is a major obstacle that refugee carers seek to overcome by offering their own ties and bonds, like in the case of Pomoc a Nádej's job manager Dobroslava:

I have asked about everyone I know if they have a job for our people. Meanwhile, I'm afraid to call anyone. Because sometimes they quit the job, or something doesn't work out, and then it's your responsibility. I have no friends anymore because of this job [laughs].

Haroun is one of the Iraqi Christians in Nitra, a man in his midthirties. He used to be a physics teacher and also worked as a painter to make some extra money on the side. His university diplomas are not acknowledged in Slovakia, and he is unable to teach in Slovak, the language he still struggles to understand himself. Finding work proved to be extremely difficult for him. Pressure on Haroun was growing when his wife was diagnosed with cancer, and he had to take on the roles of breadwinner and primary caregiver at the same time.

Pomoc a Nádej, the service organization Haroun is affiliated with, is located in an old and venerable building which not only hosts several Christian charities, but also the joinery of Ľuboš and Ondrej. The two carpenters and brothers-in-law have connections with all charities in the building and are friends with the founders of the refugee service organization as well. Habits of mutual assistance, as well as proximity, gave rise to the idea that Ľuboš and Ondrej could perhaps offer Haroun a job in their workshop. They accepted without hesitation, as Ondrej reports: "We immediately agreed. We do whatever we can to help. Those are good people; they need support and they came here to work." Haroun registered as a freelancing handyman and started assisting them wherever he could. "It is not so easy because carpentry requires training. We can't just teach him how to be a carpenter on the fly," Ľuboš admits. They tried to find him things to do, like painting doors and window frames. They did not deny that Haroun's job primarily existed because of him and his family. As Jakub explained to me when I asked him about this arrangement: "They wouldn't have needed another colleague, you know, they were getting along. They are doing this only to help Haroun."

Sometimes, improvisation produces results that are good and smart only on the surface. Ľuboš and Ondrej helped Haroun get a *živnosť* (business permit), this way he could work flexible hours, always following current demands. This benefited Haroun insofar as he could bring his kids to school and back throughout the day. However, the fact that he was not an employee of the workshop, but rather self-employed, came with a lot of insecurity. He had to pay the business fees and social insurance himself, and he never knew how many hours the brothers-in-law would need him in advance. After paying fees and taxes, what remained was hardly enough to feed his family. Ľuboš and Ondrej certainly had good intentions, but they also did not want to burden their business disproportionately by creating a superfluous job. And it was difficult for Haroun to turn the situation around: the bonds he fostered with his benefactors, his gratitude to them, the effort he invested into getting the business permit, and the argument that few other jobs would allow him the same amount of flexibility made it difficult for him to walk away. This case of improvisation produced a less-than-ideal solution which is provisional in its intentions but turns out to be very durable.

Education

Education and schooling is another area where, as practitioners agree, improvements are direly needed. The most pressing issue is certainly language acquisition. The language barrier severely limits not only access to the labor market but also the possibility of having a social life. Many learners experience the Slovak language with its intense inflection as extraordinarily difficult. The fact that the second language proficiency of Slovak citizens is statistically among the lowest in the EU (Bútorová and Gyárfášová 2011; EF EPI 2019) adds to the urgency of foreigners' Slovak language acquisition: it is in many situations the only way to make oneself understood.

While acknowledging the importance of Slovak language education, the Ministry of Education's instructions are vague and not always implemented, and sometimes the persons in question are unaware of what their respective rights and competencies are (Gažovičová 2011, 19). For example, the law obliges the district school office to organize free Slovak language courses for kids whose native language is different from Slovak. The empirical study *Vzdelávanie detí cudzincov na Slovensku* (Education of foreigners' kids in Slovakia), edited by Tina Gažovičová in 2011, has shown that this happens only rarely. Instead, the schools' teachers give foreigners' children extra lessons (paid or unpaid), or the parents hire private language instructors at their own expense. Schools often decide to integrate foreign students into years that are far below their age cohort. As a result, these students find it harder to socialize with peers, feeling stigmatized and ashamed since they are lagging behind (Gažovičová 2011, 43–44).

Current legislation explicitly stipulates that children of foreigners are not to be treated differently from Slovak children but have the same rights and obligations in every regard. This may be seen as a sensible contribution to equity and antidiscrimination. In everyday practice, however, it hinders schools from attending to the needs of foreign students, which have to be addressed to make full participation possible (Gažovičová 2011, 39). The law prohibits filing foreign kids as persons with special needs, which would entitle them to extra personnel (e.g., tutors) in class. Being held to the same examination and grading standards, even in elementary school classes, foreigners' children may have to repeat years, resulting in anxiety and frustration. This can have severe mental health repercussions.

Teachers receive no special training to help integrate children with different requirements and special pedagogical and psychological needs. Renáta, a teacher at an elementary school, feels unfit to meet the challenges connected to this task:

> We don't know where to get training for our teachers, but we would need it [...] I will never forget that Serhiy [refugee student from Ukraine, author's note] when he came, there was the anniversary of the end of WWII, so they went to Slavín [a memorial and cemetery in honor of the Soviet soldiers who liberated Bratislava in 1945, author's note] and there were things written in Cyrillic, which made him happy. And then we started talking about the war and suddenly he started acting strangely [...] I think maybe he didn't have direct experiences of the war, but the surrounding was probably uncomfortable for him, maybe it frightened him.[12] This might seem like silly things, but we are not prepared for them. We can't deal with these kids. And we don't know how much content they can handle in class, and so on.

The Slovak school system exceptionally allows schools to suspend grading for two years in well-founded cases, which teachers appreciate (Gažovičová 2011, 48). There are, however, no time slots, personnel, or funding available to provide children extra (language) training and the additional attention they need to keep up with their peers after these two years. Teachers who have foreign children in their class, like Renáta, often feel overwhelmed with the additional workload:

> Teachers don't have time to pay extra attention to the children during an ordinary class, they have 30 other students to tend to. If there was an elaborate system, that would be good. Or a personal assistant who goes to class with them. The colleague who has Amal in her class does her best, but I don't think that she will be on a level after two years that would allow her to continue like an ordinary student and get good grades.

In practice, the principle of equality is routinely circumvented: some teachers not only adapt content and grading standards to their foreign students, but they also often give them more time and attention, turning into personal mentors for all matters school-related and beyond. Other teachers often feel overwhelmed by the task of integrating foreigners into class when an ordinary school day is already difficult and emotionally draining. They tend to lower their expectations toward foreign students and prioritize the progress of the whole class (Gažovičová 2011, 52).

For Amal and Yana, the young girls in the Protestant Church's apartment, the path to school was riddled with numerous hurdles as well, and again, it was Protestant priest

---

12. She is referring to the war in Donbass following the annexation of Crimea by Russia in 2014. The family originated from that area.

Veronika and her social network that decided to help. Slovakia has a catchment area-based schooling system, meaning that district schools serve a strictly defined area. A school is obliged by law to accept any child with residence in that district. Yet, Veronika decided not to contact the respective district school but a woman from her own social network, Ivana, the head of the schools in Bratislava associated with the Protestant Church, an elementary school and the *lýceum* which Ľudovít Štúr had visited centuries earlier. Ivana accepted the two girls without hesitation. She told me that getting Slovak kids used to diversity at an early age and teaching them tolerance is one of the declared aims of her schools.

Having Amal and Yana as students turned out not to be an easy task. Especially six-year-old Amal seemed traumatized; she was extremely scared to be alone and separated from family members, as headmaster Ivana recalls:

> Our task was to teach them how to fungovať (function) in the school, which was not easy, to teach little Amal to go to school regularly and work during the whole lesson. She cried and cried. Other first graders also cry when they are away from their mums, but Amal cried much more than anyone. That must have been the stress and fear that Mum was not returning, although she lived nearby. But she needed to build a relationship with people she could trust, so her everyday routine looked like this: little Amal is coming to the second floor, controls me: "Directress, will you be here?"—"I will. The whole day." She controls the secretary, she controls the deputy, and if they are there, she is satisfied. She needs to have a feeling of security.

After one year, it was time for the older sister Yana to switch from elementary to secondary school. Since the entry-level exams for secondary education in the church-run schools would have been too challenging, she registered for their district school. But she was not accepted initially, despite the school's legal obligation to do so. It took several meetings and the tireless efforts of Veronika and Ivana to convince the school. Despite the rocky start, Yana adapted quickly and enjoyed the fact that her education was now less demanding than before.

It soon became apparent that the girls and their mother needed additional instruction in Slovak to be able to master their daily life in Bratislava. Peter from the Migration Office asked a friend of his, Laura, from the Studia Academica Slovaca, the department for Slovak as a foreign language at Comenius University. This institute usually provides language courses for foreign students, or those who aspire to become teachers of Slovak in countries where it is offered at schools (e.g., Poland, Hungary, Croatia, and Ukraine). Laura is a linguist who was preparing a PhD dissertation at the time. Teaching a refugee family with no prior knowledge of Slovak and no experience in language learning was exceptionally challenging for her and unlike everything she had done before, as she readily admitted in our interviews.

Given the lack of teaching material and the need to keep the pace and the threshold low, she improvised a lot and tried to respond to the specific needs of Reem's family. The most important task, Laura soon discovered, was to create a trusting relationship and make the meetings as fun and undemanding as possible so the women would feel safe and not too intimidated. In their everyday life, they were already exposed to high levels of stress since even the most trivial task could present a major challenge. This is why the lessons took place at home, where they felt comfortable and in control of the situation. In the beginning, they had no common language to communicate in, so she tried to involve as much body language, gestures, images, and symbols as possible and was surprised to discover a repertoire of basic metalinguistic signs that are universally understandable. For instance, 'up' or 'high' is connoted positively, meaning good mood and happiness, while 'down' or 'low' represents negative feelings like bad mood, sadness, and depression.

Movement, bodily activity, and connecting with the everyday were the pillars of this early stage of learning: she made the family cover their whole flat in Post-it stickers with the respective Slovak vocabulary written on them. Laura had the mother, an ambitious lay chef, explain cooking recipes to her, urging her to use the corresponding Slovak terms. She watched TV with the family and had the plots of Arab soap operas explained to her. One time, she initiated a project on the guitar, the girls' favorite instrument, and asked them to design a poster. The girls were excited and remained focused on the project for hours. Laura told me she had very humble and realistic expectations of the lasting impact of this activity; she wanted them to remember only two essential words: *chytiť* (hold) and *potrebujeme* (we need). She also abstained from teaching them to read or write altogether, having them note new words in phonetic Arab instead. According to Laura, avoiding frustration is of seminal importance, especially in a life situation in which everything seems scary and overwhelming. If language learning becomes associated with fear, embarrassment, and failure, students may start resenting the language, and the learning progress is in jeopardy. Laura's approach to language teaching really is bricolage—progressing in minute steps, relying on her creativity, attuning to her protégées and her gut feeling to put together new methods, and putting affordable and available, if unfitting resources to the best possible use. Often, it produces workable solutions, and sometimes, it amounts to nothing but learning experiences for herself.

She noticed that after a period of steady improvement, there was sudden stagnation: that was when the family learned that the father, Reem's divorced ex-husband who lives in Germany, had suffered a stroke. Concentrated learning was unthinkable under these conditions. Instead, Laura took the family out for trips and excursions, for walks in the city or ice skating. Even if communication in Slovak was restricted to a minimum, it strengthened their relationship.

Money and benefits

Refugees receive social benefits for as long as they take part in the integration program, which is six months for single males and females, one year for families, and 18 months for single parents with children. The benefit is provided directly by the service organization, not by the Migration Office or any other state organ. Social workers in service organizations are deeply uncomfortable with this arrangement because it introduces a delicate power imbalance into the relationship with their clients (Hlinčíková and Sekulová 2015, 67–69). Marcela, manager of ASPR, the third service organization during the time of my fieldwork next to Refúgium and Pomoc a Nádej, proposes:

> Certainly, it would be better if they got their welfare directly from the state. This way we are in a position in which we decide over the amount of money they are getting, although it's not very flexible. But it makes the relationship with the clients difficult. Because we want a trustful relationship, it takes time to build that, and it's very bad when they feel they can't tell us everything because it might affect their money.

When they start the integration program, refugees sign the aforementioned integration contract, which obliges them to visit a language course at least once a week for six months. They can reject a maximum of two job offers the organization finds for them before having their benefits reduced or canceled (Hlinčíková and Sekulová 2015, 113). Unsurprisingly, the benefits are small: in 2018, the law foresaw 290€ per month for a single person, and for families, it can go up to 570€.[13] Service organizations usually register their clients at the job center three months into their integration program, so they are entitled to unemployment benefits in case they do not find a job within the first six months. This is, as experts agree, a very optimistic time frame to be ready for the Slovak job market (Hlinčíková and Sekulová 2015, 147). The unemployment benefits are considerably lower than the integration benefits.

Since refugees often need to accept unskilled, low-paid work, starting employment can effectively diminish their net income. Another huge problem is that there is no provision for people of retirement age or invalids. Officially, they are not entitled to any pension from the Slovak state since they never paid into the system, even though they obviously cannot sustain themselves. Mothers are not entitled to maternity leave. In situations where the allotted benefit and time frame of its disbursement are too tight, clients may be eligible for a prolongation of the integration benefit. Service organizations have a say in who can apply for these supplementary payments and for how long they can receive them. But this remains no more than an emergency solution requiring intense administrative work, perpetuating dependencies between clients and service providers (Hlinčíková and Sekulová 2015, 115).

Persons with approved asylum status enjoy the same access to insurance and healthcare as Slovak citizens, but this is not the case for people with subsidiary protection. Considerable paperwork has to be filled out by doctors and clinics before they can provide health services for people with subsidiary protection. Most medical staff are unaware of this, so social workers need to guide them through the process step by step, and not a few shun away from treating them in the first place once they learn about these obligations (Bargerová, Fajnorová and Chudžíková 2011, 51–56).

Most refugees (and other migrants from third countries), especially those who did not enjoy comprehensive education in their countries of origin, or who do not get their

---

13. The Slovak minimum wage was 480€ per month in 2017, the average wage around 950€. The minimum subsistence level was calculated to be about 200€ at that time. See further statistics at https://www.minimalnamzda.sk, accessed 25.05.2018.

diplomas recognized, live in a state of permanent precarity, at least during the first few years of their stay in Slovakia. The employees of service organizations have to comply with the integration contract and the sanction regime set up by the Migration Office. This is a considerable source of feelings of guilt and shame when they realize their hands are tied in offering clients much-needed support, and hence also of frustration and grievances against the 'system' in place. Options for increasing financial help are indeed limited, with the organizations themselves being on a shoestring budget. What they can do is find alternative channels for support.

Elaha came to Slovakia with her husband and three children. They were a wealthy family in their country of origin and were threatened by local criminal organizations. When their children were harassed by actors from this scene at school, the parents realized that they had to leave. They were granted asylum and meanwhile, they have been in Slovakia long enough to apply for citizenship.

A few years after their arrival, Elaha's husband was diagnosed with cancer and had to undergo several chemotherapies. He is not able to work. While his health insurance covers his therapy, the welfare they receive is not enough to sustain the family. Elaha has tried different jobs, but they are usually short-term and part-time and pay even less than the meager unemployment benefit she receives. This is why she decided to change tracks and start her own business—a kebab stand at Bratislava's buzzing week-round market square. It is not easy to get a gastronomic business up and going while also performing the majority of parenting duties.

Having lived in Bratislava for many years now, Elaha is a familiar face to anyone working with refugees and migrants or involved in anti-racist activism in town. Weeks after the stand had opened, a wave of kebab-related posts hit the social media feeds of anyone within the liberal Bratislava filter bubble. Elaha's service organization, ASPR, kick-started the process on their official Facebook account, and many individuals who were affiliated with Elaha in one way or another followed suit. They went to Elaha's kebab stand and took photos of their sandwiches, not only praising the quality and quantity of the food but also giving heartwarming eulogies of the chef's kindness and willpower. The respective posts were enthusiastically shared and received much benevolence. Obývačka found another way to push Elaha's enterprise. They turn to her as a standard caterer whenever they have cultural activities in their community center, especially ordering her famously delicious baklava. They pay for the food with the grants they receive from sponsors to carry out community events.

Haroun has also faced a heavy blow of fate. Only a few months after having been diagnosed, his wife died of cancer. While grieving the loss of his wife together with his daughters, his financial situation deteriorated, and he turned to his service organization for advice and help. The staff members discussed the matter, nevertheless concluding that they were unable to give him an extra cash injection. It would send the wrong message to other clients, most of whom were struggling to make ends meet too. Also, unlike others, Haroun did have his job in carpentry. Some employees pointed out that the organization was already supporting the family in many other ways, if not financially, then through covering the costs for leisure or educational activities they could not afford otherwise. For example, an art therapist was seeing the two girls once a month on the organization's premises; she received payments for dedicating herself to the half-orphans. They also received help from two student volunteers who provided homework support and free-time activities for them. Those students were reimbursed for their expenses whenever they took the girls to the theater or cinema. The team found that this form of indirect support was easier to justify and agreed to focus on similar projects in the future. They offered a swimming course for the girls instead, and did Haroun the favor of offering him to participate in a religious family camp one employee was organizing in her other job.

These were just some of the ways in which refugee supporters try to avoid direct payments, nevertheless finding subtle ways of unburdening refugees financially. Again, some of these measures have a meaningful impact while others barely exceed the 'better than nothing' requirement. Some actors, especially those who do not work for service organizations and feel less bound by the Migration Office's prescriptions, are more inclined to support their protégées directly through gifts and cash. When it turned out that Reem was skipping her Slovak class at the language school, the Migration Office cut her social benefits. Veronika, however, felt compassion for the young woman and substituted Reem's reduced benefits. When the Migration Office found out about this, they made an urgent appeal to stop giving Reem financial support.

> I stepped in because I pitied her [...] I didn't see it as her fault but rather felt that she had a lot of trouble with her kids at that time, she didn't appear like an irresponsible person to me [...] I mean I got their intention [the Migration Office's, author's note], but on the other hand, I wanted to support Reem so she knows that she is welcome here, that she can really turn to us [...] But I still have this feeling that she doesn't want to cause us any trouble, that whenever there is something to *riešiť* we find out accidentally. I learn about it only when I hear other people say that there is some problem.

Favors and Community

The preceding paragraphs have shown how problems were solved or addressed because actors, as individuals, became engaged in the lives of other actors to an extraordinary degree, putting all their skills and contacts to work and crossing the boundaries between work, leisure, and the private sphere. Their engagement can be seen as individual effort bound up in a collective (morally defined) subject position. Informal practices are an important field for self-fashioning projects—they are effective channels for communicating how a person wants to be perceived by the world around her or him, and how he or she wants to relate to others. Exceeding the realm of self-serving and instrumental behavior, informal practices turn into a domain of self-realization or self-presentation. Many of the informal practices with the biggest impact are transacted between like-minded people as 'favors.' According to Caroline Humphrey, doing favors contains a "moral aesthetic of action that endows the actors with standing and a sense of self-worth" (2012, 23).

The favors that refugee supporters exchange express 'inner' attitudes that are defined both in resistance to a comprehensive 'regime' and consonance with another, subversive, communal rulebook. Favors realize the belonging of refugee supporters to an emotional community, and they support self-fashioning along this community's norms. One could also call it a moral community in parallel to what Rosenwein (2007) has described for emotion, as a social (sub-)group with a shared set of conventions on how to evaluate things as moral or immoral.[14] This group is largely congruent with those who are being denoted as (or call themselves) Bratislavská kaviareň or slniečkári—it identifies with a certain way to react emotionally to the suffering of refugees (empathetically, approvingly, sensitively), taking these affective responses as the foundation for their moral practice. Which practices exactly this commitment entails for it to be moral is very controversial, as I will discuss in upcoming chapters. The imagined 'adversary' is another point of contention. Generally speaking, this moral community aims to stand up to those people who do not include refugees in their realm of moral responsibility. However, as I showed in the previous chapter, the outlines of this juxtaposition are not always clearly defined, and thus the identification and condemnation of the 'enemy' is also not unequivocal among refugee supporters. The state's reluctance to take responsibility for refugees, for instance, is not unanimously chided. Many welcome and embrace the tasks and responsibilities that are available to them and integrate them into their lives in a way that benefits them socially and emotionally.

Yet, all these actors take for granted that a basic moral consensus unites them, potential discrepancies being regarded as inconsequential. The existence of the moral or emotional community is manifested, then, in the way those people who identify as its members interact—it is fundamentally transactional. The refugee care system would collapse without a generous circulation of courtesies among Slovak refugee supporters. The term 'favors' can be used in a context in which strict reciprocity not unlike financial transactions is expected, like in the "economy of favors" which Ledeneva observed for the *blat* phenomenon in Russia (1998). But favors can also procure more elusive, ideational rewards. In all the examples above, we see that for starting a life in Slovakia, refugees hinge upon favors that are not directly reciprocated. Ondra and Ľuboš creating a job, volunteers teaching Slovak or repairing a flat, the school principal accepting two Syrian girls and taking care of them personally, or people giving 'likes' on social media—all these commitments have their roots in ties between individuals who know each other personally. These individuals do not exchange favors only to develop or strengthen their interpersonal relationships, as would be the case in kinship networks or in societies in which subsistence depends on sturdy social relations—the relationships observed here are too loose and inessential to require this kind of confirmation.

---

14. The term 'moral community' traditionally appears in the literature in a slightly different sense than what I am describing here. Émile Durkheim (1965 [1912]) used the term 'moral community' to refer to socially as well as morally integrated rural communities. After Durkheim, the term has developed in the direction of an 'imagined community' (Anderson 2003 [1991])—a construct that imagines a certain familiarity and belonging among a group of people who may or may not know each other personally, but see the essence of their community expressed in a shared commitment to a certain morality (e.g., Lipset and Silverman 2019; Chambers 2016).

Instead, the values that are being exchanged are confirmation, belonging, and ethical self-worth. People invest time and resources to show their belonging to this community, be it through participating in a work brigade, donating money or objects, or providing positive references for refugees they know. The fact that their opinions are ridiculed or attacked by mainstream public opinion propels their desire for community building. By collaborating on projects like refugee care, they confirm and reassure each other of the validity of their views. Thus, the favors are paid to other members of the moral community as much as to the refugees benefiting from them. Refugees themselves are neither expected nor believed to be able to return favors in kind—they are cast solely as recipients.

The favors exchanged can be transformed into various sorts of capital. For some, the efforts' visibility is a marketing tool: for Veronika and Ivana, supporting foreigners and tutoring intercultural encounters make a strong claim about the kind of church community, respectively school they are, appealing to their designated audience and driving away those who they refuse to be affiliated with. Employees of service organizations know these moral commitments very well and turn to their like-minded friends first when they have to ask a favor. Dobroslava, Pomoc a Nádej's job manager, reported that "there are also people who contact us because they know that this community exists, and they want to help. They think it will be good for their own business' image to employ a refugee." For others, it is not even the particular political statement of being pro-refugee, but the sheer contentment of being alert and sensitive to others' needs that they want to experience and share with others. Veronika, volunteer for the civic organization Obývačka, explains:

> The workshop [for Obývačka's new volunteers, author's note] was the happiest moment I've had in months, I didn't want it to end. It really gave me a boost of energy to see all these wonderful, smart, active people. I don't have so many friends or family members who have this kind of awareness for bigger issues.

Another volunteer, Ján, added:

> You may not know that, but what Obývačka does is something very special in Slovakia. Most people care only about themselves and their closest family, they don't want to get involved in anything outside of their private sphere. It feels good to meet other people who want to help others. We should unite.

These individuals often describe their urge to help as a *srdcovka* (affair of the heart), highlighting its importance for their desired personal anchoring. While many people are thrown in and out of contact with refugees at their workplace for the time of a temporary integration project, a considerable number of people decide to keep following their clients through jobs. They change their employer in order to be able to continue working with this target group and with specific clients. This is one way in which people make refugee help their ground project that determines life courses and fulfills the self-imposed criteria of self-worth, showing, as I argued, that working life can be a key outlet for these deeply personal moral and emotional projects.[15]

The refugee policy's lack of formal solutions makes persons like Laura, Veronika, Jaromír, or Jakub go to much further lengths than expected, literally putting their whole personalities into the work with their protégées. They develop tailor-made solutions, considering the family's status as newcomers, past trauma, current financial and social situation, and individual interests. To arrive at these context-specific improvisations, actors not only draw from their own personal resources, especially contacts and money, but also skills they developed in their lives. For example, Laura is taking a similar approach as in her work as a teacher of Slovak for foreign university students: a good-humored ambassador of her language and culture with a predilection for playful pedagogics. Accommodating to the new task means reducing speed and expectations, one step at a time, until they are in line with what the Syrian family can cope with. Veronika persistently follows the principle of selfless service which she has become accustomed to in her work as a priest, often proceeding to help even though Reem did not ask for it.

Both women feel that their commitment to the refugees is closely connected to who they are as persons. Both express a 'need to help' which, if ignored, would lead to feelings of guilt and shame. The sense of obligation is multiplied by the certainty that there are already too few people who are doing this work, and that they cannot assume that anyone will take over, were they to stop. Their emotional involvement with the 'project' is so strong that boundaries between Reem's and their own needs get blurred. Laura recounts a day when she saw a news broadcast about Aleppo, the origin of 'her' Syrian family, lying in ruins. Laura turned off the TV in tears, made a cake, and brought it to Reem to "cheer her up." "Later I realized that I had done it more for myself because I couldn't bear the sadness and the passivity I was caught in. I needed a distraction," Laura confessed.

Arguably, Reem and her daughters sometimes felt overwhelmed by this much attention and charity, and they make efforts to break loose. Reem skipped her Slovak lessons, ditched her other volunteer whom Veronika found for her, built her own support network in the shape of Arab-speaking businesspeople in Bratislava, and quit her first job after only a few weeks without giving notice, while Veronika kept looking for new teachers and jobs. Veronika was not discouraged by this; on the contrary, she wanted to show that her solidarity was not dependent on receiving gratitude in exchange.

This personal and individualizing approach has its limits: in the long run, the strong interpersonal ties that are fostered can be excruciating for both sides, both in the

---

15. Peter, who worked at the time of my research as a social worker for the Migration Office, worked for a service organization before applying for this position; Marcela was the project manager at the service organization which was responsible for a previous cycle of integration projects, deciding to head the new project at a different organization; her social worker Monika also changed workplaces to stay close to her protégées; Erna, who was employed as a social worker at a Slovak refugee camp, left her job because of the low numbers of asylum applicants to become an education manager at Obývačka.

amount of time and effort they demand, and from the perspective of emotional invest-ment (see Chapter 5). Like in jazz music, it is a small step from ingenuity to disintegra-tion (and, for the outsider, it is not always apparent when the boundary between the two is overstepped).

I have shown that the formal order of refugee integration in Slovakia does not pro-vide comprehensive tools and mechanisms for problem-solving; as a result, informal practices prevail. When confronted with the decision of whether to follow the official protocol or look for informal solutions, refugee supporters usually opt for the latter, para-doxically scaffolding the deficient current order. The system relies heavily on individual initiative and hence on the emotional disposition and moral consciousness of individu-als. Although it is a lasting moral torment for refugee supporters that they sustain a faulty system by doing things that are not expected of them, they also find pride and purpose in providing care despite these challenging circumstances. Likewise, refugee supporters often complain about the lack of structure, but sometimes they also embrace the creative leeway it endows them with. Designating the ad hoc problem-solving prac-tices as 'improvisation' acknowledges a normative indeterminacy: improvisation may label something as imperfect, even sloppy, and temporary, as opposed to a well-thought-out and planned solution. In analogy to music, on the other hand, improvisation is also associated with artistry, excellent cognitive capacities, and tenacious practice. Refugee supporters' improvisation produces a lot of satisfying, but also many less-than-ideal solutions, the distinction between the two not always being obvious.

The refugee care system does not only rely on individuals but also on the exchange of favors among like-minded people. The economy of favors that sustains refugee care circumscribes a moral community, and the value that is circulated among participants in this economy is primarily the belonging to this in-circle.

In Slovakia, the reliance on individuals and intrinsically motivated moral communi-ties in refugee care is very pronounced. This chapter began to demonstrate that what people (want to) think about themselves, and how they navigate the vagaries of their relationships with ethical others, significantly influence how refugee support plays out overall. In the next chapter, I will look at the intricacies of these relationships with one-self and the 'Other' in more depth.

Chapter 5

ACCEPTANCE AND ADAPTATION

From Strange Guests to Dear Friends?

Štefan is a chaplain and the pastoral worker for the Christian Iraqi community in Nitra. Each Sunday he holds the bilingual mass in a tiny chapel in the local seminary. It is a small congregation with an almost familial ambience: the sermon is usually tailored for its specific audience, referring to the biographies and personalities of the group. Meeting the Iraqis and learning about their tragic life stories made Štefan appreciate his privileged life in security and peace. "Me and my family didn't have to run away, we live a calm life. When I think of them, I pray that they manage to adapt, that they feel good, because in the Middle East, the situation is terrible." For him, 'adapting' is as much about fostering an appropriate attitude to one's host country as it is about language and customs: "Integrating means dreaming about home, but also accepting life where I am and living my life to the fullest where I am. If they like life here and accept being here it will be easier for them to learn the local way of life."

The Christian faith, which they share with the majority of the Slovak population, Štefan believes, provides a good foundation for this endeavor—not least because "Slovaks are more likely to accept Christians and are less afraid of them." He is convinced that the church should stand up for refugees with everything that is in its power—not only for Christians but for all those who need it. "Of course, we shouldn't open the borders either—but we should open our doors to those who knock on it."

Refugees are, for refugee supporters, ethical 'Others' writ large—human beings whom they want to treat ethically, and who—despite their 'shared humanness'—differ from them in meaningful ways. Štefan observes how he feels when he imagines the things they went through happening to him and his loved ones and can empathize. But he also acknowledges vast differences between him and them, both biographical and cultural, and he *problematizes* them—both concerning their own well-being and indirectly to Slovak society. If we assume introspection to be at the foundation of moral practice, difference poses a lot of questions. Just how different are the Others from my own inner world? How close, how familiar can they ever get? And how to evaluate this difference—in an appreciative, indifferent, or skeptical manner? Like Štefan, most refugee supporters assume both sameness and difference—they expect refugees to be like them and unlike them at the same time. The ensuing perpetual investigation into shared and differential traits is a hotbed for contradiction and conflict. In this chapter, I describe how refugee supporters handle difference in their relationships with refugees, and I explore how these relations evolve as they move from novelty to familiarity, and from strangeness to closeness.

In Slovakia and elsewhere, charity toward refugees is often rendered as a form of hospitality—as a readiness to open one's doors to strangers "who knock on it." As I described in Chapter 2, there is widespread consensus, even in Slovakia that accommodating those who need shelter is unequivocally moral. Practiced by individuals, it is a sign of benevolence and generosity, and practiced by a community, it suggests a certain level of affluence and confidence to extend hospitality to strangers. Using the language of hospitality toward refugees who are allowed into the country sits comfortably with the move from right to favor I outlined earlier (Fassin 2011)—asylum as a voluntarily selfless act rather than a legal obligation.

Hospitality is a way to forge social relations, and also a negotiation of power and difference. As such, hospitality has aroused interest throughout the history of anthropological theory—always as a decidedly ambivalent concept (Candea and Da Col 2012). It is also a reaction to the unknown, to potentially threatening difference. Julian Pitt-Rivers described hospitality as the "problem of how to deal with strangers" in an article from 1977 which due to its lasting relevance was reprinted in *hau* in 2012. I will summarize his argument in this and the next paragraph. Pitt-Rivers observed the inherent ambiguity of being welcomed as a stranger which usually comes at a cost for the guest. The arrival of a stranger necessarily produces uncomfortable closeness in which both parties—host and guest—are at each other's mercy. Each of them, if evil-spirited, can cause the other great harm. Therefore, the stranger's presence is not simply accepted, it must be carefully monitored, whereby it is the least risky to approach him or her with prudent benevolence.

Because communities protect their autonomy to maintain their social order, status cannot be transferred from one community to another, which means that strangers need to start from scratch. This is one of the great tragedies in many refugees' stories, who lost not only their homes and possessions but also their status and profession. Welcoming rites often entail some kind of test—a way of learning who one is dealing with and, at the same time, showing the newcomer his or her place in the new environment (parallels to asylum trials can be drawn easily). The hospitality situation is also characterized by a non-simultaneity of reciprocity: the guest is kept indebted to her benefactors and must be stopped from returning the favor, since debt enforces compliance with the host's rules, preventing equality and thus rivalry. Possibly being chased away or assaulted, the guest thus also risks being incorporated beyond recognition; bereft of her or his own identity. Many cultures associate strangers with the divine and transcendental. They exert a fascination, also triggering fear and an urge to control. According to Pitt-Rivers, ambiguity can never be fully eliminated but it can be held in a delicate balance that protects both host and guest.

The most influential examination of the contradiction at the heart of hospitality was carried out by Jacques Derrida (Derrida and Dufourmantelle 2000, Derrida 2001, 2005). He distinguished the absolute law of hospitality, unconditional in a Kantian sense, from the laws of hospitality in the plural that are indispensable in guest-host relations, to arrive at an arrangement that is acceptable and safe for both sides. Unconditional hospitality would require the host to accept the stranger fully irrespective of who he or she is; the host is not supposed to ask the guest's origin, intention, or even their name.

For Derrida, the violence standardly inflicted on guests starts by making them speak the language of the host, or before that, by asking their names. If we look at actual hospitality situations, it is striking that it is never granted to a stranger in the absolute sense. The stranger needs to be somehow locatable; he or she needs to be *someone* to qualify for hospitality.

> From the outset, the right to hospitality commits a household, a line of descent, a family, a familial or ethnic group receiving a familial or ethnic group. Precisely because it is inscribed in a right, a custom, an ethos and Sittlichkeit, this objective morality [...] presupposes the social and familial status of the contracting parties, that it is possible for them to be called by their names, to have names, to be subjects in law, to be questioned and liable, to have crimes imputed on them, to be held responsible, to be equipped with nameable identities, and proper names. A proper name is never purely individual. (Derrida and Dufourmantelle 2000, 23)

Real hospitality, then, is highly conditional; it reserves the right to choose whom to welcome and whom to reject, and it prescribes a kind of (asymmetric) reciprocity, a list of rules and expectations both sides need to observe, and which Derrida, quoting Émile Beneviste, calls the "pact of hospitality." It is not surprising that it is usually the host who dictates the fine print of this pact. The laws of hospitality necessarily and perpetually violate *the* law of hospitality; but they also provide a necessary corrective, saving hospitality from "being abstract, utopian, illusory, and so turning over into its opposite" (Derrida and Dufourmantelle 2000, 79). The laws and *the* law are thus inseparable. "They both imply and exclude each other, simultaneously" (Derrida and Dufourmantelle 2000, 81). This hybridity inspired Derrida to coin the neologism "hostipitality," playing with the similar sound of the words 'hospitality,' 'hostility,' and 'hostage.' Indeed, the guest can become some kind of prisoner to the terms and conditions of the host to avoid losing her or his goodwill and protection.

Derrida himself mobilized these ideas in the context of refugees and asylum, outlining the impossibility for states to fulfill their humanitarian obligation and accept refugees unconditionally since such openness would likely lead to a collapse of the system and thus also compromise the responsibility they assumed for the refugees they already welcomed (Derrida 2001). His observations exceeded the realm of political philosophy and took on an activist dimension when he, in an interview with *Le Monde*, urged readers to be aware of this quandary and approximate "the best arrangements [dispositions], the least bad conditions, the most just legislation" (Derrida 2005, 6).

Katerina Rozakou, in her article "The biopolitics of hospitality" (2012), connects hospitality with biopolitics and examines how, in the course of asylum procedures, 'worthy guests,' are produced in a corporeal sense: harmless and needy bodies that are capable of acknowledging hospitality with gratitude. Referring to the closely related Greek term *filoksenia*, she writes:

> It sets the boundaries between outsiders and insiders, and it is a practice of sovereignty and control over the stranger. It is a one-way offer and also a means of dealing with alterity. It is an act of interest and, at the same time, one of power. (Rozakou 2012, 656)

With these theoretical abstractions in mind, it is obvious that a commitment to hospitality from refugee supporters does not provide a clear ethical rulebook, much less an instruction for how to act in any given situation. Rather, hospitality is a framework that accommodates genuinely caring attitudes as much as straightforward negotiations of power and influence.

Halfway through my fieldwork, I published an article on my academic blog in which I reflected upon the paradox of hospitality and some of its manifestations which I identified in my field.[1] Peter, the social worker at the Slovak Migration Office, who read most of my articles, apparently agreed with its content: he shared the post on his own Facebook page, adding a positive comment. At first, I was surprised about this public endorsement of a rather critical text, but upon closer inspection, Derrida's analysis of actually existing hospitality did match the self-understanding of the Migration Office as they had conveyed it to me. Employees experienced the perversion of hospitality which comes with the rigid conditions for entrance and the insistence on rules that their 'guests' find overbearing, but they were still convinced that their approach to asylum seekers was the only rational and feasible way; that they offered the 'least bad conditions' possible without undermining state sovereignty.

Two years earlier, Miriama, the head of the Migration Office, had explained to me that "integration is extremism prevention." She went on to say that this was the mantra they used to justify expenses for integration projects and stress the importance of their work toward the authorities in the Ministry of the Interior. Because how could politicians possibly deny supporting measures that ultimately protect the population from terrorist attacks? A dignified treatment of newcomers was presented as a security strategy that might stop people from turning against the local order—this argument was not only used as a rhetorical device to make it hard for decision-makers to reject proposals, but it also ran through the activities of the office like a red thread. The bureaucrats are committed to a combination of friendly acceptance and close monitoring, and through governance tools like weekly reports and regularly updated client files, they pass this paradigm on to the subcontracted integration organizations.

If bureaucrats perceive the dilemma between accepting difference and demanding accommodation, this is even more relevant for refugee supporters and their oftentimes intimate care relationships with refugees: they feel obliged to approach their clients with respect and make them feel appreciated and at home. At the same time, the paradox of hospitality obliges them to adopt a skeptical approach to difference which penetrates deep into their everyday interactions. In the detailed ethnographic vignettes that will follow, I will show to its full extent the dilemma of embracing or erasing difference.

---

1. The article can be found here: http://evamariawalther.de/evamariawalther.de/2018/11/28/guests-and-other-mortal-enemies-the-ambiguity-of-hospitality/. Accessed 04.01.2023.

Making difference enjoyable

How can one appreciate diversity and at the same time minimize the significance of difference? This question is perceived as a major challenge by the NGO workers of the civic initiative Obývačka. The main hub of their activities is their community center in Bratislava downtown. It depends on people making the trip and finding the premises to participate in their activities. They are eager to create an image of hospitality and sociability—a space where everyone is welcome, and where people can meet as individuals and equals. Martina, manager and founding member of Obývačka, states that befriending refugees while living and working in Jordan and seeing the extreme precarity and frustration of being stuck in adverse life conditions are at the root of her interest in the topic. When the opportunity arose to turn the spontaneous refugee-aid initiative Kto pomôže into a more sustainable organization, she wanted to do it right, apply all the knowledge from her studies and her experience in the nonprofit sector, and avoid all the well-known pitfalls of humanitarianism, like involuntary paternalization or positive discrimination. Her approach was to embrace the principles and ideals of decolonization and egalitarianism.

On the other hand, Obývačka's mission and *raison d'être* hinge upon the fact that not everyone in Slovakia is equal. When the team sat down in 2019 to produce a document that should state the core values and convictions that employees of Obývačka identify with, the discussion got stuck on the question of whether, and how, to include the word 'foreigner.' They tried hard to stress equal acceptance without difference—but had to admit that omitting the word 'foreigner' altogether would misrepresent what they do. The free workshops and language learning activities are meant to tackle the social and economic disadvantages foreigners are faced with, on top of the threats to their bodily integrity because of the rise of xenophobia and hate crime in public spaces. Martina told me during our first meeting that in the aftermath of 2015, public opinion turned against them. This only encouraged them to persist and provide a friendly counterweight to people's negative experiences:

> The derailment of the public debate is really bad in Slovakia. I personally know some foreigners—who are meanwhile also our *friends*—who were physically attacked just because they were foreigners, had a different skin color, or wore a headscarf. That only shows that our work is important, and we need to keep doing it and deal with it more intensely.

In other words, they find themselves in a moral paradox: they want to provide direly needed guidance, but also want to get away from the reductionist view present in the media and politics, which represents refugees either as perpetrators or as helpless and voiceless victims.

The concept of their community center relies heavily on participation: refugees' own ideas for courses and social events are strongly encouraged. One series of events they offer is titled 'An evening with […]' with the name of the person who prepares the program. The presenters often choose to introduce their country of origin, focusing, understandably, on its distinctive features which are usually also the ones that seem the most exotic to Slovaks. For example, Nasim showed some beautiful pictures of the Iraqi landscape and its cultural heritage, and Jamilah invited visitors to taste Somali food and try on traditional Somali costumes. The curiosity and spirit of discovery that visitors bring to these events are satisfied with displays of folklore in the shape of music, dress, and dance, as well as culinary treats. Food takes center stage in many of Obývačka's activities: there are regular brunches and picnics in summer to which participants are asked to contribute homemade food. Other events, like language exchange meetings, courses, and film screenings usually come with an offering of snacks and delicacies, a way to support businesses of foreigners, like Elaha's (see Chapter 4). They also organize events which are supposed to make foreigners familiar with Slovak customs, like Easter and Christmas parties that feature Slovak holiday food. Martina told me that free food is always a strong motivation for people to attend; on top of that, it is relatively easy to apply for grants with events that foster community and sociality through food.

On June 20, 2019, the International Day of Refugees, Obývačka launched a large public campaign centering on food: the slogan *Cudzincov máme plné zuby* was a witty rendering of a Slovak idiom: *Mát niečeho plné zuby* (to have the mouth [teeth] full of something), which means to have enough of something. The expression can be translated as, "we are sick and tired of foreigners," but also (literally), "we have a mouth full of foreigners." A renowned Slovak illustrator designed various merchandise items for the campaign: a tote bag with a girl munching a delicious bowl of ramen, and a T-shirt on which the slogan is accompanied by all sorts of foodstuff from different cuisines. A little later, Obývačka presented the *svetová gastromapa* (global food map) of Bratislava, indicating all the favorite restaurants serving food from the rest of the world. On the map, national categories are used, like Italian, Indian, Turkish, and Vietnamese. A special section highlights the Slovak chefs "who know how to prepare foreign food so authentically that we cannot imagine this map without them." The map also includes info-boxes specifying the various 'foreign' influences (Austrian, Hungarian, etc.) that created what is today known as 'Slovak' cuisine. Another one points out that every thirteenth inhabitant of the capital is of foreign origin. The map was launched with a public dinner at a fancy location, hosted by a well-known local food blogger. It could be bought in exchange for small donations supporting the community center. On their social media pages, Obývačka explained:

> Our #plnézuby campaign […] is here to highlight what we as people have in common. No matter where we're from, we always share common ground that we can build on. We like our phos, bureks and kebabs and have already made foreign cuisines part of our lives. Why not let the people that brought them to us become part of our lives, too?[2]

Anthropologists have long paid special attention to cultural practices surrounding the preparation and offering of food as they are an excellent indicator of social patterns, structures, and relations. Mary Douglas suggested that "the human body is always treated as an image of society" and that "[b]odily control is an expression of social

---

2. From a Facebook status, my translation.

control" (Douglas 2002 [1970], 78), which makes the way food is ingested and expelled from the body subject to rules concerning "different degrees of hierarchy, inclusion and exclusion, boundaries and transactions across the boundaries" (ibid., 61). In other words, food is always shared with others according to socially defined arrangements symbolizing distance and intimacy (ibid., 66).

Hence, it is no surprise that so many activities of the organizations I observed revolve around food—shared meals are the epitome of hospitality and a universal token of appreciation, serving to overcome distance and develop intimacy. By spotlighting migrants' culinary contributions, as Obývačka's campaign did, little hospitality situations in reverse were created: a guest taking the position of the host, even if temporarily, also means destabilizing established hierarchies. If withholding the opportunity to reciprocate is a tool of psychological subordination, the possibility to 'give back' can indeed be liberating. This transpired from the food-related events Obývačka organized around the #plnézuby-campaign, that is, dinners, cooking workshops, and garden parties which featured one or several 'foreign' cuisines. Many friends of Obývačka were eager to sign up as cooks, apparently enjoying presenting their favorite dishes to inclined Slovaks.

The ambition of the #plnézuby-campaign went beyond the immediate sociality created around a dinner table. The intention was to project the appreciation of diversity that readily exists in the culinary sector onto living human beings. 'Tolerance goes through the stomach' was the subtitle of the program, suggesting that tasting one another's food is a feasible road to mutual appreciation. The staff of Obývačka, with their higher education degrees in social subjects or the humanities, are well aware of the pitfalls of addressing difference from a position of privilege. That is why they are very alert to hidden traces of othering or orientalism in their own language.

In the #plnézuby-campaign, however, Obývačka clearly stopped discounting difference, on the contrary, they let it take center stage. In an interview on national radio that marked the launch of the campaign, Martina stressed that their goal was to show that "the foreigners who live here and function successfully, do not pose a threat to anyone, no: they even create products which we, Slovaks, really like." In the same interview, Martina elaborated that Slovakia is "one of the strictest countries" when it comes to granting asylum, given the quarantine applicants undergo before entering public space, while secret services are verifying their claims:

> The people who actually receive asylum are such *preklepnutí ľudia* (thoroughly examined/ verified people) that one can be sure that they don't present a security risk for us. They really deserve to be here and they deserve that we create a positive space for them.

Being aware of the broad audience on national radio, large parts of which may be ill-informed and frightful of refugees, Martina painted a picture of the 'worthy guests' (Rozakou 2012)—harmless and neutralized through the strict administrative procedures resembling traditional entrance rituals, willing and able to contribute something that Slovakia can benefit from—in short, strangers who are different in an 'enjoyable' way.

The cost of this strategy lies in imposing a concept of difference that does not benefit, or even encompass, all foreigners. 'Ethnic' gastronomy is the most popular by-product of immigration. From the perspective of migrants, however, the gastronomic sector takes on an entirely different meaning: a substantial part of foreigners living in Slovakia, due to their restricted access to the labor market, is forced into precarious, physically demanding, and oftentimes irregular jobs in gastronomy. Sometimes, these workplaces become community hubs where minorities and diasporas indulge in the tastes and smells of home. But much more often, staff do not prepare the cuisine they grew up with. Many refugees from all over the world find work in Pizzerias or Kebab places, which are considered Italian or Turkish respectively, or even restaurants with a traditional Slovak menu. One person from Afghanistan told me that a vast majority of people working in Indian restaurants in Slovakia are, in fact, Afghan. India, in the Slovak consciousness, is less strange and less connected to Islam than Afghanistan, making 'Indian' food a far less risky business choice. This poses the question of whether the assumed authenticity, cast in the #plnézuby-campaign as a positive by-product of difference, is really a convincing bait. In theory, a 'matching' nationality or ethnicity of the person running the establishments' cuisine is considered a warrantor for quality. Slovak chefs are singled out for 'accomplishing' authenticity, whereas it is tacitly assumed for the 'ethnic' gastro-entrepreneurs. In reality, guests are often unaware of, or simply uninterested in, the background of the people who prepare their food.

On top of that, not everyone jumped on the opportunity to deliver their new surroundings their favorite dish as a *xenium*, happy to be able to finally 'give back' to the 'hosts.' Some refugees also resisted the recruitment as culinary ambassadors when asked to cook at cultural festivals or craft fairs, because they did not see how these efforts were worth their while or (in the case of acknowledged master chefs) simply because the many requests were perceived as stressful and overbearing.

While the #plnézuby-campaign attempted to build meaningful relationships around peoples' (debatable) predilection for teaching respectively tasting 'strange' cuisines, it invoked a sense of shared humanity as a takeaway message. The campaign did not only showcase enjoyable difference, it also invited to indulge in sameness: everyone needs to eat; everyone likes tasty food; every culture can pride itself on unique and delicious culinary products. Like the usage of the legitimately suffering body trope, this rationale was chosen very consciously and in full awareness that in Slovakia, full rights and undiminished respect for foreigners are things that cannot be taken for granted but need to be legitimized based on deservingness or sameness.

Obývačka is engaging in a tightrope walk between making difference insignificant while also showcasing it. As hosts, they needed to negotiate their humanistic values, the full spectrum of guests' reactions to the hospitality situation, from eager to avoidant, and the host societies' various attitudes toward difference as something instigating either curiosity or fear. It is obvious that these quandaries can only be addressed with a certain swaying back and forth between different framings of difference. While throughout this practice, Obývačkas' employees were committed to crafting a positive and dignified image of foreigners, the goal of working together at eye level is doomed to failure (of which they are well aware). After all, Obývačka's efforts directed toward the Slovak public not only rely on their intimate, inside knowledge of the host society and the hoops they needed to jump through to make an impact—they also rely on their authority as Slovak organizations run by Slovaks. Despite being name-called as coffee-house and sun people, they are still undeniably part of the host society. Their appraising strangers and welcoming them in is hence perceived as a much less perilous scenario than if the strangers were forced to 'introduce' themselves.

While for Obývačka, difference is mainly a matter of framing and communication, albeit a tricky one, the employees of Pomoc a Nádej, in their everyday encounters with Iraqi refugees, interpret difference (read: cultural difference) as a challenge to be over-come, requiring a conscious effort to learn and adapt from both sides.

Hospitality and Hostility

In 2016, *TV Lux*, the Slovak Catholic television channel, ran a documentary on the situ-ation of Christians in a refugee camp in Sulaymaniyah. Among the people portrayed between container bungalows and dusty football grounds, talking about the loved ones they lost due to the horrific cruelties of Daesh, are some of the people soon to be reset-tled in Slovakia. Several Slovak humanitarian workers live in the camp, sent to Iraq by the Slovak Catholic Charita and the St. Elizabeth University College for Health and Social Sciences, based in Prešov. One scene shows a group of people, young and middle-aged, sitting in the cold and dim light of a residential container, with a Slovak flag in the background. A teacher teaches them Slovak vocabulary, and the group repeats in choir: "*Dobrý deň*" (Good day), "*Biela a čierna*" (black and white), "*Panna Mária, pros za nás*" (Virgin Mary, pray for us). In the next scene, the same teacher explains that "you can see they are no terrorists but beautiful human beings who lost their homes and lives." The Archbishop of Kirkuk and Sulaymaniyah, commenting on the approaching reset-tlement, states that "some years ago, you too were persecuted in Slovakia as Christians. Now it's our turn. You can understand what it means to be persecuted as believers."

Christian church leaders working with refugee communities in Iraq have been look-ing around the globe for a place their people could go to and build a new life in peace. The Archbishop of Nitra was one of the few who responded positively. In coopera-tion with the Migration Office, he started looking for an organization that would take responsibility for the new arrivals and found Pomoc a Nádej, an organization that had just been founded. The team that was subsequently put together was composed of indi-viduals with little to no experience in the field of integration services—or social work with disadvantaged groups, for that matter. I already outlined Jakub the electric engi-neer's unlikely path toward becoming the project manager as a direct result of him courting one of the team members. Most others are women who had just re-entered the workforce after years of maternity leave. Before they had worked in different fields alto-gether: Uršuľa had been a social psychologist, Dorota had studied mathematics, Adela had been an accountant in a laboratory, Dobroslava had been a businesswoman, and Mária was an agricultural engineer by training.

The Iraqis' status as worthy guests is uncontested. Their story in Nitra began with a promise of proximity. Assyrian Christians, persecuted in the Middle East for their faith, were resettled to a place where faith was an important dimension of everyday life. Their sameness in belief and worldview was meant to comfort the strangers—they were now in a surrounding that was not hostile to them, where they did not belong to a diaspora but were part of the majority. On the other side, the newcomer's Christianity functioned as a guarantee for the local population, a promise that the strangers who were about to live with them were not so strange after all. To speak with Derrida, they had a name, an origin, a pedigree; their Christian heritage meant that they were already familiar enough to be trusted. This hospitality situation was thus conditional a priori, the condition being the strangers' relative sameness.

At the outset, the team of Pomoc a Nádej also had an optimistic understanding of their hospitality, which they were convinced, would make their encounter with the Iraqis work. If clearly negotiating the terms of the 'pact,' openly communicating the temporal, spatial, and material preconditions of their host-ness, they would arrive at a fair, mutually beneficial arrangement. I joined the team about two and a half years later when the chaotic hustle of the first few months was long gone. As we shall see, a hard-to-grasp disillusionment had come to stay, and countless small, petty, and moody hostilities on both sides strain the host-guest relationship. Team members spend a considerable amount of time and energy familiarizing the newcomers with their home, meaning their city, their country, their culture, its rules and particularities. It appeared that their expectations of sameness had been disappointed, and the pact of hospitality is far from clear and transparent but constantly up for debate. The following examples show the persuasiveness of 'hostipitality' in this specific context and demonstrate how relationships, despite the best intentions of all participants, can tilt toward hostility.

Teaching the Slovak workplace

Working and looking for work were among the topics that were frequently discussed among the Pomoc a Nádej staff—one in which, according to the NGO's employees, cultural difference manifested itself in a particularly visible and troublesome way. Dobroslava had worked in a large tobacco company, but when her children were born, she did not want to return to her well-paying corporate job, looking for something meaningful instead. She is now the work manager for Pomoc a Nádej, which means she searches for fitting jobs for her clients and supports them throughout the application process. During one of my first lunch breaks in Nitra, she told me that this job was a lot more challenging mentally than her previous job. "It makes a big difference if you are talking to someone from Slovakia, from Europe, or Iraq." She needed to explain things to them that are commonplace to her—for instance, what happens at a job interview— and not explain it once, but again and again. "The worst is that they themselves don't know what they want to do," she complained. She can make suggestions, send them job descriptions, but she cannot decide for them, even if, she assures, that would be better for them sometimes. It seemed to her that nothing could really satisfy them. They turned down job offer after job offer, always finding something to complain about. She repeated the same sermon for every one of them: you need to start somewhere, get some Slovak work experience on your CV. This is going to be the only way to find a better job next time. The financial support Pomoc a Nádej offered them at the time was soon going to end, they needed to prepare for self-sufficiency. But these speeches, Dobroslava reported with a sigh, usually fell on deaf ears.

A lack of effort for both finding and keeping jobs is a common complaint that Pomoc a Nádej employees voice about the Iraqis. Supposedly, clients forget to call in sick or request holidays, causing absences to pile up on their work time accounts. They complain about demanding shift work at night and not getting enough sleep. They see doctors too often for the social workers' taste, and they are thinking about retirement already at the age of 55. In the eyes of the team, these are all examples of cultural conditioning: they assume that in the Middle East, the values of discipline and diligence were less deeply ingrained, work being merely instrumental rather than (also) a manifestation of character and virtue, as in Europe. Hence, they believe that their Iraqi clients did simply not learn to deal with administrative issues and bureaucracy since they were used to a culture of informality and clientelism. This interpretation causes agitation and frustration among the refugee helpers. Sometimes they stress the need for education, patiently explaining to their clients the obvious and subtle specifics of the Slovak labor market, urging them to adapt for their own good. Sometimes they veer toward the essentialist conclusion that all efforts were in vain since their socialization and upbringing had shaped them in ways that were impossible to unlearn.

The Iraqis usually did not get their degrees acknowledged, or could not pursue their former professions, for instance, teaching, because of the language barrier. Others arrived with little or no formal education. Things are made worse by the fact that Nitra is not a center of economic activity. In practice, that means most Iraqis get badly paying manual labor jobs at a conveyor belt or a local joinery business led by a Pomoc a Nádej sympathizer, or they commute to Bratislava or even to Germany. For people who have bigger families to feed, commuting is the only feasible way to make ends meet.

The urgency of questions having to do with refugees' livelihood exacerbates conflicts on both sides. In Ibrahim's case, tensions had built up for years and occasionally erupted in strident disputes. Ibrahim is a barber and hairdresser who had owned a successful barber shop in Iraq. He came to Slovakia with a large family, himself being the only breadwinner. In Slovakia, the barber profession pays quite well, and so the team focused on allowing Ibrahim to do what he does best. They negotiated a trainee position for him in a prestigious barber shop close to Nitra. He would get his own salary from the start, but also learn more about the hairdressing business in Slovakia. However, Ibrahim did not seem all too pleased; he argued that the wage was too low, or that his workplace would be too far away from home, indicating that he would not accept the offer. Another proposal was to let Ibrahim have a kind of hair-dressing standby duty in the organization's community center. He would wait for customers to drop in spontaneously, one afternoon per week. Ibrahim stopped providing this service after a little while, tired of the uncertainty of whether anyone would come at all. The NGO workers also tried to get Ibrahim placements in various cultural events, like street fairs and cultural festivals. They believed this to be an excellent way to promote his business and get new customers. But Ibrahim turned down most of the offers, conceding that he did not make enough money from them to justify the effort. Eventually, a local charity started a fundraiser and managed, with the help of residents, to practically donate an entire salon, with equipment, to him.

When the studio failed to deliver the expected revenue, the simmering conflict between the team and Ibrahim escalated: time and again, Ibrahim returned to the organization with requests for support or demands to find him a job elsewhere. When Ibrahim came to the office one day for one of their recurring crisis talks, I was in the room next door and heard both parties raise their voices as the conversation progressed. After the meeting, the agitated NGO workers shared their impressions with me: Ibrahim was to blame for his own misfortune, he failed to commit fully to the salon, and, more importantly, he did not take any advice or accommodate the Slovak standards for barber services. He did not fix appointments in advance, he did not ask customers exactly what their wishes were, and he did not use lotion and perfume. They also complained about his very basic Slovak after having been in the country for more than two years. The escalation occurred when one NGO employee complained about his dirty shirt: "A barber has to look *tip-top*!" Ibrahim, struck by the term 'dirty,' took offense and started in turn to insult the NGO employees himself. The fight culminated with him announcing, "Fine, I don't want your help. I'm going back to Iraq." Jakub, unwilling to respond to the stir Ibrahim apparently wanted to cause, replied with, "Fine, I'll help you book a ticket."

In this encounter, it became apparent that these actors had very different ideas of the rules and entitlements their unwritten pact of hospitality would entail. In the view of Pomoc a Nádej, Ibrahim had come close to forfeiting his right to hospitality altogether. In their view, he did not reciprocate their help with an appropriate amount of gratitude and failed to display signs of adaptation. I cannot present Ibrahim's motivations with the same depth since the language barrier prevented me from getting his perspective in detail, but apparently, he believed that as a guest, he was entitled to more extensive and efficient support than what he had received. From his statements and actions, I also think it is fair to assume that Ibrahim struggled against the role and position the hosts pushed on him and felt apprehensive about being unwillingly absorbed by the hosting community. He had been a barber all his life and was more familiar with the trade; he had to defend his way of practicing his profession for the sake of protecting his dignity. The continuous effort to meddle with his approach clearly constituted a breach of the rules of hospitality in his eyes.

The spatial and temporal extent of hospitality is usually one of the aspects of hospitality that is determined by the host. Ignorance or misunderstanding in this field can cause major offense. In Ibrahim's case, it is not a delayed, but an (announced) premature departure that leads to the affront. The deliberate withdrawal of 'guestness' is a serious threat; the fact of having failed to retain the guest cannot but reflect badly on the host.

Employees of Pomoc a Nádej clearly want to welcome the Iraqis, who were strangers to them but still brothers and sisters in faith, with open arms. But their willingness shrank on countless occasions in which their efforts as hosts did not encounter the expected levels of gratitude and compliance. Whenever the Iraqis communicated that they found life in Slovakia difficult, Pomoc a Nádej understood it as belittling all their hard work.

The Iraqis, of course, see the situation a bit differently. One day close to the end of my stay in Nitra, Manuel, Jona and I went out for an ice cream after the English class that was offered on the community center, and we stayed lingering on the town's main square, right in front of the giant modernist theater. As the light got dimmer, our conversation shifted back and forth between trivial matters and big questions about the past and the future. Manuel complained about problems with his leg which had recently been injured. It felt okay now, but he was scared that he would have a relapse if he started working again in a physically challenging job which required sturdy footwear. Jona talked about his wishes to go to university and become a teacher like he had planned to do in Iraq. He had already visited a preparatory course for university and studied one semester in Bratislava, but suddenly it turned out that he could not proceed without documentation of his previous education which is archived in Baghdad and very hard to come by. Alternatively, he could go back to school and complete the Slovak *maturita*, the high school diploma, which Jona wanted to avoid; it would be both degrading (with regard to his age) and extremely challenging to complete this degree in a language he did not know that well. Disheartened, he returned to Nitra and started working shifts at the conveyor belt to help his large family get by. "Recently I saw pictures on Facebook of my friends in Iraq who graduated," he said, suddenly overcome with emotions. "Had I stayed in Iraq, I could be a teacher now." Later he admitted that he had growing doubts about his teaching ambitions; unlike in Iraq, the job is rather low-prestige and badly paid in Slovakia.

Looking for a not-too-abrupt change of topic, I asked into the gloomy silence: "Who is your favorite social worker?" Jona explained how fond he is of Mária—even though she was not 'their' social worker (their family is usually taken care of by Uršuľa), Mária was the one who never turned anyone down but always helped the best she could. Manuel had had some time to contemplate while Jona spoke and replied with confidence: "I choose myself." Sure, some people had been helpful to him, but overall, the experience in Slovakia had been a rather frustrating one, and he blamed the institutional framework that had brought them here, not just Pomoc a Nádej but also the Migration Office and the Catholic representatives. There had been a harsh clash between expectations and reality, and in this mess, he decided he could only trust himself.

Manuel and Jona told me about the meetings they had had with Slovak representatives when they were in the camp in Iraq; they were told that Slovakia was not the promised land, but they could keep their driving licenses, degrees, and professions. They specifically told Jona that the documentation of his education he brought to the camp was enough and no additional proof from Baghdad was needed. Manuel explained that his family was in quite a comfortable financial situation at home; he had had a well-paying government job as a doctoral nurse at the hospital, and they had made plans: building a house, and organizing his wedding. Then they were displaced. When the opportunity to go to Slovakia arose, it was not only the chance to escape danger to life and limb but also the prospect of existential security and prosperity in Europe that convinced them to come here. However, none of his relatives was doing what they had learned or wanted to do, and his training as a doctoral nurse did not get him anywhere because the profession—a highly skilled healthcare worker with responsibilities exceeding those of nurses in the Slovak healthcare system—did not even exist. His father had been a driver for over thirty years. Now he was far removed from mastering Slovak well enough to pass the local driver's license test. His mother dearly missed her teaching job, but barely anyone here was interested in learning Arab.

The two young men have faith, literally. They are convinced that there was a reason why God had put them right here, right now, and that they needed to be patient and enduring. But it is clear that they still feel lost and betrayed. Elizabeth Cullen Dunn (2018) has argued that the rupture and trauma of displacement can have an equally unsettling impact as the experience of war itself. She shows that the experience of displacement, in combination with the loss of possessions, the lack of reliable knowledge of the world around them, and positive prospects for the future, produces a profound sense of disorientation (Dunn 2018, 24).

For the Iraqis, this uprooting culminates in the feeling of having been betrayed by their hosts. Like most refugees, the Iraqis struggle to make peace with the fact that they have 'ended up' in Slovakia. The fact that they themselves chose Slovakia as a destination, but partly based on false assumptions and empty promises, makes their situation all the more emotionally challenging. Reproaches for making the wrong decision compete with accusations of having been lured into something they never wanted. From their point of view, the conditions of the pact of hospitality are not being met: they have not received the treatment they were promised. They perceived the meetings in the camp in Iraq as negotiation of the terms of the pact of hospitality, but the results had not been written down. Pomoc a Nádej was not present at that time and did not feel bound by these promises, nor capable of keeping them. However, being on the receiving end of the hospitality situation, the Iraqis never had much impact on the pact to begin with. They had turned from guests to hostages quite literally: with their Slovak asylum status, they were banned from settling anywhere else in the EU or beyond without being returned back here, and if they gave up their status, their chances of being granted asylum elsewhere were slim. While these two young men are still doing their best to cooperate and fashion their own lives according to the hosts' expectations, it is clear that a sizable number of Iraqis quite simply refuse to respect their part of the pact.

In the domain of work and employment, Pomoc a Nádej intended to diminish differences and use their position as hosts to share their knowledge and help Iraqis catch up to the specifics of the Slovak labor market they couldn't possibly be familiar with. Lingering differential understandings of work-related things caused irritation, but what really sowed the seed of hostility were the different ideas on how much support, and how much accommodation was expected of each of them. The laws of hospitality are not guaranteed by any superordinate authority; their implementation cannot be claimed at any court and they are not even codified in legal documents. Guests and hosts can only hope that they have equal knowledge of their unspoken agreement.

Often enough, that is not the case. The team of Pomoc a Nádej and the Iraqis both were convinced that they were overfulfilling their own obligations while the others were failing to meet theirs. They were, however, very hesitant to address what they perceived as the other side's transgressions, rather harboring resentments and assuming ill intentions even where there may have only been misunderstanding.

Cultural difference and privacy

The issue of work and livelihood represents an unequivocal mission for Pomoc a Nádej: in their view, clients are not taking it seriously enough and need to be pushed toward adaptation, in their own interests as well as their hosts'. With other issues, a sense of hostility, more precisely, an instinctively negative appraisal of 'cultural difference' is present, but less easily translated into moral practice. Conflicts about family management, gender relations, and religiosity are clearly bordering the intimate sphere of guests which hospitality encounters are supposed to leave untouched. At the same time, they pose the question of whether, as Karl Popper stated in his Paradox of Tolerance (2003 [1945]), too much tolerance can indeed have repression as a consequence.

Team members accept the fact that some of the illiterate women above 50 years, who had never been formally employed, would never enter the workforce in Slovakia. More problematic in their eyes is a bias they perceived in decision-making power in most households. This was particularly salient for the families who chose to give up their Slovak asylum status and return to Iraq. It was usually the father of the family who implemented this decision, with other family members tagging along even if they would have preferred to stay. The unequal allocation of responsibility and deciding power within households pose difficult challenges to social workers. They hesitate to interfere in private affairs within the family realm. On the other hand, gender equality seems like a non-negotiable property of European law, and teaching newcomers to respect these values is considered an essential part of integration.

Some families had (through the intense mentoring and mediation of Pomoc a Nádej) secured mortgages and purchased and renovated their own homes. Purchasing property is seen as particularly meritorious and as a milestone in the integration process (see Chapter 7). Slovakia is among the European countries with the highest rates of home-ownership and lowest rates of rental housing. Receiving a mortgage and building a home for one's family is *the* standard life plan, succeeding to do so earns one the respect and acknowledgment which most young people aspire to. Jakub does not grow tired of defending the Iraqi's right to plan their future and pay off their debt "like everybody else" and praises the exceptional dedication and cultural adaptation that such clients display by investing in a future in Slovakia.

Therefore, the team applauds families like the Issa couple, with their four sons between teenage and adult age, who decided to purchase a small, run-down house in a village outside of Nitra, and repair it themselves. Jakub was especially proud of the head of the family, Noah, and his undeniable talent for practical tasks which he constantly yielded in his new life in Slovakia, while his wife Marina seemed less oriented. She had received a more comprehensive education and used to be a teacher. The man's practical drive, however, also caused problems: the walls of the old house were moist and likely to grow mold. Pomoc a Nádej asked a sympathizer who was very knowledgeable about DIY construction to have a look at it, and he recommended a procedure which, according to Jakub, would have required a few days in terms of draining the walls and isolating them in a manner that would last. Noah, wanting to save time and money, decided to skip that step: he isolated the respective walls with the help of tar, then clad them in wood, resulting in a pungent smell causing headaches. The team was appalled that Noah ignored the expert's opinion (whose verdict they endorsed naturally). They also speculated that Noah had not yet fully understood the climate conditions in Slovakia, with cold and moist weather almost year-round. On top of that, Marina cried out her suffering on Mária's shoulder, complaining about the terrible smell that made the place nearly uninhabitable, and her stubborn husband who refused to listen to her or the boys. Also, she never wanted the house in the first place, as she preferred living in the city.

They were desperately looking for a way to make Noah aware of the alleged careless-ness and unsustainability of his decision, without telling him upfront what to do with what was now undeniably his own property. Mária did her best to explain to him the implications of his plans but to little avail. At the team meeting the same week, Dorota suggested finding a male who could talk Noah out of this idea. The team eventually dismissed the plan, after all, Noah had not listened to the expert either and the damage had already been done. Notably, on moving day less than a week before, the judgment had sounded a bit less fatalistic: Jakub seemed happy with the result, accepting that they preferred a quick fix over lengthy preparations and that they could remedy the remain-ing problems one after another.

The boldness of Noah's decision-making breached certain ethical (and legal) prin-ciples NGO workers regarded as commonly accepted in Slovakia, like the equality of men and women and the idea of shared responsibility of both spouses in a marriage. When we were discussing the topic of religious and cultural difference, team members repeatedly referred to Noah as the prototype of a patriarchal man from the Middle East. This ostensible cultural difference breaches the boundaries of tolerable difference for at least some team members. Others prioritize the protection of the intimate sphere of their guests as long as the consequences will be confined to the family circle and not cause conflictuous encounters outside of their respective homes.

The reflex is to interpret different gender constellations as less civilized and progres-sive, but after two years of rubbing up against one another, alternative interpretations also came into view. The following conversation took place when only the female team members were present in the office. Uršuľa explained:

> From our culture and from our perspective they [the Iraqi women, author's note] seem oppressed, but when you look closer it is more complicated. The woman has the say at home. It's almost like the separation between the minister of the interior and the minister of foreign affairs. The minister of foreign affairs has to represent. But the minister of the interior directs everything from the inside and is actually more important. Women are in charge of the house and the family and thus make all the significant decisions and men do as they're told.

Adela nods and adds:

> If you think about it, there is *more* respect for women than in our culture. Men do more work, women work a maximum of six hours, if at all, and they don't have to do all the housework on top of a day job like is expected of us. From all the things we are usually

expected to do *na kolena* (with our last strength), Iraqi women are only expected to do maybe 30 percent of that, the rest is done by the man.

Dorota also confirmed her approval: "If an Iraqi woman is sick, she is not required to do anything, if we are sick all they say is 'Oh, well can have the car so you can drive to the doctor.'" All sigh in agreement and are silent for a bit, as if recalling the endless series of episodes when they felt overwhelmed dividing their attention between jobs, children, family, and spouses.

It speaks for the deep entrenchment of looking at problems in their relationship with the Iraqis from the angle of cultural difference that in a potentially de-orientalizing moment like this, rather than drawing parallels between patriarchal orders deeply affecting both their own and their guests' life worlds, the women stuck with a comparative scheme that highlights alterity and cultural difference.

Although it does not always affect their evaluation of their Iraqi clients, team members do acknowledge and accept religious variety. They remind each other of the fact that Christian faith and spirituality can take various shapes in different locations. They are also aware of the local specifics of Catholicism in Nitra and Slovakia. When debating differences in levels of public display of religious affiliation, the following exchange occurred:

Adela: The community in Nitra is particular. Everyone belongs to the Catholic bubble, without exception. In Bratislava, it looks completely different already. Here it is extreme. Maybe it's because it is new for everyone that religion is so strong. After all, it used to be oppressed for a long time.

Uršuľa: It was maybe nicer under socialism than today because faith was a personal conviction. After 1989, there was this big 'religion boom' and all these big organizations are fighting for ground and exerting pressure and pushing political agendas.

Mária: It was nicer back then because faith was about quality. Only those for whom their faith was truly important made the effort to hold it up against the adversities.

Adela: For me, it is also new that my kids are going to a church-operated school—when I was that age, I was in socialist youth organizations [giggles] I even was a pioneer!

At that point, the topic of the conversation changed to socialist youth organizations. With tangible nostalgia, they recalled the different statuses that could be achieved, the scarves they made for themselves, and which family members had enjoyed the honor of taking part in the *Spartakiáda*[3]—which had been everyone's dream.

This conversation shows that the expectations of the Iraqi archbishop were not fulfilled—the Slovaks in Nitra do remember the time when they were oppressed for their faith, but they remember it with a certain nostalgia. Again, they do not draw a parallel

---

3. The Spartakiada was a gymnastics parade that was held every five years in Prague between 1955 and 1985, commemorating the Red Army's liberation of Czechoslovakia in 1945. See Petr Roubal's *Spartakiads* (2020) for more information.

to Iraqis' experiences. Like the 'rift' imaginary in Slovak society, the assumption of cultural difference has a self-perpetuating force that glosses over certain similarities. However, the assumption of sameness—in the religious domain—also belongs to the unshakeable convictions of the Pomoc a Nádej staff. Trying to reconcile their expectations of sameness with the supposedly insurmountable difference they experienced in their work, they had arrived at pitting religion against ethnicity. The differences that had come to be labeled as negative are standardly identified as 'Arab,' belonging to the 'Arab' world overriding the association they might have with Christian culture.

There is a large variety of Christian faith groups in the Middle East, with crisscrossing ethnic designations. Not an expert in this field myself, I inquired about the Iraqi's ethnic self-identification. Did they consider 'Arab' to be an identity label for themselves? They all reacted very dismissively. Elizabeth stated that part of why she decided to stay in Slovakia despite all difficulties was that there were so few Arabs, read Muslims. If their experience of persecution and displacement had taught them one thing, it was that Christians and Muslims are not meant to be neighbors. Lukas, when asked what he thought of the label 'Arab,' just pulled his crucifix necklace from underneath his sweater and stated, as if offended: "You thought I was an Arab?! I know more about the Bible than anyone here." Manuel was kind enough to provide a slightly more elaborate response:

It's complicated. This word—Arab—it's not really clear what it means. It can be used for someone living in an Arab country, speaking Arab, or having Arab ancestry. Historically the term has its roots in the core Muslim land from which expansion started, others who converted to Islam later don't count. Christians prefer not to be called that because—well, they are Christians. If you take Arab as ethnicity, I am more likely Syriac, which denotes the descendants of the original Christians. There are three words in English: Syrian, Syriac, and Assyrian. When the media reported on us, our group, coming to Slovakia, they always wrote about the Assyrians from Iraq, but that is not entirely correct, the minority of us were Assyrians. The priest who was seeking out the families in the camp was Assyrian and he was looking mostly for those, but then he started including families with sick kids too, so it is diverse.

He continued saying that he did not mind being called Arab because he grew up in an Arab country, but then again, these kinds of categorizations did not mean much to him: "You should look at the individual person. Either you are a good person—then we get along—or not."

"Or else does hospitality begin with the unquestioning welcome, in a double effacement, the effacement of the question and the name? Is it more just and more loving to question or not to question?" Derrida (Derrida and Dufourmantelle 2000, 29) asks in his lectures on hospitality, concerned how much knowledge of and familiarity with the stranger is required, or recommended. One may ask what impact it has to call someone by a false name. If, as Derrida argues, a name is never merely individual, then a false name carries with it a whole set of false assumptions, designations, preconceptions, thereby subsuming persons under one all-encompassing category of strangeness. Once a false name is acquired, it is difficult to erase it.

In the things pertaining to the private sphere, Pomoc a Nádej perceived substantial difference between themselves and their guests, identifying them as 'cultural' (while arguably overlooking substantial similarities). Unlike the domain of work and employment, where it was easy to evaluate difference concerning a clear goal, finding suitable jobs, the domain of religious practice, family affairs, and couple relationships was much harder to evaluate. Pomoc a Nádej employees saw themselves in a double bind causing a veritable moral torment: the respect and sanctity of the private realm, which is supposed to be off-limits in an ideal hospitality scenario, and their obligation as social workers and hosts to instruct them on core values of their own community, enforcing, if necessary, non-negotiable rules. While they were confident that they had the authority to determine which degrees of accommodation could be expected from refugees, they were hesitant to act on these judgments. They are testing and redrawing the boundaries of interference according to Mattingly's laboratory model, sometimes resorting to minimally invasive, sometimes to quite disruptive measures. Now I will examine how these trajectories of (non)interference shifted with growing knowledge and familiarity.

From Hospitality to Friendship

The Iraqis, since their arrival in Nitra, had changed in a way that made them look a lot less like strangers: they were getting more confident in using the local language, they settled down in their own houses which were beginning to resemble true homes, they were a lot more knowledgeable about Slovak and local conditions and could manage larger parts of their everyday lives on their own. Because of this growing autonomy, the reliance of clients on their social workers had grown less absolute, and the hierarchical distance between them had diminished. Nevertheless, clients remained dependent on institutional help in a great number of matters. The relationship between refugees and helpers had taken on a different quality. They spent considerable amounts of time together, had better insights into the other's private life (although more so in one direction than the other); they stood together in crises and solved countless problems; they even occasionally participated in shared leisure activities, like picnics and excursions.

As Martina had done in our first interview, many refugee supporters liked to refer to their protégées as their 'friends.' It sounds, of course, much nicer than the bureaucratic 'client,' or alternative geographical ('Iraqis') or legal ('refugees') designations. Calling someone a friend means acknowledging him or her as an individual rather than a representative of a category, and as a holistic personality rather than an assembly of characteristics and needs. The term reflects positively on the user, it credits him with the ability to affectionately relate to others at eye level, be they objectively disadvantaged, or not. When refugee supporters use this term, I think they want to benefit from the positive connotations of its usage, as well as express the genuine closeness they perceive toward their clients-cum-friends.

In a popular understanding, friendship is an optimistic concept associated with several very positive properties: it is a relationship between free and equal individuals, "based on spontaneous and unconstrained sentiment or affection" (Carrier 1999, 21). It is free of any strategic and calculating intentions; the key motivation for maintaining the relationship is mutual appreciation. Starting from Montaigne's essay "De l'amitié" from 1580, there is a strand of philosophical thinking throughout the centuries that supports this image, by stating that friendship is like a refuge for the wretched individual; it is a space that is free of restraint and expectations that shape other spheres of life, like kinship relations or the workplace, and it is ancillary to these because it allows people to develop themselves freely. Contemporary proponents of this narrative also announce a global golden age for friendship as traditional social structures weaken (Paine 1969; Giddens 1992; Spencer and Pahl 2006).

Anthropological accounts of friendship usually start by juxtaposing it to kinship (characterizing it, as noted above, as a less structured type of relationship). However, I want to pit friendship against the relationship one has with a stranger, connecting it to the previous deliberations on hospitality as a solution to the question of 'how to deal with strangers.' The evolution from stranger to friend is gradual and possibly also never complete. As a logical consequence, hospitality and friendship can be imagined as consecutive evolutionary stages: hospitality is understood as friendliness you extend to a stranger while friendship applies to a familiar person.

But the two concepts may be less distinctive than one assumes, as they may be seen to be merely existing on a continuum based on their composition out of either shared or distinct properties.

Let us stick with the idealized public imaginaries of both concepts for now (Bell and Coleman 1999; Carrier 1999; Paine 1999). These see both hospitality and friendship as benevolent ways of relating to others; both contain a form of unspoken consent, an obligation to a certain degree of mutuality, although the contents of the respective pacts may vary widely. However, they also differ: hospitality is a handbook for arrival and beginnings while friendship pertains to staying and continuity; hospitality is characterized by conditionality while friendship is an expression of free will and choice; hospitality comes with a promise to respect privacy while friendship demands authenticity, disclosing one's true self to the other, exposing fragility. Although a guest can become a trusted person because of their non-involvement in local affairs, intrigues, or rivalries (Sorge 2009), it is usually the friend who is expected to be most open about their thoughts and feelings, expecting the same degree of transparency and honesty in return. It remains, of course, a risky deal that is prone to exploitation and betrayal (Paine 1999). This is just one of the reasons why the transition from 'more of a stranger' to 'more of a friend' is carefully managed.

These observations, taken together with the refugee supporters' language policy, seem to warrant the hypothesis that friendship is the more ethical way of relating to another person, for two reasons: it is a more equal relationship, with both parties sharing the same level of liability and obligation; and it is less prone to exploitation and manipulation, with instrumentality being regarded as absent or excluded (Bell and Coleman 1999).

Ethnographic accounts complicate both assertions. Concerning equality, studies have shown that friendships do occur more frequently between individuals from similar socioeconomic or ethnic backgrounds (Allan 1989), which makes sameness a precondition for friendship rather than a result of it, serving to reinforce social groups (Dyson

2010) and underscore existing inequalities by accumulating social capital within one's circles while excluding others (Carrier 1999).[4]

When talking about friendships and aspects of instrumentality, the usual assumption that the pursuit of material or strategic interests necessarily spoils friendships has also been disproved. The preceding paragraphs have listed multiple ways in which people may benefit from friendships in terms of finding approval, escaping coercive structures, maintaining social status, preventing conflicts, and so forth. It is hard to discern at what point such "instrumental" expectations begin to overshadow the required "spontaneous and unconstrained sentiment" (Carrier 1999, 21) of friendship.[5]

Less has been written about the 'dark side of friendship,' forms of constraint and the exertion of power that are realized with friendly means (Bell and Coleman 1999; Allan 1989). The assumption that the relationship is based on affinity and trust and that one's friend wishes nothing but the best for oneself means that individuals can substantially impact their friends' lives, to the extent that the friendship becomes harmful for the other. This can happen consciously when the affective bond has disintegrated. It can also be an unintended side-effect of well-meaning interventions, for instance when the friend's needs are misidentified or conflated with one's own motives and interests.

When two people's relationship moves from hospitality to friendship, developing higher levels of familiarity and intimacy, this may come with waning feelings of strangeness but not necessarily a dissolution of difference. For refugee supporters, the difference remained a challenge in treating refugees as ethical Others even when they became very close to one another, and they needed to carve out new ways to evaluate and manage differences in their encounters.

Closeness and interference

Employees of Pomoc a Nádej claim that they maintain a professional distance both to their clients and their work—mainly as a measure of self-protection, to avoid getting too emotionally caught up in their clients' hardships. One day I confronted Jakub with some of the nice things clients told me about him in his absence, for example, that he had a "heart of gold." Jakub laughed it off and explained to me that "friendship is good, but it is much better to have a professional relationship." According to him, it was only natural that one developed a deeper connection with some people over time. However, a personal relationship could tilt suddenly—you could get along splendidly, but then one day you did or said something wrong and destroyed the friendship. As a social worker,

---

4. It needs to be said that this is not always the case, especially outside the Global West and North. Friendship can also be an arrangement between two individuals with the explicit aim of bridging social divisions (see, for example, Barcellos Rezende 1999).

5. Again, it points at a certain Eurocentrism in classical accounts of friendship that gifts and favors come to play a crucial role in friendships around the world without hollowing out the affective aspects, for example in Chinese *guanxi* (Smart 1999) or interethnic friendships in the Amazon (Santos-Granero 2007). It is also often overlooked that Western or European friendship frequently contains multiple dimensions of reciprocity and personal benefit.

one needed to maintain flexibility and professional distance to be able to demand things that may be unpleasant but ultimately in the client's best interest.

Despite this mantra of professional distance, unsurprisingly, the team members do get along better with some clients than with others, and some clients are more friendly and appreciative of the organizations' work than others. Spending countless hours together, some client-social worker pairs have developed into special relationships that are based on mutual affection and include shared activities that exceed the integration agenda. "If you don't pass your math exams, we're not going to be friends anymore," Jakub said jokingly to his favorite boys from the Issa family who were supposed to enter secondary school. Lukas is Mária's platonic date when she needs one, for example, when attending the annual ball of a local charity. Uršuľa grew very close to the Karah family after the mother grew sick with cancer and she accompanied them to numerous medical appointments, becoming an invaluable source of optimism and hope for the devastated family.

The most 'popular' client in terms of personal relationships is probably Magdalena. A mother of four, the young woman is very eager to learn Slovak and communicate with the team on matters both work-related and beyond. Next to the Issas, her family is one of the first to buy a house in a nearby village, and she attends driving school and Slovak language classes. Requiring substantial assistance, Magdalena and her family are still presented as a particularly successful case, owing to their willingness to cooperate and adapt to the cultural template for a satisfying life in Slovakia, including a job, a car, and a house. Magdalena is also an outspoken and straightforward woman; she enjoys conversations with the team members and uses them to vent her frustration about things that were not going so well and the problems she encountered. Unlike most other female clients who are more hesitant to speak out for themselves, Magdalena is a transparent client; the team appreciates that they do not need to guess what her concerns are but that she clearly states what she needs help with.

Magdalena has a special relationship with Mária, 'her' social worker; they call each other even when Mária is on holiday just to exchange news, and Mária occasionally watches after Magdalena's kids. Of course, there is an instrumental side to their relationship, with no particular effort to conceal it, especially from Magdalena's side. Her all-too-clear communication of demands and expectations (due to her personality but probably also to her limited capability to express herself more eloquently in Slovak) occasionally amuses the office: "Magdalena called, and when I told her I don't have the car today she just said, 'okay then I don't need you anymore' and hung up," Mária reported to the team one day. Bursting into laughter, Dorota commented: "Your relationship is really based on pure, unselfish love."

The comment was supposed to mock Magdalena's calculating approach to sociability (and also carried a little side sweep against Mária's overly good nature). In the moral community Pomoc a Nádej, it was apparently desired that the relation between carers and Iraqis, although necessarily instrumental, should at least take on a disinterested pretense. But Mária and Magdalena do like each other, they feel obliged toward one another, which interferes with their professional relationship in complicated ways.

One day, Magdalena complained to Mária about her neighbors' two big dogs, of which she was afraid. She and her family had moved into their new family home a little over two months earlier. Mária made it her project to purchase a fence with Magdalena. I accompanied the two to the hardware store. After a long search, they found a rather cheapish fence and were on their way to the cashier when they ran into a shop clerk. Mária explained the situation to him, and the clerk said that they did not have the correct wire for it. He suggested checking other stores for lower prices. Mária agreed and carried the fence back. Magdalena had not understood much of the conversation and Mária explained in simple Slovak that she thought the fence was too low, also they had no wire, and they should go and check another store. Magdalena agreed. We went to another hardware store, but Mária needed to find a parking spot and had to make some phone calls, she told us to go inside alone but not buy anything yet, as she had discount cards. Magdalena seemed quite distressed and insecure. We found some fences, but they were too long. Not knowing what to do, Magdalena called Mária and her husband, in turns. Together, we built up the courage to talk to a shop clerk (my knowledge of construction props vocabulary was not much better than Magdalena's). The clerk, thankfully, was very patient and showed us a shorter fence. But Magdalena was still undecided and increasingly impatient. She wanted to postpone the purchase or drop the project altogether. She called Mária again who was waiting outside.

After that, Magdalena and I attended a driving class with some other Iraqis. When the driving instructor announced that the second class of the week was canceled, Magdalena sighed in relief and told me that her prayers had been heard. In between the renovation works, her four children, the PC lessons, and driving school, there was hardly any time left for herself. After the 90-minute lesson, we rejoined Mária who was still fence-hunting. We went back to the first shop and found a few similar fences. Mária and Magdalena walked up and down the shop pondering. Finally, Mária suggested buying the cheapest fence and, since it was a bit low, attaching it in two layers. She told Magdalena that it was up to her to decide though. Magdalena agreed. They paid, and Mária put the receipt in a folder in which she kept all the other clients' receipts in case they needed to return anything. When Mária dropped Magdalena at her village home, her kids were already getting ready for bed.

Tilo Grätz (2004) writes the following about the emergence of friendship in social settings:

> From an individual perspective, it is a small but quite decisive difference, whether somebody supports another person because he recognizes him as a friend, or, the other way round, somebody recognizes another person as a friend because of the support he may expect from him or vice versa (I help you because you are my friend' or you are my friend because you help me). (p. 112)

I believe that in practice these two paths are hard to distinguish and can lead to equally cordial relations, even if the latter seems to fall into the category of friendship 'compromised by interest.' In the case of Mária and Magdalena, friendship and support are indissolubly connected, and their relationship is very close. Magdalena is particularly fond of Mária because Mária always goes the extra mile to help her. Her appreciation of Mária and the respect for her help go so far as to occasionally throw herself into passivity. It is hard to reject such generous help, even if one is tired and weary and believes that the maximum amount of effort appropriate for purchasing a few meters of fence has been reached hours ago. The least she could do to make up for Mária's labor was patient gratitude.

Mária is also deeply caught up in the relationship with Magdalena. Her knowledge of Magdalena's situation, the financial hardship her family was suffering due to mortgage payments, her fear of dogs, and her high opinion of Mária's person prevented Mária from letting Magdalena down. She felt unable to stop searching before the perfect fence was found. Magdalena was so used to this all-inclusive care that she was reluctant to take any steps independently. The emotional investment in each other and the mutual obligation kick off a spiral of reciprocity that oftentimes benefits neither of them, on the contrary: Magdalena's dutiful and quiet gratitude triples Mária's workload, and Mária's over-engagement causes Magdalena a headache.

The entanglement went so far as to affect Magdalena's child-rearing practices. Magdalena's two elder kids who go to elementary school have a very hard time there. Since they live in the village, they need to get up very early to go to school and are hence constantly exhausted. They also have trouble learning the Latin alphabet—they are terrified of having to read out texts in front of the class. They had both been put into classes where most children were one year younger than them. Mária was in touch with the headmaster of the school and learned that they also often forgot their utensils and were at risk of losing another year by not being transferred to the next grade.

At one of the team's weekly plenary meetings, Mária vented her frustration. She felt that all her appeals were in vain, the children did not remember much of what she explained to them. One day, for example, she showed Hamza, one of the children, how to pack his bag properly, and the next day it was "complete chaos again." She also discussed this with the parents, but it ended in a farce. What else was she supposed to tell them, that they needed matching socks? Jakub supported Mária, saying that they, as social workers, could not ignore the issue just because it was the parent's task to teach their kids and they should know how to do it properly. Uršuľa disagreed passionately: even though they could try to adapt, they would never become as structured as Mária, or as Mária would like them to be. Rather than lecturing and putting pressure on them, she should leave the education of the children to their parents and give them the chance to learn from their mistakes. Mária, offended and confused, maintained that obviously, Magdalena and her husband did not understand the consequences, and besides, it was not exaggerated to advise parents to tell their children to pack their bags. Indeed, Magdalena was asking for help. Uršuľa intervened, again with full confidence, that she, Mária, could not interfere with people's private family life like this, and on top of that, educating was not her but the parents' obligation, her task was, at most, to inform. As the debate had grown quite heated at this point, Jakub cut it short by saying that there was a common ground: they should give clients an understanding of the basic foundations of 'Slovak culture,' without pressurizing them into any particular decisions.

The week after, Jakub and Mária went on a joint mission to a 'crisis talk' with Magdalena and her husband, to urge them, with some emphasis, to send the children to a special needs pedagogue, and be more attentive to their kids' performance at school. They felt this setting with the two of them in tandem and the fixed appointment was necessary to convey to them the seriousness of the issue. They had prepared everything carefully, even agreeing on a "secret code word" to drop when they felt the other one was going too far. A little later Mária arranged a meeting with the special needs pedagogue.

The way Uršuľa, whose personal and emotional relationship with Magdalena is far less developed, promoted non-interference, pointing out that barely any other family received that amount of care (although bad grades were common) speaks to the fact that friendship encourages significantly higher degrees of insight and involvement. Magdalena's language proficiency, her inclination to entrust her contact persons with her fears and problems, and the compassion this stimulated in some team members, make her friends feel obliged and entitled to intervene. They had her best interest at heart, of course, but were little aware of the power differential that characterized their relationship despite all closeness, making it hard for Magdalena to reject their well-meaning advice. Firstly, because she did not want to disappoint her friends, but also because she was still dealing with the representatives of an organization that had considerable influence over her quality of life.

As clients and carers grow closer and develop mutual affection, the leverage of refugee supporters over their clients may shrink. But it also opens up channels for the exertion of influence and control. My ethnography shows that the emergence of friend-like relations leaves hierarchical orders largely intact. Mutual trust and openness, leading to greater knowledge of each other's problems and concerns, and an increased sense of responsibility, propel refugee supporters to choose more drastic means of influencing their clients' lives. They declare it not just their professional task but make it a deeply personal project to nudge clients in a direction that is best for them, often projecting their own imaginaries of a 'good' life. Both clients and refugee supporters capitalize on their friendship with each other to warrant the other side's approval and support and pursue their own personal projects.

Jokes with a double bottom

While undergirding hierarchies, the closeness and intimacy of the friend-like relationship *also* provide channels for relief and contestation, namely in the shape of joking and mocking. "Learning the laughing lines, getting the jokes, coming to share a sense of humor is perhaps the central yet strangely nebulous heart of understanding, and belonging, within social relationships" (Carty and Musharbash 13, 2008). Understanding the jokes in a foreign surrounding, like in another country, is indeed like a benchmark of belonging, as it requires a high degree of cultural knowledge. Explaining jokes, thus, can be a tiny ritual of initiation. From a more structural perspective, Alfred Radcliffe-Brown (1940) observed a function of humor that runs parallel to the management of difference we have identified in both hospitality and friendship: it is a kind of pre-emptive measure to express mutual benevolence and diffuse potential conflicts. In what Radcliffe-Brown calls "joking relationships" certain individuals, occupying particular positions in a kinship structure for example, are allowed or even compelled to tease each other (one-directionally or mutually) in a friendly way without having to fear negative consequences. This tacit pact is supposed to prevent hostility and thus secure the stability of the social order.

Carrying out conflicts under the protective disguise of humor, mocking, and banter, is a feasible way to avoid open confrontation. Since it does not address the root causes of hostility, it is a strategy of avoidance rather than a solution, although a highly effective one. Mary Douglas (1968) states that joking "brings into relation disparate elements in such a way that an accepted pattern is challenged by the appearance of another which in some way was hidden in the first" (Douglas 1968, 365). It is in this unearthing of hidden possibilities, in the vital, subversive, and spontaneous attack on a stiff order that humor has the potential to transform social relationships. Many ethnographies have described humor as the preferred means of expression of the suppressed, excluded, and marginalized; making fun of their abusers offers an outlet for frustration and can even become a bedrock for resilience and resistance (e.g., Goldstein 2003; Carpio 2008; Alexeyeff 2008).

I want to show the dual role of expressing belonging and jumbling power relations that humor played in Slovak–Iraqi relationships in Nitra. Mocking and pranking emerged as a popular tool, especially for young Iraqis, to engage with the members of Pomoc a Nádej, in ways other than acceptance and compliance. It allows them to try other roles and test the permeability of hierarchical relations.

Manuel, whose training as a doctoral nurse has not been acknowledged in Slovakia, was sitting in the office, waiting for a job briefing by Dobroslava. "I can become a doctor in Iraq easily, you know," he told Adela and Dorota who were at their desks. Dorota picks up on it, and the following dialogue takes place:

> *Dorota:* "You can become a doctor here too."
> *Manuel:* "But here I need to study."
> *Dorota:* "And there it's possible without studying? I think I will go there and be a doctor."
> *Manuel:* "But you need money."
> *Dorota:* "I need, or I will get? I expect that I will get money there."
> *Manuel:* "You will if you work for the government or some political party."
> *Dorota:* "Okay, I can do that. Do you have contacts for me?"
> *Manuel:* "I don't have a party. I have principles, you know."
> *Dorota [in played puzzlement]:* "What is that?!"
> *Manuel:* "Moral standpoints, you know?"
> *Dorota:* "What is moral?!"
> *Manuel:* "I decided that I need some, maybe. Yesterday evening." [laughs]
> *Dorota:* "Well, you need a change sometimes, so it doesn't get boring."

This scene presents a reversal of roles in multiple ways. Manuel and Dorota take on positions that are quite the opposite of the usual ones in their relationship: Dorota, usually complaining about a lack of effort and honesty in clients, pretends to be the slacker who believes that everything is for sale, and Manuel, usually the one being instructed about the Slovak ways, plays the lecturer, providing intimate insight into local customs and particularities. During my fieldwork, little mutual mockeries like these were very common, especially in which clients made fun of team members, usually leading to collective laughter or witty comebacks.

Some jokes, however, leave the realm of harmlessness far behind; the closer the relationship, the more likely it is for more daring punchlines to be made. The young Iraqis found a friend and ally in Štefan, the chaplain. On their first summer in Slovakia, they participated in a spiritual summer camp titled 'missionary holidays' which Štefan organized; they have fond memories of the time full of sociability and laughter. This was before Štefan was made responsible for the Iraqi 'congregation.' Somehow, maybe because of his being unaffiliated with Pomoc a Nádej and the many frustrations of administrative labor, the young crowd grew quite close to him, and he grew fond of them. Especially of Hana. Hana is a young Iraqi of 17 years who is doing just fine in Slovakia: she is a talented volleyball player and an excellent student. She also managed to learn Slovak at an admirable pace and talks so quickly that even the locals squint. But her youthful self-consciousness takes turns with certain identity quests and insecurities. Hana confided to me that talking quickly was partly a conscious strategy since she hoped that if she only talked fast enough people would also overhear her mistakes.

Hana does not only talk fast, she is also (in)famous for her quick-wittedness. "Bold, bolder, boldest, Hana," that is how Štefan sums it up, but with an affectionate tone. Hana, in turn, sends Štefan pictures of her McDonald's Latte Macchiato because "he loves coffee." She would like to go to McDonald's, a place associated with young sociability and leisure, more often, but "the Iraqis don't have time, and with the Slovaks, I wouldn't know what to talk about."

One Sunday in April (the first of April, to be precise), I passed Štefan and Hana after mass; they were engaged in a visibly emotional conversation. "I believed you," Štefan said with a mixture of reproach and exasperation. He was pale as death. Hana, for her part, could not wipe a somewhat devilish grin off her face while she enjoyed her successful prank. She had told Štefan, right before mass, that her father had decided to take her and her two siblings back to Iraq, as soon as possible. Štefan, sick with worry and unable to make sense of this sudden turn of events, had had trouble focusing on the service. A little later, Hana experienced a hint of a bad conscience; she saw that Štefan was aghast. But she still giggled when she retold me her naughty deed. It was a highly efficient April's fool joke: she not only performed emotional manipulation, making someone else experience unpleasant sensations of insecurity, rage, and helplessness (which she was well familiar with); putting others in a tight spot gave her a feeling of authority and superiority which she was often lacking. The successful prank was a confirmation of herself as a person. There could barely be a better affirmation that her presence in Slovakia was wanted than Štefan's concern and worry about her alleged departure.

As the Iraqis later explained to me, as a result of being shaken by killings, terrorist attacks, bombings, and kidnappings almost daily, black or gallows humor became a common occurrence on April Fool's Day and other occasions in Iraq. It is customary to shock friends and relatives with horrible tidings and then dissolve the other's terror into a burst of redeeming laughter. Although their lives are not at stake anymore in their new home in Slovakia, these jokes seem to follow a similar pattern for Iraqi refugees: in an everyday life that often seems like a never-ending string of setbacks and adversities, it provides a certain relief to imagine a much worse scenario for a moment, then rejoice in its fictionality. Consciously or not, the confrontation with this humoristic form demands a certain degree of cultural adaptation from the Slovaks, who are used to much tamer practical jokes. Pranks can convey a hunch of an idea of what it feels like to be in this kind of situation. It gives Slovak refugee supporters an understanding of the dimension of the difference between them and their Iraqi friends—a difference that is not primarily cultural but pertains to an entirely different horizon of life experience, which includes war, displacement, trauma, and disorientation. Nudging Slovaks into an empathetic re-enactment of these experiences bears the potential of deeper understanding and intimacy—of course with varying outcomes.

One day I was driving with Mária, Lukas, and his mom. Sara, the mother, needed to catch an appointment for X-raying her knee at the local hospital. They were running late, which is why Mária got out of the car with Sara, leaving the nerve-racking hunt for a parking spot to Lukas, who recently received his Slovak driving license. When we finally spotted an empty space, it was very narrow. I anxiously advised him to keep looking, but Lukas maneuvered the car into the tiny gap without problems. On the way to the hospital floor, Lukas announced that he was planning to prank Mária. We saw her standing behind Sara who was filling in the visitor's form. "Eva, I need to tell you something," Lukas said with his head bent and a guilty voice. "We wrecked your car while parking, and another car as well." Mária immediately turned to me to ask if Lukas was joking, both disbelief and concern were already written on her face. Trying to stay neutral, I murmured "I don't know," while Lukas repeated his story with more emphasis. "I am so sorry, Mária." Mária's facial expression spun out of control for just one moment, then she regained her countenance and told Lukas "*Nevadí. Uvidíme*" (It doesn't matter. We will see). Now Lukas stepped out of the role of the beat dog and told Mária it was just a joke. Mária shook her head in overplayed disbelief, then punched Lukas in the side jokingly. Lukas was slightly disappointed; he had expected a more desperate reaction from Mária's side. Mária explained that she always acts by the maxim "Don't turn it into a problem unless it is a problem."

Humor is not just how the boundaries of authority are tested, and alternating positions are tentatively assumed, it also serves as a means to confirm the existing relationship and reassure oneself of the others' loyalty. Making an offensive or exaggerated joke is a gamble: if the prank goes too far, its teller is at risk of losing the target's goodwill—which, in Lukas's and Hana's situation, would be a quite serious scenario. If the prank goes well and both sides are united in laughter, it does not only create a moment of carefree commonality. It is also an extraordinary personal affirmation showing "You have made fun of me and yet I approve of you; you are allowed to talk to me this way because I trust that the intention of the joke was not to hurt but to give us both something to laugh about."

This chapter has shown the difficulties that occur when looking for an approach to alterity that stays true to ethical imperatives of tolerance and friendliness, yet also eliminates the 'risks' of difference. Hospitality and friendship, both considered to be particularly moral ways of relating to others, entail caring and supporting practices as well as the exertion of influence which may or may not have boundary-violating qualities. The evolution of client-carer relationships, going from professional distance to a more friend-like mode of socializing, reshuffles the relations between guest and host, tolerator and tolerated, but not enough to dissolve the hierarchy altogether. Quite the contrary, emotional closeness can boost levels of involvement and thus strengthen power differentials. Humor can expose, ridicule and challenge, but never transform these structures. The ethnographic material has shown that impulses to accept and to correct, emerging from the ambiguous nature of both hospitality and friendship, take turns in directing refugee supporters' actions, confusing refugees long-term on whether they are accepted as they are, or expected to adapt to a particular ideal image. I have also shown that refugee supporters problematize this, taking reflective stances toward their own and each other's practices and trying to lay new ground rules for how to balance acceptance and interference in their work.

In the theory chapter, I have introduced emotions and morality as embodied appraisals—evaluations either about what is right or wrong, or what is good or bad for the perceiving subject. In the question of difference, we see how much evaluations of a sociopolitical nature converge with very personal impressions, sympathies, hostilities, and vulnerabilities toward groups or even single individuals. These influences are not merely sideshows to a culturally and politically defined spectrum of opinions on cultural difference. They are at the very core of the work refugee supporters do. The way difference is evaluated as enrichment or nuisance is inseparable from the relationship in which it surfaces. From the cultural repertoire of reactions to difference, actors pick that which best aligns with their relationship at a certain point in time.

What these relations look like, and how they evolve, is not a matter of chance or a product of circumstances. Advancing guest-host-like relationships into friendships requires conscious commitment, from both sides, over extended periods. Refugee supporters opt for this because as a ground project, building a true connection and offering veritable support for refugees has the potential to deliver joy and validation—the kind that may support an entire personhood. This commitment is meaningful because it also entails accepting the risk that Martha Nussbaum sees as its indelible part: incursions of luck that may cause the loss of the person one has invested trust and effort in, being disappointed, hurt, or abandoned by this person, or causing this person harm in one's own right. Actors move from a hospitable to a friendship-like relationship not automatically but because *they want to* and accept the vulnerability, emotional turmoil, and moral peril that comes with this decision. These consciously crafted relationships are one of the reasons why it is important to study migration (also) through the lens of emotion and morality. Independently of policy papers and legal regulations, acceptable and unacceptable levels of difference are always determined in concrete relations, in practicing refugee care—and not necessarily in a more permissive way than the regulations demand.

If refugee supporters consciously craft relationships of mutual affection and intimacy, the opposite is also the case. In a different trajectory, they carefully maintain relationships that withhold unconditional trust (and mistrust!). The next chapter explores the rationale and the strategies behind ways of relating to one another that refrain from definite judgment and commitment.

Chapter 6

TRUST AND MISTRUST

Negotiating Trust and Mistrust

During an integration meeting, Mohamed was asked whether he had any opportunity to talk Slovak in his day-to-day life. Mohamed answered through his interpreter that he had Slovak friends he could practice with. "Slovak?!" Sofia commented incredulously, looking at the others with raised eyebrows. After the meeting, Nina told me she also had a funny feeling about these 'friends.' She expressed worries that they might be associated with the local drug scene. At the next meeting with Mohamed, Nina tried to find out more about the mysterious friends. Casually, she asked him how often he met them and how old they were. Mohamed answered her questions and added with a giggle that they shared a joint sometimes.

The revelation that Nina's immediate suspicion was not too far beside the point made me painfully aware of my own subconscious assumptions. The team's intuition that those people accepting Mohamed as a friend could not be entirely kosher seemed cynical to me. I had brushed off Nina's scenario of him spiraling into drug abuse and petty crime as too pessimistic—and it probably was. Yet it still astonished me that Nina's instinct about the involvement of illegal substances, the possession and consumption of which is punishable by severe penalties in Slovakia, was correct.

My misjudgment both of Mohamed's integrity and of Nina's intuition was one of those fieldwork moments that made me acutely aware of the delicacy of "negotiated trust" (Loizos 1994): How to approach the refugees' and NGO workers' accounts and my own assumptions with some caution while building trust at the same time? Trust is the basis of ethnographic fieldwork, especially in organizations. A modicum of trust needs to be there to build any kind of relationship; if we cannot believe that people's accounts of themselves hold at least some value, and that the information they convey is by and large in consonance with what they take to be true, ethnography as a method would essentially be worthless. Participant observation, with close attention to the thoughts, speech, and actions of those in the field, can approximate knowledge, but never produce certainty. Also, ethnographers must work toward being regarded as trustworthy. One day I hung out with the Iraqi teenagers in Pomoc a Nádej's community center when Hana exclaimed, "Eva is always taking notes, she's a spy from the Migration Office!" Panic rushed through my veins. It was a gag, and it eventually became an inside joke between them and me which fostered rather than inhibited intimacy. But if anyone took the threat of me secretly working against them seriously, it would mean the collapse of those relationships and, in a tightly knit organizational setting, very likely the end of this kind of fieldwork.

To complete the circle, anthropologists have learned to mistrust themselves. We are held to constantly interrogate our evaluations, opinions, the accuracy of our notes, and the things we believe to be true. Trust and mistrust in fieldwork are not polar opposites, one being the foundation of any benign relation and the other its enemy. Negotiating trust means not a gradual replacement of mistrust with trust, but constantly balancing one with the other. This moment of introspection allowed me to develop a better understanding of the NGO workers oscillating between trust and mistrust toward their clients.

Throughout the day, refugee supporters were constantly evaluating their clients in terms of trust, investigating whether or not they could achieve, in Guido Möllering's words, "a state of favorable expectation regarding other people's actions and intentions" (Möllering 2001, 404). Making these judgments was an intense moral and emotional labor. Trust is a sought-after ideal in client-carer relationships, but placing trust where it is not *deserved* is seen as neglectful or unfair. Refugee supporters were concerned that refugees were fabricating stories to receive more money or practical help, while others, due to the scarcity of these resources, were not getting their fair share. The seemingly mechanical and bureaucratic acts of resource allocation hinge upon highly subjective evaluations of trustworthiness. Time and time again, refugee supporters even deliberated if clients should be mistrusted as much as suspecting them to become a threat to themselves or Slovak society. In this chapter, I examine how refugees and refugee supporters negotiate trust—how highly volatile trusting and mistrusting attitudes translate into action.

The theorists on whom I draw in this chapter build the bridge between seeing (mis) trust as attitude and as practice. Trusting and mistrusting are predominantly seen as everyday practices based on both cognitive and intuitive, embodied judgments, tying in with my practice theory approach to morality and emotion. There is a tradition in social sciences, dating back to Simmel and Luhmann and continuing to the present day, of treating the subject matter of trust in normative terms, understanding it as the foundation of any fair and functioning society, economic order, and political system (Luhmann 2009 [1968]; Simmel 1990; Giddens 1990; Stolle 2002; Corsín Jiménez 2011). Generalized trust, according to more recent accounts, is especially important in immigration countries, since it "facilitates life in diverse societies, fosters acts of tolerance, and promotes acceptance of otherness" (Stolle 2002, 398). Mistrust, on the other hand, has been described as a real threat to peaceful conviviality, being linked to undesired phenomena such as conspiracy myths, manipulative media, expert and elite hostility, proneness to populist rhetoric, and the like (Mühlfried 2019).

The argument that mistrust erodes social cohesion is particularly present in early analyses of the postsocialist[1] societies in Central and Eastern Europe in the first two

---

1. For approximately twenty years already, scholars have asked how long it is appropriate and epistemologically salient to use 'postsocialism' as a temporal designation, and whether it bears any analytic value to compare the economic, political, and demographic circumstances of the formerly socialist countries by pressing them into the same ill-defined scheme (Hann, Humphrey and Verdery 2001). In my opinion, the designation 'postsocialist' retains validity

decades after 1989. Scholars like Piotr Sztompka (1999) diagnosed post-Transformation societies (in this case, Poland at the turn of the millennium) as suffering from a "symptom of distrust," stemming from the unreliability of the public authorities under state socialism and the chaotic transition period. Hosking diagnosed postsocialist countries with a persistent "crisis of trust" (Hosking 2005, 252), which needs to be overcome to strengthen democratic rule and civil society (s. also Rose-Ackermann 2001). In *Trust, Property and Social Change in a Southern Slovakian Village* (2003), Davide Torsello describes villager's tactics to assert control over their life circumstances in the 1990s, including an (over-)reliance on personal contacts and a strategic ambiguity toward authorities and institutions, remaining skeptical while still allowing cooperation. The notion that socialism fostered a lasting culture of general mistrust, exempting only the most intimate circle of family and friends, still yields a lot of support, also among my participants who blame Slovaks' reservation toward strangers on this legacy.

A more recent strand of social theory claims that mistrust is not a social abomination at all, emphasizing instead its productive and knowledge-procuring qualities. Referring to Nietzsche, who coined the equation "the more mistrust, the more philosophy" (Nietzsche 1954 [1887], 211 as in Mühlfried 2018, 13), scholars like Florian Mühlfried, Mathew Carey, and others make a case for mistrust as a virtue and a means of critique. These accounts contest mistrust's reputation as 'trust's evil twin,' taking Niklas Luhmann's work on trust as a starting point and developing their argument in demarcation from his conclusions. Luhmann (2009) argued that both trust and mistrust function to reduce complexity; they engage with the problem of risk, either dismissing or including it in the course of unfolding action. Mistrust stimulates precautions for potential misfortunes. Nevertheless, Luhmann is convinced that without trust, respectively measures to limit mistrust, society slowly but surely descends into chaos.

Florian Mühlfried confirms Luhmann's observations of the anticipation of risk but maintains that, while reducing complexity in some respects, mistrust *enhances* it elsewhere (Mühlfried 2018). Unlike what is commonly imagined, mistrust does not result in paralysis or lethargy, but it stimulates cognitive and practical activity. He who mistrusts anticipates unexpected outcomes; she uses her imagination to envisage the things that could go wrong as well as thinks of alternatives to avoid negative scenarios (Bürge 2018). Hence, we could say that mistrust means embracing messiness.

Accordingly, mistrust can lead to the intensification of social interaction rather than the other way around (Bürge 2018, see also Bognitz 2018)—due to the need to 'keep an eye' on people, procure information, check compliance, and so on. Translated into

---

as long as people deem it a significant aspect of their present lives. When studying the allocation of trust in a country like Slovakia, the narrative of mistrust as a socialist legacy is ubiquitous from an emic perspective. I take these interpretations seriously while maintaining a critical distance. The widespread argument that mistrust toward refugees in Slovakia results directly from a particularly postsocialist cultural constellation, for instance, seems to be abridged: as stated below, mistrust in refugees is a rather universal phenomenon, increasingly common in countries that are destinations of asylum seekers, like Italy, Greece, France, or Germany.

refugee care work, more mistrust also means more supervision, more meetings, more questions, and more bureaucracy.

Matthew Carey is another proponent of the rehabilitation of mistrust. In *Mistrust: An Ethnographic Theory* (2017), he focuses less on mistrust in its generalized shape but on an individual practice. He argues that as such it is an unavoidable response to the freedom of others and their ultimate impenetrability (see also Gambetta 1988, 219). Carey claims that mistrust contributes "to a philosophy of rugged autonomy and moral equality that assumes other people to be both free and fundamentally uncontrollable" (Carey 2017, 25). He shows this using the example of friendships among villagers in the Moroccan Atlas Mountains, who, even though close and fond of each other, always maintain a certain distance and discretion in relations. Rather than overburdening relationships with unconditional trust, making them susceptible to disappointment and violation, applying a combination of trust and mistrust leaves room for imperfections and forgiveness.

Some of these scholars call for mistrust and trust to be studied separately (Brand 2018; Pelkmans 2018) while others argue that they should be seen in relation to one another (Mühlfried 2018; Mühlfried 2019; Bürge 2018; Schiocchet 2014), curiously making a similar point, namely that mistrust is not merely the absence of trust nor its natural antagonist. The authors contest the commonsense moral dichotomy outlined earlier, trust being a valuable property while mistrust threatens relationships and should be overcome. Rather, trust and mistrust have their own moral logics. They are separate but inevitably linked practices that are carried out simultaneously, sometimes informing, and sometimes disrupting each other.

Having introduced these accounts, I do not assert any one normative moral evaluation of trust or mistrust but acknowledge the moral complexity refugee supporters navigate regarding questions of trust. Refugee care in Slovakia and elsewhere has a built-in institutionalized disposition toward mistrust that permeates every encounter. Following the pattern established in previous chapters, I will analyze these systematic pressures and then continue to look at what happens beyond them, in everyday practices of trust and mistrust which balance and evaluate reason and emotion, knowledge and uncertainty.

Institutionalized Mistrust

Politics of suspicion

Systematic suspicion is, to a large degree, a political creation which has come to dominate refugee care across contexts and countries. Refugees have been associated in migration studies with a "disposition towards suspicion" (Schiocchet 2014, 112). In asylum trials, this becomes particularly visible: numerous ethnographies, not just post-2015, have shown how officials put asylum applicants' stories to the acid test to an extent that resembles an *in dubio contra reum* approach (Tužinská 2009; Cabot 2014; Ticktin 2012; Griffiths 2012). Miriam Ticktin describes a political climate in France since the 2000s in which reducing the number of immigrants is imperative, the baseline assumption being that most asylum claims are fabricated. Officials automatically dismiss stories they have heard before as fraudulent, and only exceptionally shocking, or emotional cases are recognized as authentic (which, tragically, provides asylum seekers with the incentive to make up particularly striking stories). In Heath Cabot's case study of Greek legal aid organizations (2014), NGO workers automatically mistrust "good storytellers," while successful applicants often pride themselves on being "good actors." The interplay between performative and unveiling prowess in asylum procedures produces "pervasive uncertainties that manifest in an endemic climate of distrust and which, for workers, reflect the epistemological problem of how to know, really, about those whom they must judge" (Cabot 2014, 113).

Helena Tužinská's ethnography of asylum courtroom hearings in Slovakia (see also Chapter 4) shows that suspicion is boosted when there are so few asylum trials that there is heightened (political, not public) attention to every single case as each of them might set a precedence: Slovak judges are extremely reluctant to accept even well-documented claims that applicants would face persecution in their home country, even if, as in one case, they were imprisoned for no apparent reason or, in another case, their daughter was murdered by regime supporters.

This mistrust is mutual, which is nicely encapsulated in the title of E. Valentine Daniel's and John Knudsen's 1995 anthology *Mistrusting Refugees*: refugees on their part have good reason not to take every bit of information from officials at face value. Firstly, the experiences that precede forced migration often entail uprooting and the shattering of trust and certainties, making it hard for many refugees to trust again, especially authorities (Dunn 2018; Schiocchet 2014). Secondly, refugees' encounters with state power take on highly inconsistent, non-transparent, even random forms; different authorities may offer contradictory information or no information at all; bureaucracies may mess up or lose their data; judges may ask irrelevant questions or make outrageous decisions; all of which can only lead them to conclude that the immigration system is pitted against them (Griffiths 2012; Daniel and Knudsen 1995).

Comparing Tužinská's findings about mistrust in Slovak asylum hearings with my ethnography, it seems that the maxim of mistrust introduced in the initial stages of the asylum procedure is sticky and continues to dominate the relationship between state and refugees for years to come, even in successful cases. The asylum process, legally speaking, ascertains their neediness according to the parameters of the Geneva Convention, obliging Slovakia to offer them a predetermined measure of support and protection. The case studies in this chapter have in common that the seeming finality of this decision is illusory. Since the popular assumption is that deserving, "legitimately suffering" refugees—worthy guests—would do whatever it takes to fit into their host community, and if they do not, they cannot really have been so miserable before, doubts about their neediness are tacitly revived.

Mistrust in the Slovak refugee care system

Mistrust is not just a generalized attitude, structuring the encounters between refugees and the state; it is institutionalized in the way the official integration projects are written by the Migration Office and implemented by the service NGOs. There are several built-in mechanisms to measure deservingness and confirm or reject entitlements, which ASPR, Refúgium, and Pomoc a Nádej needed to implement. The first tool is sanctions which are defined and imposed in the project description. If clients miss more than two sessions of their language course, for example, or more than two scheduled meetings with the NGO in a month, their financial benefits are cut in the following month. In addition, benefits may be cut successively over time. If clients, for 'legitimate' reasons, need extra time to find a job that can sustain themselves or their family, they receive less financial support. It is reduced in consecutive steps as an additional incentive to prioritize their job hunt. A second powerful surveillance tool is auditing. Employees need to write weekly reports about their work with the clients, as well as *kazuistiky*, client files, in which each encounter and each significant event in their clients' lives is recorded. The purpose of the reports is not immediately clear, but they do give the Migration Office extensive insights into clients' 'progress' regarding the predefined integration goals. Both measures are arenas of negotiation between NGOs and the Migration Office. It is difficult to combine them with the empathetic approach social workers endorse.

NGO workers complained about their extensive auditing tasks on a nearly daily basis. Not only is report-writing a rather nerve-racking task that comes on top of their huge workload, but they are also worried that their clients' privacy and data protection rights might be violated and, not least, that they too are being monitored. Sofia confided to me that over the years, because of these concerns, her style of report-writing had changed significantly. When she first started working for the NGO, she attempted to give faithful and detailed accounts, whereas now she has become a lot more pragmatic and briefer. Reporting every minor inconvenience that occurs in their interaction with clients to the authorities feels like another factor eroding the thin layer of trust between her and her clients. On the other hand, as social workers of all NGOs discussed at a schooling I attended, reporting also serves self-protection: should there be any serious complication with a client, it is wise to have a paper trail of measures and precautions taken to defend oneself against accusations of negligence. It is the only way to prove that all their legal obligations have been fulfilled.

The legal sanctions also cause ambiguous feelings among NGO workers. Refugee supporters ask how they are supposed to be the refugees' confidants and expect honesty when they are also executing the most harmful measures—the cutting of benefits. Social workers often argue that clients are not straightforward with them but fashion all their interactions to maximize or at least not jeopardize financial support. "I'm sorry, but I don't make the rules" is what clients usually hear right after the bad news that their benefits are being cut. Several workers in service NGOs mentioned that they envied organizations like Obývačka which had nothing to do with social benefits and could approach clients in a more carefree way. Indeed, Martina told me that the foreigners who frequent the community center sometimes tell them things 'their' service organization does not know.

However, social workers are not entirely dismissive of the sanctioning system either. It makes relationships with their clients more manageable; it is one of the few tools of micro-governance that they have at their disposal. If clients do not attend meetings or refuse to communicate, it prevents refugee supporters from doing their job properly. In the initial months, refugees might still not understand that they need to report to the job center, make a routine health check before starting to work, and pay the electricity bill or the garbage disposal. Nudging clients into timely cooperation is for their respective best and saves social workers time and effort. The threat of financial cuts is providing an incentive for clients to stay in touch with their social workers.

Sanctions and audit obligations insert the criteria for 'deserving' refugees into the work of nongovernmental actors and leave little other choice but to regard clients with skepticism. Refugee supporters are in the paradoxical position to not only determine whether certain criteria are fulfilled but also to be responsible for making people correspond to the predefined ideal. What they really audit is their own efficiency in implementing integrative measures. This presents social workers with difficult moral dilemmas: cut benefits to incentivize self-sufficiency, or find legitimizations to continue payments and help people get their feet on the ground? Exclude small hiccups from report-writing, or include them for hindsight accountability?

Practicing Trust and Mistrust

The institutionalized mistrust determines much of the framework of client–service organization interaction. As we have already established for other issues, the distinction between refugee supporters who are committed to building trusting relationships, and state policies sowing the seeds of mistrust is an oversimplification. Refugee supporters sometimes endorse controlling and supervising measures, even placing trust in institutions like contracts and reports to protect them against accusations from both clients and state authorities. Also, as we shall see, they engage in control and supervision to an extent that exceeds the delivery of obligatory services to the Migration Office. A skeptical attitude determines the way refugee supporters talk among themselves about their clients, and how they presented the challenges of their everyday work to me.

Mistrust is present when social workers repeat the date and time of the next meeting three times, slowly. It is tangible when the Slovak teacher assumes that no one did their homework. It is noticeable when social workers fill out forms for their clients instead of letting them do it at home. It arises when they voice their 'astonishment' that client XY is sick *again*. It is audible when they say "Just as I expected" after a client misses a meeting. It materializes when they complain about clients asking for money for things they "know very well" are not refundable. It is there when they blame short and snappy answers on impoliteness rather than limited language skills. It is palpable in their tacit assumption that clients could not solve any problem they themselves could not solve.

All these minute acts and utterances go back to the same attitude that Mühlfried and Carey developed in their appraisals of mistrust: there is a shared sense that maintaining an attitude of mistrust, even though it requires extra work, is morally correct because it aids fairer resource allocation and prevents misjudgments and even dangerous or threatening situations. Maintaining mistrust means maintaining the capacity to act sensibly in undesired scenarios, acknowledging that one can never fully anticipate another person's actions. Refugee supporters would rather be generally mistrusting toward clients, hence upholding a functional working relationship, than have their "favorable expectations" disappointed. Of course, while this mistrust is upheld, actors need to simultaneously establish, confirm, expand, and demonstrate trust.

How do actors, on an individual level, decide on the right course of action if performing evaluations in terms of trust and mistrust is an ongoing and infinite process? Once again, a plenitude of different factors—intuitions, deliberations, knowledge and the lack thereof, institutional constraints and internal convictions—create a messy situation in which it can be very hard to assess the significance of certain information and events for refugee supporters' actions. Like in Mattingly's definition of moral laboratories, they need to maintain mental images of several scenarios simultaneously, preparing both for favorable and less favorable outcomes—more specifically, protecting relationships, building trust, but also reserving room for the option that expectations may be disappointed or one's placement of trust betrayed. In the following sections, I analyze the practices refugee supporters engage in to manage this internal discrepancy, and how this plays out in concrete encounters. Indeed, I argue that there is no clearly defined threshold between deliberation and action at all, but the undecidedness and oscillation between trust and mistrust are directly reflected in action, sometimes very consciously and transparently so. The practices I describe all enable this laboratory mode—until a reduction of complexity and a decision to either trust or mistrust is the only way to get forward.

A language of indeterminacy

The balancing act between trust and mistrust encourages a certain mode of communication which, due to its binary character, has been called "doppelbödig" (Brand 2018) (German for with a double bottom), "doublespeak" (as in George Orwell's novel 1984), or "duplicity" (Mühlfried 2019). Scholars who have observed these figures of speech usually maintain that the mistrust is tacit, below the surface—it is not expressed in speech acts, at least not willingly. Brand sees this as a kind of skeptical response to claims based on "the rights-based definition of victimhood, according to which being a victim constitutes legal entitlement and a source of power" (Brand 2018, 85). It is quite common for social service providers of all kinds to accept claimants (like, in Brand's case, victims of domestic violence) with open arms while, at the same time, scrutinizing whether their accounts of abuse and brutality are genuine. The task is not to share one's suspicion with the claimant (which might turn potential precautions ineffective) but also to keep open the possibility of successively eliminating one's mistrust and taking a genuinely supportive stance.

Contrary to this, I claim that there are other figures of speech that aim not to disguise one's uncertainty, but exactly at making it explicit—to communicate that the claimant should not be too sure either of one's trust or mistrust. An attitude of mistrust is sometimes too obvious in the NGO social workers' behavior to ignore; instead of hiding it from the clients, NGO employees rather aim at legitimizing doubts so as not to lose clients' trust altogether. They are eager to explain their clients' entitlements to them in a way that makes the allocation seem strict but fair.

They do so by acknowledging measures of institutionalized mistrust that control access to certain entitlements and, in the next sentence, explaining empathetically why these thresholds of deservingness are nonetheless justified. For example, Sofia reacted with compassion when Ali could not have his foreign driver's license acknowledged, forcing him to repeat the course and the test in Slovakia, but was quick to add that traffic rules differ significantly between countries and safety should be a priority. Dušan, the organization's legal advisor, spelled out the complex procedure for obtaining Slovak citizenship to his clients and admitted that the chances of succeeding, on the first attempt, were rather low; but then he went on to explain that citizenship is "the highest thing a country can offer to its inhabitants" and that it is understandable that it guards this threshold carefully. NGO workers try to convince their clients that these displays of mistrust are by no means meant to harass them personally but to maintain general standards that everyone, even them, would want to be guarded.

Of course, reservations are mutual: many clients do mistrust the NGOs, as they are more than skeptical that their best interests will be served by them. Some respond to this uncertainty with a minimalist mode of communication—they turn to the NGO only for the most basic and harmless tasks and refuse to disclose anything about themselves beyond what is absolutely necessary. Others are less certain about what they are supposed to think about the NGO, clearly fighting their own inner struggle between trust and mistrust. They are torn between appreciating the hard work of the social workers and being the grateful client on the one hand and questioning the limits of their entitlements as they are presented to them on the other.

Salma is a middle-aged woman with two kids with mental handicaps, and she fits into the ideal refugee label in many respects: her husband used to be a scholar and she had enjoyed being a housewife, but despite this privileged social background, she had managed, as one social worker phrased it, to "swallow her pride" and accept a work offer at a local laundry service to support her family. One day I interviewed Lucia, Salma's volunteer Slovak teacher, who quite surprisingly voiced harsh criticism of the NGO. She made it clear that she thought of the details as confidential, but that the relationship between Salma and the organization was deeply problematic. I was really surprised to hear that, after all, according to my own observations, Salma was always smiling, polite, and undemanding when meeting the NGO staff. Was Lucia ill-informed? Or did both the social workers and Salma put on a duplicate performance whenever they were meeting in the office space?

Subsequently, I was listening out for a hidden second layer in their conversations and came to understand that Salma was indeed strongly suspicious of the NGO and Slovak refugee policies overall, expressing this not overtly but subtly. The NGO responded with equally subtle suspicions and accusations. At one meeting she enquired, together with her interpreter, what had happened with the financial grants for driving licenses which had been announced several months prior. She had applied for that money and had not heard back. Sofia explained to them that this was an initiative of the Migration Office and they had nothing to do with it, but if she had not received a response by now, her query had probably been unsuccessful. Sofia obviously expected that Salma would leave it at that, but Salma was persistent and asked what kind of criteria had been considered when distributing the grants, and why she had not received one. When Sofia could not answer that question, she suggested calling the responsible Migration Office worker, Boris, right away, taking advantage of the presence of the interpreter. The interpreter explained on the phone that the family needed the license urgently, as the husband went to work every morning and the children needed to be brought to school, Salma wanted to be independent. They learned that the application had been indeed rejected, as only those who were willing to take the course and test in Slovak had been considered—there were insufficient funds for allowing any support or interpretation into Arabic. But Boris still promised to investigate what he could do.

After they hung up, Salma insisted that she had never asked for a translation into Arabic and that she was also willing to do it in Slovak. Sofia said that she understood how important the issue was for Salma, but that she needed to also understand the Migration Office's skepticism. "Look, we are always solving issues, even minor ones, with an interpreter." The driving exam encompassed very technical and complicated vocabulary. "The money will be gone no matter if you pass or not, so the Migration Office wants to make sure that the money is spent where there is a chance of success." She also stressed that this is all the more important because being an active participant in motorized traffic is a huge responsibility. So, in line with what I have described above, Sofia started by establishing empathetic rapport, expressing doubt in the next sentence that Salma would pass the driving exam. She also used the traffic safety argument for broader legitimation. This time, she did not even defend her own actions, but rather the Migration Office's which was responsible for the decision not to fund Salma's license.

Salma remained quite unimpressed and let Sofia know via her interpreter that she would bring all her willpower to attaining a driver's license and try the best she could. The strategy to make mistrust transparent and digestible apparently does not always work out as planned. Even more so, it is often completely unclear whether the mistrust packaged nicely achieves its intended effect, maintaining an honest and transparent mode of communication, or quite the opposite, in that clients turn their back to the NGO and adopt a habit of 'doublespeak' themselves.

Leaping to action

While doublespeak leaves addressees in uncertainty as to whether they are trusted or distrusted, that does not necessarily mean that the speaker is undecided. While absolute trust or distrust is rare (Pelkmans 2018), so is perfect indifference without any inclination toward trust or mistrust. Returning to the concept of hospitality, the host can entertain several levels of precaution without suspending the hospitality altogether. In the case of refugees, the perils of hospitality being destroyed, and trust being abused, are commonly imagined as severe, as their preemptive categorization as 'suspects' shows (Stephen 2017, see Chapter 2).

Even though refugee supporters regard such worst-case scenarios as extremely unlikely, they are constantly engaging with the problem of risk, for example in Mohamed's case. The episode with the joint was not the only occasion at which the team was suspicious of him: he missed scheduled meetings and language classes and did not make any effort to find a job, although his financial support had almost ended. He also was not very talkative and released only little information about his life after and before coming to Slovakia. There was also an incident when Mohamed stormed out of the office unexpectedly, in the middle of a conversation with Sofia. A little later, he apologized, explaining in basic English that he was "not okay in the head." In meetings, Mohamed reported with the help of an interpreter that he suffered from anxiety and had trouble sleeping. Linda, the organization's psychologist, pointed out that a restricted memory capacity is one of the symptoms of post-traumatic stress disorder, which would explain his many absences. In their encounters with Mohamed, the social workers thus attempted to carefully balance two contradictory approaches: protect Mohamed as a particularly vulnerable client *and* be particularly wary of moments of irritation.

The team did take Mohamed's side occasionally, and quite decidedly so. One day, Mohamed was evicted from the bus by a ticket inspector. Mohamed readily admitted not having had a ticket when the inspection took place, he wanted to buy a ticket from the driver but got into the vehicle through the middle doors, not in the front, as he should have. He reported having been screamed at and aggressively dragged out of the bus by what seemed to be a typical curmudgeon Slovak *revízor* (ticket inspector). Hearing this story, the employees of the organization were convinced that Mohamed had been the victim of a racist assault. They tried to comfort him and urged him to file a complaint with the local public transportation company.

Lucia, the youngest employee, accompanied him to the office of the transport agency and defended Mohamed against a stoically unfriendly clerk who did not believe Mohamed's story because the ticket inspector of the bus in question was female. "So what? Are you saying women can't behave in questionable ways?" Lucia commented, also mentioning her suspicion that a xenophobic sentiment had triggered the harsh reaction. Finally, they were asked to fill in a complaint form, but Mohamed, unnerved by the whole procedure, uttered that he would rather just pay the fine. *Chudák* (poor him), Lucia told me as we walked back to the office without Mohamed. "Now he has to pay for being treated inappropriately."

A lot of trust is involved in this specific interpretation of the events. There were no witnesses present to confirm what happened to Mohamed on the bus, and no sources to draw from except his agitated account. Still, the social workers believed his story rather than assuming that he was making things up to evade a fine, exaggerating, or just fantasizing. They based this evaluation not solely on Mohamed's credibility, but on the plausibility of the story. The scenario of a man from the Middle East being bullied out of a bus in a Slovak town sadly seemed all too familiar and thus believable to the women in the NGO office. Of course, they did not miss out on reminding Mohamed to purchase a ticket immediately the next time.

The decisive cognitive operation when investing trust into someone, Guido Möllering (2001) maintains, is an act of suspension: blind spots, uncertainties, and knowledge gaps are consciously and temporarily brushed aside while the limited available knowledge is taken as a measurement for future levels of trustworthiness. This terminology confirms Simmel's argument that trust always entails a dimension of "faith," a somewhat elusive phenomenon that is "both more and less than knowledge" (Simmel 1990 [1968], 179, as in Möllering 2001, 405). Möllering reads this as a call not to neglect a transcendental or illogical element that can be just as important as rational 'good reasons' in the process of establishing trust. Ergo, "trust can be imagined as the mental process of leaping—enabled by suspension—across the gorge of the unknowable from the land of interpretation into the land of expectation" (Möllering 2001, 412). This happened when the social workers, despite a lack of evidence, decided to treat Mohamed's story as if they knew it was true.

The refugee supporters of Refúgium have built a moral laboratory here, carefully guarding their indeterminacy while entertaining several scenarios for the future. They evaluate the impact of each of their steps for both versions: What is the worst thing that could happen to them if they trust Mohamed, and what is the worst thing that could happen to him if they distrust him? It is a complex and exhausting procedure, occasionally producing confusion and uncertainty on the side of the clients.

Zigon's moral breakdowns are caesuras that mark the transition from one paradigm for action to another, intending to reduce complexity and return to a state in which moral decisions happen relatively automatically. Maybe we can conceptualize this as the moment in which the scale tips to one side and ends the balancing act between trusting and mistrusting practices. Mistrust or trust, in this situation, is actually used to reduce complexity. Although the reasons may not always be logically graspable, actors arrive at a point at which they pick a side quite consciously, hoping to simplify future decision-making: fewer scenarios must be considered, and fewer precautions made. In any case, I think it is possible to identify not only 'leaps' to trust but also to mistrust—occasions at which impulses to trust are suspended and a latent disposition toward mistrust becomes dominant. This may trigger actions that make this evaluation irreversible.

Although supporting Mohamed to stand up for himself in the face of racist discrimination, there was nevertheless a growing mistrust toward him, translating successively into active precautions, especially when Mohamed picked up the habit of texting Sofia random pictures of cute babies and flowers, but also more puzzling ones, like veiled women, flags, and a gun. The team had been swaying between seeing Mohamed as a slacker or a particularly traumatized and indigent individual. A suspicion crept in through the enigmatic sequence of pictures, although never made explicit, that was more serious: the vague allusions to (violent) religious extremism in his messages was the straw that finally broke the camel's back. Feeling responsible toward the Slovak public, and toward other, more compliant clients, NGO workers informed the Migration Office of their suspicions.

Little later, two Migration Office employees came to town for one of their control visits. They took part in a meeting with Mohamed in which he was asked to be more diligent regarding his communication with the social workers. The conversation was translated by an interpreter. Mohamed seemed calm and remorseful, explaining the missed appointments and language classes, by pointing out his mental health problems. He repeated that he slept a lot, had trouble retaining new information, and occasionally suffered from anxiety attacks. He requested to be reminded of appointments one hour prior, but Sofia insisted that he receive the same treatment as all the other clients.

After this meeting, social workers continued approaching Mohamed as before, making him job suggestions and finding him a private Slovak teacher, but it seemed that they had made up their mind: *Nedá sa integrovať takýto človek* (It is impossible to integrate a person like this), Sofia relayed to me on one occasion. A little later, Mohamed left Slovakia without prior notice, after less than a year in the country.

In this case, we see a basic level of trust bordering on pity, as well as mistrust, being simultaneously present but constantly alternating—until it did not. Calling upon the authorities to decide over Mohammed's fate is a step with irrevocable implications. Considering that the main trigger for this change was a series of pictures from a private chat which did not need to become public, one can hardly interpret this solely as a result of institutional mistrust. Sofia came to mistrust Mohammed on the same private level on which he addressed her, likely influenced by the association of refugees with terrorism which dominates the public discourse and political arguments against accepting refugees. Even though she and her colleagues disapproved of this kind of populist rhetoric, as well as of the Migration Office's penetration of clients' private lives, a creeping "what if" managed to tip the scale in the opposite direction and change the paradigms of evaluation and action permanently.

Trust Between Rationality and Emotion

The breakdown of trust in Mohamed poses the question of aspects that go beyond hard facts or documentable realities. I cannot say with certainty whether the cooling relationship between Mohamed and the Slovak institutions was the ultimate reason for his departure. It is, however, uncontested that the situation deteriorated because of an odd 'vibe' or 'feel' that had spread throughout the team following the messaged photos and other incidents that caused irritation. Sofia had anticipated his imminent departure on several occasions: "I don't know why. I just feel he wants to leave." Refugee supporters refer to their own intuitions as a valuable source of insight and they defend their right to follow their gut feeling when talking to clients. They claim that through their experience, they have developed a reliable sensor for the problems or intentions clients might not make transparent.

We can understand this 'sensor' as a kind of embodied knowledge, rooted in memory and accumulated experience. Trust is associated with certain physical sensations, evoking sentiments of bodily comfort and calm, while mistrust is linked to increased alertness to impending danger. Instinctive feelings of repulsion or attraction regarding a (potential) recipient of trust are of paramount importance for somebody's evaluation (Hörlin 2015; Lahno 2002). Trust or mistrust may involve cognitive operations, a critical engagement with the problem of risk; however, they also must be subjectively *felt* to be effective.

The staff of Obývačka, the NGO that trains volunteers and matches them with refugee "buddies," intensely engages with this quandary in their volunteer program: a trustful relationship is the groundwork of successful volunteering, but it can only be engineered to a certain degree. In the compulsory training session, which all volunteers need to attend before being matched with their partners for the program, they are instructed on how to create favorable conditions for trust. In one of the workshops I attended, Helena explained:

> The target group is really sensitive when it comes to trust. The most important things are regularity and duration. Schedule a meeting in advance, and try to find a rhythm, even if you don't have time that often. And try to hold out, even if the first few meetings are dragging on and you find no rapport. Growing accustomed to each other takes time.

Obývačka does not leave it to advice only; they also established an administrative framework to increase transparency and accountability. Volunteers and foreigners sign a contract at the beginning of the program, which clearly states the mutual obligations. In addition, there is a series of volunteer meetings and supervisions to exchange experiences and confidentially discuss problematic situations. But even so, the matching of volunteers and foreigners fails frequently. It is not unusual for volunteers to go through several 'matches' before they find one where everything 'fits.'

Anna, who belongs to one of the first cohorts of volunteers of Obývačka, was first matched with a family from Donetsk. Anna's husband is from Western Ukraine, which Obývačka saw as an advantage. But to the family, his origin may have been an obstacle to trust, Anna suspects; they soon started postponing and canceling meetings with bogus excuses. Anna was disappointed with this first experience and asked Helena to find her another match. This time she was paired with an Afghan family with a rather secluded and traditional lifestyle. The father had been in Slovakia for seven years and had applied for citizenship, while the mother had only limited social contacts and spoke barely any Slovak. Anna was excited about this match; she is a well-traveled woman and had hoped to get in touch with people with a distinctly 'different' cultural and religious background. Her task was to keep the wife company and practice Slovak. Anna's husband also got involved and stayed with the man and the children while the women conversed. This arrangement worked for a while—until it did not anymore. The Afghan family broke off contact quite abruptly. Anna is convinced that there was a specific event that must have shattered their trust because the change was very sudden; it was most probably something they could not understand—her best guess is that she inadvertently violated gender norms or rules of politeness.

In this case, Obývačka's attempts at encouraging trust were only partially successful. They were aware that guidelines and cultural training could increase the likelihood of the emergence of trusting relationships, but there was no way to guarantee that the assigned partners open up to each other. Their only chance is to admit and explain the paradox that revolves around the intentionality of trust: you need to believe that the rational parameters for trust are met to achieve it, but it cannot be exclusively intentionally constructed; it can be easily undermined by an elusive element of instinct or feeling.

John Dunn circumscribes the paradox in the following way:

> Since at the moment of experience it is necessarily unchosen, trust as a passion cannot be in any way strategic, though of course like any other psychic state it can in practice prove to have either good or bad consequences [...] As a modality of action, however, trust is

ineluctably strategic, however blearily its adopter may conceive the circumstances in which he or she comes to adopt it, and however inadvertently they may carry through the adoption itself. (Dunn 1988, 74)

Even if emotion and cognition are indissolubly linked, the proportion of these two components varies depending on the type of relationship they are applied to:

Like the affective bonds of friendship and love, trust creates a social situation in which intense emotional investments may be made, and this is why the betrayal of a personal trust arouses a sense of emotional outrage in the betrayed. (Lewis and Weigert 1985, 971)

To a large degree, the suffering and anxiety of refugee supporters when deciding whether to trust or not to trust is caused by the fact that they have very close, sometimes even friend-like bonds with 'their' refugees (see Chapter 5) which must be, at the same time, professional relationships between service provider and recipient. Refugee supporters strategize on how best to reconcile these personal relationships with the state's demands for control and supervision. Their strive for pragmatism and efficiency which suggest mistrust in many situations also has structural roots: the scarcity of time and resources compels them not to entrust refugees with critical tasks themselves (see above). The emotional component, for its part, puts to work personal, individual experiences, opinions, grievances, and so forth. If we look at the actions guided by suspicion, we see how many of them do not (directly) aim at catering to the state-enforced paradigm but reflect refugee supporters' own sentiments as professionals and as private persons. Their agency, their declared aim to create trustful relationships is thus not only challenged by institutional constraints but also by their own sentiments, feelings, passions, urges, impulses, or whatever else you might call the less controllable movements of the mind. I will provide some examples of how such predispositions impact the allocation of trust and how they interact with structural factors.

Dorota does not hide her disappointment and frustration when she complains about the limited interest events and opportunities attracted among the Iraqi community, given that it takes her, the manager of the community center and volunteer programs, a lot of time and effort to develop them. In the first year, for instance, they organized a summer camp for kids with a program of games and outdoor activities that lasted a few days. The refugee kids were invited to participate, free of charge, they only required the mothers to prepare lunch for everyone. The mothers, however, hesitated, asking if they would be paid for it. Dorota had been excited about offering the children something nice basically for free and was still upset when retelling this episode.

Similarly, Dorota convinced some of the women to sell the decorative artifacts they produced in a weekly workshop led by a Slovak artist at a local crafts fair. It was a hot day, and around midday, Dorota came to visit the women with a popsicle for everyone. She was stunned to learn that the women had already left, claiming that they did not sell enough. Other sellers had spread out their items to cover the gap in the middle of the fair. These experiences both made Dorota reflect on her clients' and her own moral behavior in a bigger context. They were a kind of moral breakdown because they meant a rupture of everyday, automatized moral behavior in which the questions "What is right? What is expected of me and what do I expect of others?" were actively posed. Of course, Dorota's willingness to trust clients is influenced by how much she likes them and in how far they meet her expectations. Having perceived a lack of both, Dorota is inclined to suspect self-serving or effort-avoiding motives behind clients' actions, which impacts her readiness to provide support.

The way refugee supporters' personhood is tangled up with practices of trust and mistrust is crucially influenced by an unspoken "moral economy" in Michele Rivkin-Fish's sense (2011). This term delineates that in exchanges in which services are offered 'for free,' as in many charity initiatives, alternative forms of reciprocity and 'payment' need to be found, like forging a "sense of satisfaction that derives from helping deserving others" (Rivkin-Fish 2011, 192). For refugee supporters, next to the recognition and approval circulated among like-minded people in their 'economy of favors' (see Chapter 4), positive feedback from clients becomes an important source of validation and purpose. Clients' dissatisfaction, on the other hand, becomes a trigger for both personal offense and resentment. Like the Migration Office worker in the opening scene of this dissertation, they ask themselves whether it is really 'not enough' what they have to offer.

Often, deeply felt frustrations arise from a discrepancy in social capital or economic status. For social workers who spend their time helping clients with the most basic everyday tasks, it is somewhat unintuitive that those same clients may have had more social capital than themselves before their forced departure. Global studies of migration have pointed out, again and again, that since poverty severely restricts freedom of movement, the wealthier members of any society are more likely to migrate (Haas 2008). When Iraqis are eager to move into their own house with a separate room for every child, they strive for a standard that many Slovaks, possibly including those active in social work, may never attain. (Of course, on the other hand, the organization's explicit encouragement to do so might have been a major motivation for said families.) For many of the refugees, buying a car or getting a driver's license is a major priority for starting a new life in Slovakia properly. Refugee supporters are aware that some refugees had good education, prestigious jobs, and may have enjoyed a significant degree of affluence prior to becoming refugees; they can rationally acknowledge just how hard it must have been for them to lose all that. They also know that in the countries of origin, certain status symbols like cars are valued even more than in Slovakia. But the logic of the moral economy of charity sometimes overshadows these insights. A feeling of unfairness or pretentiousness is another emotional response which, semiconsciously, plays into the negotiation of trust and distrust.

Leaving Slovakia for another country is perceived as the ultimate expression of ingratitude from the refugees' side. The suspicion that refugees might have intentions or make plans to exit the country is a common one affecting many layers of refugee supporters' personhood. Whether they had a close personal relationship or not, social workers do not acknowledge the departure of former clients with indifference. Once refugees have attained asylum or subsidiary protection, they are not entitled to seek asylum anywhere else in the EU; they are also not allowed to change their country of residence. Their only chance to do so legally is after receiving Slovak citizenship, which implies becoming a citizen of the EU.

Although integration facilitators have neither the competence nor the intention to thwart refugees' westward journeys, refugees usually make such plans in secret. And although there is de facto little they can do about it, except warn refugees about potential legal repercussions and the possibility of being transferred back to Slovakia, social workers spend a considerable amount of time speculating about expected departures. Jakub makes fun of those Iraqis who claim that life is hard in Slovakia: "I've already been living here for over thirty years, and I plan to stay another thirty. That's almost heroic!" This cynical remark also contains a pinch of wounded pride: as I outlined above, refugee supporters often name the love of their country as motivation for working with refugees; they also often report that they think of Slovakia as a good place to live, a country with great potential for the future. It hurts them to see strangers so unhappy with what their country has to offer. It confirms certain negative stereotypes as a less worthy and accomplished member of the European community that they are trying to disprove.

They also see it as a further disregard for their tireless labor and effort. When NGO workers investigate suspected departures, they are also asking the question of the sufficiency and effectiveness of their own work. Stakes were high for Pomoc a Nádej: the presence of Iraqi Christians in Nitra had attracted a lot of public attention from the outset, and the Migration Office was eager to present it as a heartwarming success story. The project would have had to be declared a failure if they had departed to Western Europe in large numbers. The fact that nearly half of the group returned to Iraq was judged excusable—after all, Daesh had been pushed back, granting an explanation for a return home that seemed to have nothing to do with the achievements of Slovakia as a host country (although friends of the returnees reported that a deep sense of disillusionment with life in Slovakia was certainly present and not entirely irrelevant to their decision).

Disappointment, feelings of injustice and a lack of appreciation as well as abandonment are all frequent emotions in the everyday work of refugee supporters which have eroded their emotional disposition toward trust, slowly shifting their parameters for ethical behavior. A chain of unsatisfying or disapproving experiences forms the backdrop of memories from which mistrusting attitudes emerge on a personal level. In rare cases, the discontent with certain refugees' behavior far exceeds these subtle frustrations, creating compelling reasons for embracing mistrust. Those are the cases in which NGO workers experienced disrespectful or even threatening behavior from their clients. In one instance, social workers insisted on their right to withdraw trust entirely, leading to the dismissal of a client from the project. When Sofia told me about the incident, she was visibly shaken; the memory was still disturbing her. The client had asked her on a date before and sent her inappropriate text messages, both of which she responded to with friendly rejection. One day, when she was alone in the office with him, he started screaming at her, throwing things, and threatening her. Attempts to appease him failed. She was convinced that he was prepared to use violence. Sofia managed to retreat into the back office, block the door, and call the police. After a few minutes of verbal abuse, the client finally withdrew.

Sofia was deeply affected by this experience—she was anxious when walking alone in the street and worried that the client might find out where she lived. Then, to her great surprise, she found herself in an interview-style situation at the Migration Office a few weeks later. She justified their decision to expel the client from the project with the argument that sexist, aggressive, or violent behavior is not tolerated—as is even written down in the integration contract. The integration contract, with its unmistakable and immutable rules, became something she could place her trust in in this unpleasant situation. She also referred to the weekly report in which she had documented the inappropriate text messages. The Migration Office urged her to let the refugee re-enter the program, barely responding to her account of the events. "They denied me the help and support I would have needed after a traumatic experience," Sofia told me.

From her point of view, this had been an opportunity to apply mistrust productively, as a precaution to safeguard the staff or other clients from harm. This mistrust, she felt, derived from a highly comprehensive combination of rational motives and emotions: the client had severely transgressed the laid-down rules and thus it was only consistent to let him face the consequences. Additionally, the foundation of the carer-client relationship was irretrievably damaged after this unpleasant confrontation; she would never be able to 'choose' to ignore her deeply seated mistrust. She also grappled with a lasting sense of betrayal and even considered quitting her job. Instead, she detached herself mentally from the Migration Office—convinced that she would have to get along without the support of this institution, she gained a new clarity; she would adjust her behavior accordingly and be prepared, should a similar situation ever occur.[2]

This example shows NGO workers being more proactively mistrustful than the Migration Office, supporting the claim that mistrust does not solely derive from state authorities' insistence on it but from the social workers' needs and emotions as well. It also demonstrates the deteriorating dynamic that a leap to mistrust entails: the relationship between the NGO and the Migration Office certainly was not characterized by unconditional trust before—it was rather a diplomatic and situation-specific negotiation of trust and mistrust. After this event, however, this delicate balance was destroyed, and the damage that was done took a long time to repair.

Trust and Certainty

The cases I have described above show how actions tilt toward distrust on both the clients' and refugee supporters' sides, but they also show the moral torment triggered by this. Each time actors decide rather not to trust, they do so with great reluctance.

---

2. Coincidentally, the Migration Office workers referred to the same incident in an interview I had with them. They were still very upset about the NGO's refusal to continue working with this client "because he didn't stick to the rules" and portrayed it as an occasion in which the NGO had squandered the trust it had invested in them.

Since trust represents a morally superior position, they always wonder if they *really* have enough evidence and legitimacy to distrust. Such evaluations are ever incomplete and remain on the level of speculation, as I will show in a final segment of the chapter.

Trust is crucially based on knowledge, but it is also about drawing conclusions from incomplete knowledge. The rational side of trust imposes an imperative to accumulate as much high-quality information as possible while the emotional side demands the courage to deduce from assumptions that are not yet certain. As I have shown, these two processes are at least partly decoupled—there is not a definable threshold of knowledge that mechanically engenders feelings of trust or mistrust. Rather, accumulating facts and evaluating them emotionally take place in parallel, and they require developing parallel scenarios for the future. All these scenarios are taken seriously and require preparation. Available knowledge is applied to arrive at predictions, expecting a degree of continuity between current certainties and things to come.

In line with the Aristotelian tradition of understanding emotion, trust is a judgment performed with the purpose of guiding action. Trust puts present action and future outcomes into conversation; Matthew Carey explains that "[s]ympathy is trust in the present and trust is sympathy extended into the future" (Carey 2017, 64). If both trust and mistrust mark the absence of certainty, these projections into the future are of varying quality, depending on the available material. The following case poses these complicated questions: What if the knowledge is fragmented, contradictory, and of questionable provenience?

Abed is a 22-year-old man, the oldest of four brothers with a single mom, and he is, as a friend of his confided to me, entirely disenchanted not only with the Slovak refugee support system but with the entire Western world. The friend told me that instead of choosing the line of least resistance and enjoying the freedom a lack of attention would warrant him, as many of his fellow clients do, he adopted a proud and confident attitude: he makes a point out of not asking for things and still pushing through his own interests by presenting his supporters with *faits accomplis*. The NGO does not assume this to be a conscious strategy, but the trust-mistrust pendulum is certainly swinging toward the mistrusting side. Abed had made the NGO invest quite a lot of futile effort. He was determined to become a doctor and had insisted on visiting a gymnasium, but his limited Slovak language skills made him fail most entrance exams, except in the case of one bilingual private school. The NGO had fought hard to exempt Abed from the tuition fees and was not amused when he stopped attending lessons and was eventually expelled from the school. The NGO offered to get him into another school type, but Abed refused, instead taking up part-time work and attending qualification courses in software programming, paid for by the NGO.

About a year later, Abed approached the NGO with a new idea: no gymnasium would ever accept him, he was growing older, and was impatient to support his family financially, so he needed to get his *maturita*, the university entrance diploma, in another way. He did some research and found a school in India that was, as he formulated it, "willing to help." He would prepare for the exam at home with the help of books, then attend the exams in India and return with the diploma two weeks later. He had already contacted the Indian headmaster as well as a lawyer, the only thing that worried him was how to travel without jeopardizing his or his family's asylum status. Purposefully, Abed did not ask the NGO anything while presenting his plan, and he did not show particular interest in their opinion either.

Sofia had some severe objections against Abed's endeavor. Importantly, she had serious doubts that the *nostrifikácia*, the process of getting this Indian degree acknowledged in Slovakia, would be successful. But there were more weighty implications with helping Abed realize his dream. "We have to bear in mind the risks," Sofia explained at the ensuing team meeting, "and they are considerable." Firstly, she was afraid that they would end up with a large workload—arranging his visa and the trip, followed by the nostrifikácia process, and then he would probably want to be exempted from the university tuition fees which, him being a foreigner, would also require their intervention. Secondly, there were serious ethical issues with his plan—the Indian schools were likely after his money, selling him, in the end, a *"kúpený diplom"* (bought diploma).

She also stated that the organization should be very careful about offering financial support for the nostrifikácia (which usually amounts to about a hundred euros) since this resource was intended for "deserving" people who had studied hard in their country of origin and were desperate to maintain their status in Slovakia, even if the project plan did not stipulate that only diplomas gained before arrival in Slovakia were eligible for free nostrifikácia. She also felt uncomfortable writing Abed another recommendation letter, knowing about his past educational ventures and his failed maturita. Comparing him to 'model' client Aila (the gynecologist in training) in terms of achievement, Sofia believed that Abed would not be able to handle the challenging subject of medical studies—"Aila sometimes doesn't answer the phone when I call her because she's studying so hard."

The risks Sofia was talking about, in other words, are both of a practical and moral nature. Approving a foreign diploma would have finicky ethical implications for their further work with clients. The most sensitive issue, however, was Abed's deservingness of valuable resources—the financial support for the nostrifikácia process and the NGO's time and effort in tackling administrative tasks. Much depended on making the right judgments—about Abed's overall sincerity and whether his intentions could be trusted, but also the NGO staff's own image as recipients of trust with an interest in staying trustworthy for their other clients in the future.

One week later, there was a second meeting which was attended not only by the two main social workers and psychologist Linda of the NGO, but also by a social worker of the Migration Office, and a lawyer from the Human Rights League that supports refugees in all issues regarding legal status and permits. At the beginning of the session, Abed surprised everyone with the assertion that he did not feel fit to study medicine and wanted to become "a successful IT engineer" instead. After explaining his India plan once again, everyone in the room voiced doubts and warnings. The Migration Office worker suggested visiting an IT course that builds upon his last one, with the perspective of getting an internship at a local IT firm after successful completion. He also mentioned several personal contacts he could mobilize to ensure Abed a future in IT. "I think this is a fantastic offer," Linda commented. Abed, however, explained that a lot of IT-focused businesses insist on a diploma, as he had experienced during interviews.

He rejects most of the objections with arguments that seem more or less plausible, visibly disheartened but determined to stay steadfast. "Come on, you can tell me *ako chlap chlapovi* (between us men), that you are already decided, aren't you? You're a free man and we can't hold you back," the Migration Office employee finally commented, which brought the discussion to an end quickly.

After the meeting, Sofia was in a fretful mood. She felt that Abed's 'friend' from the Migration Office had been steering the conversation to a good end converging with Abed's intentions, using an "among men" and "free man" vocabulary. He had also asked Abed how many years he would spend in India, although he knew that he was not really intending to study there. She suspected that the two men had made arrangements before the meeting and had prepared a performance to let Abed look good.

Is assuming a conspiracy the appropriate way to tie together the many loose ends of this story? Abend's account indeed raised various questions, all of them having significant implications for an evaluation of his deservingness of trust. Abed's friend had told me that the reason why he failed the private school was that his family's financial support had been cut, and he had to find a side job as a result. The kazuistika of the NGO stated, however, that the benefits had only been cut after his dismissal from school. Did no other school accept him because of his bad grades, or because of his insistence on an individual study plan for home study, as he did not want to attend lessons with his much younger colleagues? How could the teacher of his IT course praise him for his extraordinary talent while the same teacher complained about him missing several sessions of the course (as Sofia recalls)? The Migration Office social worker was also under the impression that the NGO had not managed to get Abed into a specialized school while the NGO claimed it was Abed who refused any school type except gymnasium. How is one supposed to interpret the fact that Abed was chasing the dream of being a doctor all this time just to switch to a much more accessible career as a programmer while nevertheless maintaining the plan of graduating in India? Is it true that for finding work in the IT sector, formal education is not a must (as the panel of the meeting tried to convince Abed), or is it strictly required (as he reported to have heard from representatives of the industry)?

The fact that this convoluted narrative is the best I could do to summarize many pages of field notes on the case 'Abed' is telling. No matter the degree of involvement, it was difficult for everyone to keep track of the current status of the relationship between the client and the NGO. The case of Abed shows that the intensified contact and social exchange that is part of this mistrusting practice does not increase certainty—indeed the opposite seems to be the case. The trajectory was changing so frequently that there was barely any time to evaluate current positions, the key problem being that reliable information is difficult to come by: Which information gets changed or lost in the transfer between different carriers—and languages? Which information is consciously adapted or even falsified? How to weigh contrasting statements or contradictory sources of information? How to deal with the obscurity of intentions or motivations? I have stated above that trust or mistrust cannot be willfully manufactured since un- and semi-conscious evaluations play an important role. Refugee supporters engage in strategic indeterminacy in order not to narrow down their range of action before a satisfactory degree of informedness is reached. But in the end, they nevertheless pursue solutions with a certain finality. Ruling out uncertainty, hence reducing complexity, means both fairer and more ethical care, and less work. Suspicion means labor, as the lack of certainty requires social contact and communication, and cognitive activity in the shape of taking precautions and anticipating various scenarios. The simultaneous juggling of both trusting and mistrusting practices creates a situation of constant temporariness: there is always the aspiration to arrive at a final evaluation, which is, however, constantly delayed by the unfathomable complexity of everyday life.

I have shown that refugee supporters not only need to reconcile the state authorities' skepticism with their desire for trustful relationships. They face fundamental uncertainties that engender a categorical suspicion. Actors practice mistrust and trust simultaneously, although their actions usually suggest a prevalence of either one or the other. To explore what is behind this simultaneity, and how people arrive at trust despite uncertainty, it is necessary to understand trust's characteristics as an emotion as well as a rational operation. The emotional side of trust, which feeds on individual refugee supporters' experiences, their past joys and fears and disappointed expectations, plays an equally important role in the maintenance of suspicion as institutionalized measures of mistrust. A focus on emotion also shows the intense personal investment and struggle involved in going to and fro between trust and mistrust. The futile attempts to overcome the emotional limbo between trust and mistrust cause lasting discomfort—moral and emotional torment intersect. On the side of refugees, these quandaries cause anxiety, feelings of abandonment, a lack of planning security, and often enough basic goods and services. The responsibility for these shortcomings can, as this analysis suggests, sometimes be attributed more clearly to specific individual's predicaments than the complicated surrounding circumstances suggest.

In the emotional practices of trusting and mistrusting, individual-biographical and structural-discursive factors are particularly tightly entwined: the very personal feelings of disappointment, insult, unfairness, and so on, which influence refugee supporters' inclination to trust are a product of their embedded knowledge—of which common refugee tropes in public discourse, the negative one of the 'good storyteller' and the positive one of the 'legitimately suffering, grateful guest,' form important parts. It is thus equally important to examine and problematize these tropes on a political, semantic and discursive level—as the scholars I referenced have done before me—and to describe how they are put to work in dealing with everyday dilemmas, that is, messiness. To continue my investigation of the latter, I will now turn to 'integration,' another term that has been understood in various ways that carry opposed moral implications.

Chapter 7

EMANCIPATION AND PATERNALIZATION

The Difficulty of 'Letting-Be'

Elizibeth and her husband Milad are among the Iraqi families who took out a loan to buy a little house outside of Nitra. But while the family feels very comfortable in their own home, it comes with new challenges: the villages around Nitra are predominantly commuter areas. People commonly travel into town by car to work. Elizibeth's husband, however, works in Germany for several weeks at a time, taking the family car with him. Not just jobs, but also education and health facilities are concentrated in Nitra. Elizibeth has to travel from their settlement to the center almost every day, to attend driving classes and to bring her four-year-old daughter Lana, who has Down syndrome, to a daycare and rehabilitation center.

Having her long-term adaptation and 'functioning' in mind, social workers wanted to teach Elizibeth to go to Nitra by bus. They showed her where the bus stops were, and explained to her the connection, schedule, and where she had to change. Elizibeth was unenthusiastic about the proposal, to say the least. The bus goes only once an hour and takes, unsurprisingly, significantly longer than the car. But the social workers argued that many Slovaks rely on public transport daily, so they could expect Elizibeth to tolerate the inconvenience and do the same. Elizibeth claimed that the bus ride was a stressful and straining experience for Lana and that her daughter's restlessness could affect the other passengers. Anyone who ever accompanied Elizibeth and Lana on the bus (including me) got a rather different impression, namely that Lana, generally of calm and introverted nature, was not too bothered by the ride and the other passengers. "If a doctor or health professional confirms that it is bad for Lana's development to go by bus, then that's a different issue, of course," Jakub explained, immediately adding that he was rather inclined to see it as an excuse. Elizibeth also complained that she had to carry Lana in her arms due to her difficulties with balance and coordination. The NGO promptly addressed this problem by providing Elizibeth with a secondhand stroller. Once, Elizibeth missed the bus but elegantly saved the day by calling her acquaintances from the village, asking them to give her a lift. The second person she called promptly agreed to take her to town because she had to run errands as well. This was seen by the NGO as proof of her ability to cope. But Elizibeth just could not make peace with this arrangement. Every time she went to Pomoc a Nádej's office, she complained about how straining the commute was for her and Lana. She always finished with a relenting *Skúsim to, uvidíme* (I'll try, we'll see).

"I'm not a psychologist here, I am a taxi driver," Uršuľa told me in a serious tone when I asked her if she liked her job. "Driving people around and all these little services take up a lot of my time." Nevertheless, she offered Elizibeth a ride on several occasions. Indeed, various members of Pomoc a Nádej drove Elizibeth to and from her village regularly, finding all sorts of reasons for diverting from their own paradigm. Either someone was going that way anyway, or it was raining, or they had recently had a disagreement with Elizibeth and wanted to show some goodwill. Why did the well-reasoned objective of teaching Elizibeth how to use public transport independently so often take the back seat, as Elizibeth climbed on the front seat of a car?

The other side of the coin was the following: the activities Elizibeth went to Nitra for increased her scope of action and participation. Firstly, bringing Lana to the rehabilitation program thrice a week helped the little girl improve her physical and linguistic skills and also gave Elizibeth some time to herself. The second project Elizibeth pursued in the city was driving school. Elizibeth was adamant about wanting to get a driver's license, which she saw as an important milestone connected to many big hopes: they could get a second car for the family, so she could finally move around freely and independently. Then she could bring Lana to rehab five times per week instead of three, and she could drive her other kids to German and English language courses in town so they could get good jobs in the future. This begged the question of whether driving Elizibeth around, enabling her to take the best advantage of these improvement projects, was the greater contribution to her eventual integration. Jakub also argued pragmatically that "the school year is almost over, and next year Lana might go to a regular kindergarten if we manage to find one, so should we really invest so much effort and discussion into changing her habits?"

Elizibeth's assertion that the bus was an unbearable imposition for her was equally shaky and wrought with contradictions as the NGO's response. The goal was clear ('integration'), but the means were not always so apparent, and sometimes the perspicacious approach was sidelined for a spontaneous display of pity and help toward a mother who is usually taking care of three kids all by herself, one of whom is bodily and mentally challenged.

Cases like Elizibeth's urge NGOs to spell out parameters they regard indicative of good or successful integration. Which skills and knowledge should stand at the end of an integrative process? What has to be prioritized, individual clients' well-being or adjustment to the host community? In the social work literature, this dilemma is referred to as "double mandate" (Böhnisch and Lösch 1973): being in the service of both the welfare of clients and society at large, social workers must not only care empathetically, but also define expectations and ensure that they are being met.

NGO workers understand that it is their job "to integrate people," conceptualizing their integrating work as a proactive way of relating to clients and attuning their behaviors to their eventual benefit. In other words, social workers engage in an act of *care* in which 'integration' is both the method and the outcome. When I say that 'integrating' is an act of care, I take as my starting point the same broad definition of caring as Lisa Stevenson applies, namely "the way someone comes to matter and the corresponding ethics of attending to the other who matters" (Stevenson 2014, 3). In Stevenson's ethnography, as in mine, this definition comes to encompass both the state's welfare directed toward those who are placed in its care, and relationships between carers and those cared for. In this chapter, I examine the different modes of care engendered in integrating practices. Looking at how 'integration' is commonly understood (and criticized), I show that opposing impulses are already deeply ingrained in it. The contradiction pertains mainly to the emotional scope of the relationship between carers and those cared for: a detached, pragmatic, and an attached, empathetic mode may both appear morally superior.

There are various examples in the anthropology of care of situations in which withholding or limiting direct, physical care means that actually one 'cares' deeply (see also Han 2012): for instance, Jarrett Zigon describes how in Downtown Eastside of Vancouver, a neighborhood with high rates of drug addiction, the former and current drug users create a non-judgmental space in which users are not 'reformed' through corrective interventions, but rather acknowledged and accepted as they are, which leaves room for community and actual healing. This inspired Zigon to develop the concept of "attuned care," a way of relating to others that is characterized by "being-with" and "letting-be" (Zigon 2018, 108). Attuned care is not exclusively, or even primarily, the redemption of an obligation or an agreement.

> Rather, an attuned connectivity—or simply attunement—is better understood as an ontological responsivity through which the being of diverse existents becomes intertwined such that what is at stake is not interest or obligation but the very existence of this intertwinement. (Zigon 2018, 151–152)

These thoughts are at the same time an extension of and a move against the anthropological commonplace that providing care for others is the quintessential path to moral becoming. Annemarie Mol, Ingunn Moser, and Jeanette Pols describe the particularity of caring practices as a "specific modality of handling questions to do with the good" (Mol et al. 2010, 13). The joy and affirmation of being needed and providing life-sustaining care has been described as the source of moral accomplishment (Kleinman 2012). As Nussbaum argues, being meaningful to the people who are meaningful to us is a major source of joy and validation, and this joy, again, is dependent on the fragility and neediness of others. Hence, refraining from offering care and 'letting be' can be a very painful effort.

NGO employees generally think of emancipation as a challenging, sometimes counterintuitive, but worthwhile task. The social worker whose goal it is to make him- or herself superfluous as quickly as possible is the standard they compare and hold themselves and others to. They understand paternalism as a deeply problematic approach, reasoning along the same lines as many anthropologists do in their critiques of humanitarianism and charity, which I have sketched in the subchapter of the Introduction "Themes and Topics in Recent Research on Refugee Care," (p. 10): it deprives recipients of (parts of) their individual agency, and in the worst case, it even forecloses the formation of autonomy by prescribing a narrow path and making sure protégées stay on it. It is a goal they strive to achieve in a veritable virtue ethics approach, requiring constant self-observation and adjustment: Employees are reminded at almost every team meeting to refrain from any "delivery of services" clients could well handle themselves.

Jakub stressed the importance of mutual supervision because one can easily overlook one's own inclination to offer excessive support: "I always see how Mária solves problems that are a far cry from what is obligatory or even necessary, and then I go on and do the same thing the next day, and I think to myself 'What am I doing here?'" Sofia explained to me that the trick is to help clients in a way that not only teaches them how to do certain tasks but also gives them confidence. For instance, some people do not like talking on the phone to make an appointment with the doctor and come into the office hoping that Sofia might do it for them. In such a situation, Sofia asks them to call the doctor themselves while they are in the office with her. This way, she can step in if they really do not understand but also deliver proof that they are capable of doing this task without any help the next time. Jakub from Pomoc a Nádej applies a very similar strategy: "I go with them once, twice, maybe thrice, for instance, to pick up medicine or buy a bus ticket. After that, they should know how to do it alone."

But as Elizabeth's case suggests, this shared conviction is difficult to put into practice. NGO workers slide back into offering support that, according to their own definitions, is to be judged as superfluous or hampering independence. Trying to navigate through each day, the goal of fostering independent individuals gets sidetracked easily. "Full service," is oftentimes the less time-consuming and costly alternative. Do they really want to let the young client fill in the form of the telecommunication company alone, if he can easily make a mistake that will set the issuing of the service back for weeks? Or do they really want to go through the form together, question by question, to make sure he understands each of them, instead of filling it in themselves in a few minutes?

Critiques of Integration

While negotiating these details, refugee supporters refer to 'integration' as a known entity or a defined goal. This stands in contrast to the semantic nuances and also the political struggles that revolve around the buzzword 'integration' (in the context of migration) today.

When asking social workers what they regard as successful integration, most list particular achievements, like having housing and a job, or finishing an education. Some declare cultural competence in the Slovak context as the endpoint. Most see leading an independent life as the target of the integration process. Others elevate the discussion to a more abstract level, explaining that a person is integrated when becoming a full-fledged member of a society, able to recognize both the obligations and rights that come with it. The accounts differ significantly, but they also have some striking common features.

All of the above qualifications assume that integration is something that has to come from the foreigner: it is a debt vis-à-vis the host country which he or she is obliged to repay gradually. Further, it is also taken for granted that the help and guidance of proficient others is needed, constituting the 'care'-dimension of integration. In the responses social workers gave me, integration is very much associated with action and interaction—clients who preferred not to engage in economic or civic activity were regarded as insufficiently integrated (although similar life choices are not uncommon among Slovaks). Integration also assumes a positive vision of coexistence and cohabitation which is redeemed by merging formerly 'different' individuals into the 'majority.' This abstraction from refugee supporters' utterances converges with popular understandings of integration in Slovakia and beyond. Politicians and practitioners widely use this proactive, adaptive notion of integration with minimizing difference and maximizing harmony as its goal. Whenever the term is not discussed specifically or no working definition is provided, this is usually the 'default' understanding of integration, even in scientific surveys.

But 'integration' has also become the target of increasingly intense critique by scholars and by those affected by it, attacking both the term in its current usage and the (state and non-state) projects designed to promote it. These critics form an approach to issues of migration from a perspective that refuses to essentialize nations and nation-states as having fixed characteristics, producing hierarchization and exclusion. They urge scholars to discard still prevalent "methodological nationalism" (Wimmer and Nina Glick Schiller 2002), or a "national order of things" (Malkki 1995) and instead to "de-migranticize" migration studies, focusing on entire populations including migrants without problematizing them a priori (Dahinden 2016, 2210).

Similarly skeptical of the juxtaposition of national communities, and migrants, Willem Schinkel (2018) argues that the target of integration is based on skewed assumptions, as it is often conceptualized as the return to an allegedly pre-multicultural past devoid of fragmentation and conflict. 'Society' is thus posited as inherently harmonious, and any problems occurring have external (migrant) roots and will disappear once respective migrant populations 'merge' with society. Schinkel observes that in the context of migration, the term 'integration' loses its meaning as a positive characteristic of a social whole (being homogeneous and well-rounded), and comes to mean instead a property of an individual—one either is or is not 'integrated.'

> But this individualization of integration is entirely without theoretical underpinnings. Instead, it rests on commonsensical notions of "society" and its individual "members," and on the historically particular plausibility of the individualist (neo)liberal assumptions of this society as consisting of individual members to whom any 'misfit' between the two can be one-sidedly attributed. "Integration" thus changes from a system state to a state of being of an individual. (Schinkel 2018, 3)

In a similar simplification, migrants of a particular geographic origin are imagined as a group, and the integration or lack thereof is projected indiscriminately on all its members. Schinkel identifies as the main problem the fact that the concept of integration is "purified of notions both of class and race" (Schinkel 2018, 4), although only certain subjects, namely those racially identifiable as 'non-white,' are regarded as amenable to integration measures; white persons are often granted "dispensation of integration" (ibid.). By defining someone as 'other,' and normatively imposing a target they need to approach in a developmental logic, integration can be called a neo-colonial technique, according to Schinkel (2018, 10).

Integration thus proceeds in an abstracted and likewise personalizing direction simultaneously. Migrant subjects are problematized twice: collectively, through their assumed belonging to a group with anomaly status, and individually, through their 'integration backlog' that they are expected to diminish but can never fully eliminate. As we shall see, both dimensions are picked up on in practices of care.

Scholarly research, in Schinkel's opinion, has done a poor job of dismantling the problematic assumptions in integration discourses. Indeed, research has contributed to the proliferation of these assumptions, through scientific projects defining an 'ideal' approach to integration in a given setting. Projects evaluate local initiatives, 'measure' integration in terms of quantifiable parameters, and propose refined policy tools, always guided by normative concepts of integration. These approaches mirror national interests and are often initiated by or carried out in partnership with public governing bodies (Meissner and Heil 2020, 4–5). Many scholars by and large agree with the tone of this critique, rejecting especially the discriminatory sociopolitical implications of the integration terminology. Some have suggested revisiting common definitions of integration, conceptualizing it not as a policy concept, but broader (Penninx 2019). Others abandon the concept of 'integration' entirely, developing alternative terminologies that are less charged with normative and (neo)colonial connotations (Klarenbeek 2018; Meissner and Heil 2020).

Recently, the term 'integration' has been inspected, questioned, and (re)appropriated by those who have been affected, respectively (in their view) objectified by it: migrants and their descendants but also members of other groups that are commonly perceived as needing adaptation to the mainstream. A migrant critique of integration is getting increasingly audible in countries such as Germany, which established its status as an immigration country at the latest in the 1960s when *Gastarbeiterverträge* (guest worker contracts) with Italy, Portugal, Turkey, Spain, Greece, Yugoslavia, and others brought many migrants to the country. There was no notable effort to develop integration policies until well into the 1990s, long after it had become clear that a lot of these 'guests' had come to stay (Oltmer 2012). The *Gastarbeiter* generation, which was seen as only suited for hard, blue-collar work with low salaries, established role expectations toward migrant workers which the young generation is now struggling to shake off. In a controversially discussed anthology titled *Eure Heimat ist unser Alptraum* (Your homeland is our nightmare, 2019), the editors Fatma Aydemir and Hengameh Yaghoobifarah give voice to a generation of young Germans *mit Migrationshintergrund* (with a migrant background) who feel tired and humiliated by the double burden of being structurally discriminated against and expected to be especially compliant and hardworking. They reject the notion of 'owing' anything to the German 'society.' Jewish author Max Czollek counters overbearing expectations toward minority groups with a call to de-integrate (*desintegrieren*) instead, a subversive practice he defines as "acknowledging society as a locus of radical diversity" (Czollek 2018, 56, my translation). Aladin El-Mafaalani, son of Syrian immigrants, disenchants the wishful image of the harmonious society standing at the end of successful integration, claiming instead that more controversy, more negotiation, and more conflict are inevitable outcomes of diversification, which he sees as a catalyst for much-needed social change (El-Mafaalani 2018, 76–77).

Migrant critics of integration in Germany aim to challenge the one-sided, normative, and objectifying undertone in common understandings of migration. In doing so, they usually emphasize their ethnic and class identity rather than arguing that it is irrel-evant. They inhabit their racial identity to call out racism; they stress that the 'migrant experience' of everyday life in Germany differs from the experience of Germans who do not look 'foreign' or have 'foreign-sounding' names; they want to be seen as collective(s) with particular interests other than seamless assimilation into 'German' society. If we compare this debate to the way integration is discussed in Slovak society (which I am about to describe), we see that integration critique pertains to, and emerges in, particu-lar historical, social, and political contexts and cannot be easily generalized.

In Slovakia, migrant voices that engage in identity politics and stand up to assim-ilative pressures are almost completely absent, and a corresponding subject position would be hard to assume. Migrants who do participate in the public debate often take great care to show that they are very well capable of fulfilling the Slovak expectations or conforming to set standards.[1] A contribution to the debate that is particularly vis-ible is migrants stressing that they are self-sufficient and even eager to 'give back' and help Slovakia flourish. For instance, during the onset of the COVID-19 pandemic, Obývačka did a recurring feature on their social media platform where they intro-duced foreign-born 'heroes' working at the frontlines of Slovakia's battle against the virus. Hamid, a medical student from Afghanistan and a volunteer at a testing center explained how his experience of needing help as a refugee now obligates him to help others whenever possible. A campaign video of Ivana, cofounder of the Human Rights League and a progressive candidate for the 2020 parliamentary election, featured the testimonials of her former clients from Bosnia, Vietnam, Afghanistan, and Zimbabwe, all of whom Ivana helped gain citizenship as a lawyer. They all stressed how they study, work, and start a family in Slovakia; and that they vote for Ivana because they have become proud citizens of the Slovak Republic, caring about the future of the coun-try. Nastaran Motlagh, a Slovak stand-up comedian originally from Iran, finishes her program by telling how she was once praised for speaking better Slovak than Andrej Danko. The pride she feels for beating the famously ineloquent politician and chairman of the nationalist party *Slovenská národná strana* (Slovak National Party) when it comes to Slovak language proficiency makes for a hearty, harmless laugh, fostering identification rather than alienation.

---

1. Of course, the communicative strategy to claim belonging and rights by stressing that migrants do integrate is very widespread, even in immigration societies such as the German one. This defense strategy against notorious accusations of migrants causing problems rather than contributing to society has been internalized by many. For example, following the ter-rorist attack of a right-wing extremist shooter on a Shisha bar in Hanau, the mother of one of the victims, in tears and grappling for words, stressed that her son completed professional training and wanted to work "for Germany"—as if she felt she had to prove the killer wrong by showing her son's eagerness to make a contribution. The fact that the TV station chose this quote to be included in a 2:30-minute clip on the victims' social surroundings is tell-ing as well. https://www.zdf.de/nachrichten/heute-journal/hanau-in-tiefer-trauer-100.html. Accessed 03.10.2020.

A survey based on questionnaires and focus discussions carried out by a research group around Slovak sociologist Michal Vašečka shows that an ethnicized understanding of 'being Slovak' is very dominant among the population. Respondents conceptualize Slovakia as 'the country of Slovaks,' labeling even recognized national minorities like Hungarians and Roma as 'foreigners.' Access to the 'we' group is thus defined in terms of ethnic Slovakness, which normalizes Slovaks' privileged access to certain entitlements and renders any effort by migrants to achieve full parity and belonging through integration futile (Vašečka 2009, 88).

Under these circumstances, it is easy to see why non-Slovaks think establishing a self-confident, assertive migrant discourse would be pointless, even counterproductive. Rather, communicative efforts are channeled into defeating negative stereotypes and increasing levels of acceptance and belonging to improve migrants' life chances. A telling example is the Vietnamese community, one of the largest groups of people with migrant backgrounds in Slovakia and Czechia. Most of them arrived as students or workers from the 1950s onward, based on an agreement between friendly socialist countries, and later through family reunions. After 1989, they were among the first to lose their factory jobs due to the economic transition so they often founded small businesses, especially bistros and convenience stores, to maintain resident status. They are now regarded as 'model migrants' because they are economically independent—and otherwise largely invisible. Inside this community, there is a widespread behavioral code of 'flying under the radar,' as the ethnologist Miroslava Hlinčíková found out while doing fieldwork among Vietnamese families in Bratislava. Her work contains the following quote from a woman of Vietnamese origin:

> Under normal circumstances, if I was home in Vietnam, I would allow myself to get upset, to say what I think, but I realize that they look at me with different eyes, so I try to control myself, simply to express myself neutrally. I thus got into a state where I no longer appear as a person, but people notice very much that I am a foreigner, that my features are Vietnamese, that—she is—the Vietnamese are like that. (Hlinčíková 2015, 46)

Another group excluded from Slovakness is the Roma minority. Roma, despite their century-long presence on the territory that is now Slovakia, are always presented as unintegrated, as needing integration—or, more precisely, as needing to show more effort in terms of integrating *themselves* into Slovak society (Podolinská and Hrustič 2015). The position of large proportions of Slovakia's Roma population at the margins of society has been historically (re)produced: integrative measures have always coexisted (and often intersected) with discriminatory segregation policies (Belák et al. 2017; Filčák, Szilvasi and Škobla 2017; Donert 2017).

Recent studies suggest that the situation of Roma seems to deteriorate rather than improve, owing to a complex set of factors, but most of all to the harmful stereotype of the lazy, violent, and criminally inclined Roma which effectively blocks any real social participation (European Commission 2018b; Kozubík et al. 2020). One of the most contested current government measures is the so-called work activation program. The long-term unemployed (often Roma) carry out auxiliary and low-skilled tasks several hours a day and receive a particular kind of payment on top of state unemploy-ment benefits—as of 2023, 86.80€ per month. It is not surprising that refugees, espe-cially after a prolonged unsuccessful job search, are also transferred into this scheme. Anthropologist Jan Grill has observed that municipalities (ab)use this policy mainly as a source of cheap labor. They rarely facilitate the transition into the regular job market (Grill 2018, 115–116). The approach to integration that transpires from these historical and contemporary policies shows that 'unadapted others' are supposed to integrate. At the same time, there is a comprehensively low expectation toward their ability to do so. The goal of their adaptation is always defined in relation to Slovakness: difference must be neutralized or tamed, while non-Slovak collective ethnic or cultural identities are viewed with suspicion.

Let us note for now that the conditions for integration in Slovakia are markedly dif-ferent from the societies in which the critiques I summarized are commonly voiced and which they address—simply because migrants are a significantly smaller phenomenon in numbers, and choose different modes of visibility and public expression. I will return to the importance of this difference at the end of the chapter. At the same time, the way integration is understood and practiced in Slovakia exhibits all the points of critique mentioned above. The imagined, racially and ethnically defined entities of migrants and minorities are exempted from, and posited as a threat to, an equally imagined 'integrated' societal whole.

These harsh demarcations are also at the foundation of the integrating care work refugee supporters engage in. They—indiscriminately—designate persons in need of integration as a target group of social policies and recipients of 'integrating' measures. Since the target of these measures is an imagined hegemonic 'Slovakness,' the same integrative process is supposed to lead anyone to this same goal. At the same time, understanding successful integration as an individual achievement also raises expecta-tions toward those who accompany this process. They can easily come to feel obliged to provide intense and tailored mentoring along this path.

I argue that this twin logic inherent in common understandings of integration corre-sponds to the different models of care I have observed in refugee supporters' work: one is detached and de-personalized, following the principles of equity and disinterestedness, the other is engaging and cognizant of each case's contexts and characteristics. I will analyze the first mode using Lisa Stevenson's concept of 'anonymized care.' The second one I call 'personalized care' or 'paternalizing care.' I use these two terms to account for the fact that these practices, although very similar, appear different depending on the perspective from which they are looked upon, and the respective normative evaluation attached to them.

Anonymized care

The precondition for anonymized care is to guarantee institutional and ultimately political accountability toward those who are placed in the state's care. It is supposed to secure a fair and auditable allocation of care measures. In other words, it is essen-tially what happens when the Weberian characteristics of bureaucratic management (originally published in 1921), especially hierarchy, impersonality, and adherence to fixed rules and regulations, are applied to the organized provision of care (Weber 2015). Anthropologist Lisa Stevenson shows, through the example of the Inuit in the autonomous Nunavut territory, how Canadian state authorities fulfill(ed) their welfare obligations toward their citizens in the tuberculosis epidemic in the 1950s and the still ongoing so-called suicide epidemic. She shows how anonymized care, although well-intended, seems cool or even cruel with its calculating and utilitarian logic. The concern of the responsible authorities is to have an absolute minimum of "dead Inuit," thus intervening, even against the wish of the affected and their dependents, with life-preserving measures.

Anonymous care, then, is all about configuring reproducible protocols of care that specify measures, also defining the right time and order for them, and applying them uniformly to all those who are made recipients of that care. Stevenson explains that anonymous care means caring about

> others, without knowing who they were—to care indiscriminately, professionally, and anonymously. To care anonymously requires being able to care intransitively, to be able to say, "I care" without specifying for whom. (Stevenson 2014, 83)

Slovak NGO workers try always to maintain a professional distance from clients, although sympathy and trivial factors such as Slovak language proficiency naturally forge closer, sometimes friendship-like relationships with some individuals—Chapter 5 has dealt at length with the intricacies of these relationships. But even if NGO workers admit that they relate to some refugees in friendship, they still maintain that the care they provide is fairly distributed and disinterested and claim not to let personal sympathy or apathy impact the treatment of respective clients.

Not least because of its apparent contradiction with their close and friendly relationships with some clients, NGO workers feel obligated to performatively affirm the anonymous character of their care work toward outsiders. On a house visit to the social housing estate where some of their clients were accommodated, Sofia asked the housekeeper if he was aware of any problem or conflict. Hesitantly but with an audible grudge, the elderly gentleman told how "the black guy," one of the inhabitants, could be seen leaving and entering the house with a martially looking training device, an expander with a metal spiral. According to him, this prop resembled a weapon and scared the residents of the women's shelter located in the same building. To illustrate, he even took a baseball bat from under his desk, "See, I can't walk around with that, it would scare people." Also, this person was often drunk. Sofia was visibly amused by this alarmist account and instructed the housekeeper that "I can't tell them what to do, they are all their own people" and that neither working out nor drinking was against the law. The concierge was not convinced, he uttered, "But you are responsible for these people." Sofia interrupted him, maintaining that they are responsible for themselves and that if he ever feels seriously threatened, he should just call the police. "Are you sure?" the housekeeper replied with a surprised and skeptical expression on his face. "Of course, I don't want them to be treated any differently from anyone else."

Next to showing the difficulties many people have in understanding the relationships Refúgium has with its clients, this episode is an example of how an anonymous approach to care delivers a detached stance toward clients' troubles. Sofia could have taken the opportunity to call the housekeeper out for his racist prejudice—her decision not to do so seems to suggest a certain indifference toward her client. She insists that the same rights apply to this client as to anyone else living in Slovakia. This statement is also meant to counter the common accusations in conspiracy myths, that migrants or refugees receive preferential treatment or stand 'above the law.' It is her organization's official policy not to offer protection to clients who behave in socially intolerable manner or break the law just because they are—arguably—less familiar with local customs or rules. In the social workers' eyes, this approach does not stand for the abandonment of clients but rather means acknowledging their autonomy and dignity by trusting them to take responsibility for their actions.

Using the example of a particularly anonymous form of care, a suicide prevention hotline, Stevenson shows that anonymous care, although impersonal, does not have to be detached or cool. It can follow the instrumental logic of 'caring for' as much as the sentiment of 'caring about.' She maintains that caring anonymously, being reduced to an unspecified human being relating to other human beings through care can be a connection to the "sublime," which, according to Talal Asad, involves a "dissolution of the self" (Stevenson 2014, 87).

Sofia was anything but indifferent toward the client she had just denied responsibility for. His name was Paolo, he was one of the 'oldest' clients, who arrived in the country almost thirty years ago when it was still called Czechoslovakia. Paolo was one of the 'challenging' clients; he was diagnosed with manic depression, and Sofia could tell numerous anecdotes about how his psychotic episodes had brought the two of them into precarious situations. Like that one time when he screamed "You have ugly legs!" at a woman on the street. Sofia quickly pulled him away and told him at the next street corner that he could not behave like this. "I can't? But why? After all her legs were really ugly," Paolo replied dead serious. Sofia reported these incidents with amusement. "*Je s ním sranda* (It's great fun with him)," she used to conclude her narrations.

Unfit for regular employment, Paolo participated in work activation programs designed for the long-term unemployed among the Roma (see above), entailing low-skilled work in maintenance in exchange for social benefits. Paolo had worked as a janitor in a shopping center a few hours per day for several years, a job he both excelled in and depended on for his mental health. However, when he forgot to take his medication in spring, he entered a manic phase and was unable to work his allotted amount of hours. The *Úrad práce* (job center) then cut his benefits and sanctioned him with a temporary prohibition to work. The NGO tried to lift the sanctions, but unfortunately, they could not point to his medical condition because his diagnosis had never been recognized by a general practitioner. While Sofia tried to fix this omission, the trajectory shifted drastically as Paolo's case worker at the job center announced that if diagnosed with bipolar disorder, they would need to withdraw his work allowance permanently. The mental illness would cast general doubt over his ability to follow routines. In other words, without the doctor's certificate, the benefits would remain cut; with a certificate, he might lose his job altogether.

The state's welfare institutions were obviously unable to take Paolo's individual health problem, a temporary manic phase, into account. In the state's system of anonymous care, individual characteristics only become meaningful when they cause a reclassification of the person involved. With the diagnosis of manic depression becoming official, the question was whether to shift Paolo from the category 'long-term unemployed person who does not take his work assignment seriously enough' to the category 'mentally ill person incapable of working.' Both entail a certain caring presumption: the sanction and the temporary prohibition to work were supposed to be an educative measure aimed at making Paolo a more reliable worker, and the permanent prohibition to work was a precaution against possible threats against himself and others which might emerge from his diagnosis. Yet, both evaluations worked to his disadvantage and ultimately prevented what arguably *is best* for Paolo: a strict daily work routine and a forgiving attitude in those rare instances of a psychotic episode.

"Implicit in the system of care is that the object of care must learn to mime the caregiver's attitudes to time and to care," Lisa Stevenson explains (2014, 134). That means staying abreast of the bureaucracy, keeping appointments and being on time, being transparent, and not demanding too much attention. Caring (in all its shapes), according to Stevenson, is a way of making individuals predictable by fixing them to a particular subject position. The forms of anonymous care she observes attribute to the recipients of care the role of a subject whose interest (staying alive) converges with that of the state, which can take appropriate measures and show some leniency in their implementation. If clients do not assume this subject position, the scope of care measures to help them is severely restricted.

Refugees in Slovakia face similar demands; they are expected to fit themselves into the subject position of an autonomous migrant whose aim is to be self-sufficient, working actively toward achieving increasing levels of economic success and 'integration.' Clients like Paolo are thus assigned a position they cannot realistically occupy: he depends on social welfare and has no drive or intention to change this. Social workers who abandon the trajectory of anonymous care operate outside the territory of state-sanctioned welfare, which restricts their possibilities. Of course, Sofia did not always stick to the protocol for anonymous care in Paolo's case: she tried to reach Paolo's case worker at the job center, the one who announced that a diagnosis of bipolar disorder might cost him permission to work, and convince her, as a person, of the temporariness of Paolo's indisposition. She used the specifics of the case to incite sympathy and ask for an exception, which is exactly the opposite of anonymized care.

A telling illustration of how the subject position of the autonomous migrant produced by anonymous care leads to miscalculations and simplifications is how it was applied to me. One day I reported to Dorota that the English class for Iraqi teens had been canceled because none of the students had shown up. "You are here more often than any one of them," Dorota said, adding with a smile, "You should be refug [...] Iraqi of the year!" Her spontaneous switch to the even more absurd denomination as 'Iraqi,' making for a better pun, speaks for the humorous character of the remark. However, on other occasions, Iraqis told me, visibly frustrated, that social workers had mocked them for not speaking Slovak as fluently as Eva.

As a 'migrant' (however temporary), I fulfilled the conditions for integration (speaking Slovak, attending courses, making efforts to socialize) better than others. Disregarding context and biographical details, I was a foreigner who was particularly committed to blending into the Slovak and NGO framework. Of course, this comparison was completely nonsensical, as the Iraqis noticed without difficulty. I was young, familiar with the Indo-European language family, able to study Slovak in an academic setting, having literally nothing else on my schedule other than to follow the NGO's integration measures at close range. And, more importantly, the 'migrant' subject position I was assigned glossed over enormous racial and class-based differences: most Iraqis had no other choice than to work shifts in manual jobs, and many had also not received much formal education before coming to Slovakia. Securing their existence and advancing their integration through language courses were mostly seen as separate projects, with the first one taking precedence over the second.

Moreover, being a white EU citizen, I benefited from the 'dispensation from integration': rarely did anyone expect me to integrate (more), either because my willingness to adapt was taken for granted, or because my eventual non-integration was not perceived as a threat or nuisance. Indeed, I was asked very often why I bothered learning Slovak at all, while refugees were always reprimanded for their alleged lack of commitment to language learning. The moral dilemma of my presence setting a precedence for the subject position of the autonomous migrant that was unachievable for many refugees, harming their relations with their carers, was almost impossible to resolve. My attempts to explain my privileged background to NGO workers were interpreted as likable humbleness and contributed to enhancing my status rather than having a compensatory effect.

There are huge differences in how difficult it is to assume the subject position of the autonomous migrant. I was seen as occupying it by default, for Paolo it was basically unattainable. This differential access shows that anonymous care is not as neutrally bureaucratic and equitable as its proponents claim. It is, like the concept of integration, interspersed with normative assumptions about its potential beneficiaries of a racial, ableist, or class-based nature. Before this grim backdrop, refugee supporters' frequent recourse to paternal and personal care did not appear as a diversion from their "we empower them"—self-fashioning project. Rather, it engenders a second mode of moral practice—a more intuitive, affect-based one which is realized in parallel—or in turns—with emancipating efforts.

Paternal(izing) care

"Sorry that the presentation will be in Slovak because I still haven't managed to learn Arab," said Jakub while setting up the computer and projector. He had spent some nights designing a little website which he was now presenting to the Iraqi women assembled in the community center. The website would function as an e-shop for the crafts and decoration items the women produce in their weekly meetings with the help of Slovak handicraft maker Sára. Meanwhile, Dorota walked around collecting the last products of the handicraft group, colorful wreaths made of paper, paid the women the piece price that Sára suggested, and handed them a receipt. Thus far, most items had been sent to a US American charity which supported Pomoc a Nádej with grants. This organization offered them on its website as "goods made by persecuted Christians." Jakub clicked through his brand-new makeshift homepage, showing short profiles for the respective sellers, which then linked through to the 'products' the respective person offers. There was a photo of Elizabeth with her husband, and Lana, smiling in front of one of Slovakia's many fortresses, another showed a cheerful portrait of Ibrahim, the headstrong hairdresser.

Jakub repeats that he just wrote down some random information and that it was not public yet, but he would like all of them to share a photo and some personal info, about their family, their kids, where they come from, and so on. He explained that people bought things more easily when they knew something about the seller. The aim was to enable them to produce more and sell more, thus also creating a higher revenue. He also assures that there would be no contact details like a telephone number or address so that buyers could not get in contact directly. All the women needed to worry about was to craft their products. After that, Pomoc a Nádej would buy the items from them, so they get the money immediately. The NGO would also handle the photographing, packaging, and shipping of products as well as communication with the customers.

The group's response was not exactly what Jakub had expected: the women showed they understood the Slovak presentation and nodded at the mention of higher revenues; however, they did not immediately sign the agreement stipulating the publication of their photos but asked for more time to think it through.

A little later, I was in the car with Mária and Magdalena. Magdalena is not part of the handicraft group but witnessed the presentation because she had a meeting with her voluntary Slovak language tutor before. She was puzzled by what she just saw: "They're no good," she said brashly about the rag dolls, earrings, and decorative wreaths the other women produced. "The things are not so nice. My daughter does stuff like that at school. Who will buy that?" Mária laughed and explained: "Some people may want to help refugees. Then they do not care if it is nice or not, they will buy it anyway to support a good cause." Magdalena asked, half-jokingly: "These people exist in Slovakia? Are they many?" Mária laughed again, replying, "Maybe not too many. You met almost all of them."

Although Jakub never mentioned words like 'pity,' 'goodwill,' or 'help,' it was quite clear to Magdalena that compassion would be the only possible motive for people to buy the little handcrafted items. The other women were probably also not convinced by the business plan. Were they so hesitant because they hoped their work to be taken more seriously than being distributed as thank-you gifts for donations? Did they feel like Jakub was making fools of them by presenting them a charity initiative as a legitimate business model? Would they have wanted a greater say in the development of the web-shop idea? Or were they simply concerned about the protection of their personal data?

The kind of care practiced here is not categorically anti-emancipatory—one could argue (and Pomoc a Nádej did) that this was a means to the end of helping Iraqi women become economically active and have more money at their disposal—but it assigns recipients an entirely different subject position. It does not require or presuppose the clients' own initiative or the capability to recognize what *is best* for them. The subject position for the providers of this form of care is that of benevolent superiority—an arrangement reminiscent of patriarchal kinship structures. Familiar with the many battlegrounds of his clients and the fatigue most of them experienced, Jakub assumed that it would be too complicated and tiresome for his clients to become involved in the sales, marketing, shipping, and programming of their little business venture. He did not even deem it particularly important that they understand the premise the business was built on.

On countless occasions, the assumption to be (preliminarily) better in recognizing clients' needs and appropriate measures to meet them means that the step of explaining options and getting consent is skipped in the problem-solving process. When Nina helped Malek apply for disability benefits for his two mentally challenged children, she was still fairly new on the job and filled in the form without having met the kids. With the intention to reap the largest possible benefit for the children, she ticked the boxes for all extra grants, including 'orthopedic shoes' and 'subsidies to make housing barrier-free.' Malek had not seen the list before entering the civil servant's office at the social insurance. The civil servant remarked that to claim these benefits, they needed to provide proof of the children's mobility restrictions. Malek did not understand the conversation fully but took a picture of the form with his cell phone. When they went outside, Nina was full of regrets, she translated the information she had received into English and admitted remorsefully that she had not only filled in the form without consultation, she also was not informed of the fact that a medical recommendation was compulsory. Malek explained that his children were indeed not restricted in their mobility. Therefore, claiming these benefits was beside the point.

To be fair, confrontations like this occur rarely. The failure to provide information or discuss possibilities usually goes unnoticed or is even greeted by clients, who are happy not to be burdened with decisions that remain opaque to them. On another occasion, Lucia advised Malek's wife Salma at a job consultation meeting where she was supposed to choose between two vocational training courses. Lucia presented the contents, guessed the level of difficulty, also language-wise and evaluated how the dates and time scheme would fit into her daily routine. Salma was paralyzed, constantly repeating "I don't know," "It all sounds good," and "What does Sofia say?" throughout the meeting. She felt unfit to make up her mind, and Lucia felt unfit to take this responsibility away from her. But when half an hour had passed and the conversation had not moved forward at all, she started to ask more suggestive questions, accumulating evidence to accelerate the process: "Wouldn't these dates be better for you? You like baking, don't you? You'll hang in there with the vocabulary, right?" Salma and Lucia seemed equally relieved when the application was finally sent out, but certainly not perfectly satisfied with how this encounter went.

As I explained in the opening paragraphs, caring for someone in love and dedication is commonly regarded as a moral good, but so is overcoming the impulse to care and setting the person cared for 'free.' Anthropologists have studied the moral implications of care extensively and commonly know that seemingly selfless and disinterested acts may have a dominating or calculating side. There is a self-serving dimension even to loving and affectionate practices, as follows from an application of the anthropology of gifting to the 'gift' of care. Marcel Mauss is the first to forcefully make this point in his seminal essay on *The Gift* (1990 [1954]). Gifts can thus have a coercive effect as they—*nolens volens*—push the gift recipient into a position of inferiority and indebtedness. The fact that gift-giving is so thoroughly positively connoted in common-sense understandings means that it is almost impossible to give without demanding or receiving something in return; like gratitude, moral credit, status, a clean conscience.

In humanitarian discourse, gifts are considered problematic for the same reasons: they create unequal terms and impose (possibly) unwanted obligations on the recipients. Katerina Rozakou accompanied a group of Greek activists working with refugees for whom gifts or donations were taboo. Activists hoped, on the contrary, to get invited and offer refugees the possibility to host and 'care for' them (Rozakou 2016, 190). This practice slowly cracked when in 2015, the number of refugees and thus also the perceived level of 'neediness' rose to unprecedented levels. A few years earlier, when the Greek middle classes went through the economic crisis, they were forced to sacrifice autonomy for debt and learned that debt should not be necessarily perceived solely or primarily as an obligation but as relief from immediate need. The moral operation paternal care requires is to weigh what is more severe: Is it the pain caused by misery and destitution needing relief? Or is it the pain caused by the loss of status, independence, or dignity that comes with accepting this relief?

Rarely can this question be answered easily. Many clients are clearly unhappy about how much they depend on the NGOs' help. They are aware that they are trading help for dignity or autonomy, but they often have no other choice while dealing with their own acute needs. One client once brought the pharmacy receipt of the medication he purchased to treat his wife's cold, asking Sofia if it was eligible for a refund. When Sofia informed him that only medication received through a doctor's prescription would be covered by the project, he immediately, in one smooth movement, crumpled the receipt and threw it into the office bin, as if trying to erase the incident entirely, leaving no trace of his (degrading?) request for financial help.

Obývačka has a systematic and rather radical approach aimed at preventing situations like these. As I mentioned above, it is their philosophy to support foreigners while encouraging them to contribute something of their own, resulting in a form of solidarity not unlike what Rozakou describes. They rally against all avoidable hierarchization and urge their volunteers to take this imperative to heart. Volunteer training is considered a cornerstone of their endeavors, and they are proud of their pedagogical concept. At the beginning of one of the training sessions I attended, after an introductory round, Helena asked everyone to remember a time when they helped someone. The girls exchanged their stories in small groups, reporting the feelings of pride and affirmation they experienced when providing unconditioned help on the most diverse occasions.

Then Helena asked them to recall a situation in which they had received help. Some girls described acts of random kindness. Another girl told how a woman helped her settle in when she went to study in Britain. But after a while, her new acquaintance's sense of responsibility for her became suffocating, as she felt she was being shown around to her friends like a fancy accessory. The relationship improved again when she found something she could help the woman with in return, and they were able to relate on eye level.

The purpose of the exercise was, for one, to reflect on the powerful impact of even minor instances of care. Helena was careful to attenuate volunteers' exaggerated expectations and motivate them at the same time. "Don't think that your mentee will be perfect at Slovak or have a great job after a year thanks to you. Sometimes it is enough just to be there, to spend time with them and show an interest." In addition, the exchange was aimed at making participants aware of the 'dark side' of care, based on their own experience. Volunteers were encouraged to remember moments when they felt helpless, unworthy, or even ashamed of receiving care, and understand the psychological dynamics that underlie an existence that is dominated by receiving help from others. Because of this, Obývačka's team considered presents a "big no-go": Helena asked the volunteers to empathize, for example, with a struggling father who is working hard but still cannot afford his daughter's most fervent wish, a bicycle. Now, here comes the "miracle auntie" from Slovakia who is fulfilling this wish without much ado, and the bike they never thought they could own is suddenly standing on the doorstep. Besides the temporary joy such a gift would obviously bring, its paternalizing dimension may throw a family dynamic out of balance and do severe damage to the breadwinners' sense of self. Helena suggested that instead, Obývačka could perform the role of an institutional middleman: if volunteers recognized an acute need or one object that one family is conceivably lacking, they could give it to Obývačka's staff and they will then pass it on as an anonymous 'donation.' Compared to a personal gift, fraught with intimacy and pressures of reciprocation, this anonymized giving is much less momentous and socially exposing.

Pleas like these are not always heard by volunteers, however. Many volunteers embrace the role of the 'auntie' and find great joy in giving refugees little and larger gifts. As I discussed in Chapter 4, members of the moral community of refugee supporters transact favors and services in exchange for a feeling of purpose and belonging. They are ground projects for them in which doing good and feeling good are entwined. The anonymization deprives the act of giving of its interpersonal, human dimension and thus seems pointless to many. Next to examining which subject positions are adequate for subjects to integration, one should also look at which positions carers or 'integrators' can be expected to occupy without feeling alienated or replaceable.

Volunteers, NGO workers, and also clients occasionally challenge the virtuousness of letting-be. They argue that it is cruel to both sides, while intense involvement makes them feel worthy and connected. Having acknowledged the 'dark side of care' that gets too overbearing, the next section looks at non-anonymous care from a more benevolent angle, highlighting the mutually validating effect of personal care.

Personal care

Abi was an invaluable asset to the NGO community in Bratislava. Not only did he have a good command of the Slovak language, but he also had an extraordinarily dramatic story which he shared with the most diverse audiences. Abi comes from Herat in Western Afghanistan, his parents were both killed in a violent conflict, and he was raised by his grandmother. When the security situation in Herat worsened due to frequent attacks of suicide bombers, it was his grandma who convinced him to leave the country and join his brother who had been living in Germany and Holland for years already. With the help of expensive traffickers, he traveled via Tajikistan, Russia, and Ukraine and broke his leg shortly before crossing into the EU, which forced him to return to Russia for another six months. At the second attempt, after hiking for days and being close to exasperation, he finally reached the Eastern Slovak town of Hummené. His joy was short-lived; he soon learned that he had two equally unappealing options: applying for asylum in Slovakia or traveling on, risking deportation out of EU territory if stopped. After his extraordinarily exhausting journey, the second option was what Abi wanted to avoid the most, so he decided to stay in Slovakia. The asylum process came with new humiliations: the investigators did not believe he was a minor, adding three years to his legal age. His claim for asylum or subsidiary protection was rejected twice. Fortunately, the NGO Human Rights League took over his case and brought it to the Supreme Court where he was finally granted subsidiary protection. Ever since, he has had to prolong his residence every two years.

Because of missing documents, he was only able to find unpleasant work against poor payment, sometimes the employers did not pay him at all, and he did not dare to complain. He also started going to school again, but since the Slovak authorities did not validate his Afghan education, Abi, meanwhile a young adult of 18 years, needed to attend the eighth grade of a local elementary school. Being much older than his classmates, with teachers not taking his extraordinary situation into account whatsoever, Abi came to hate school quickly.

When Abi and I first met, he was excited to talk German to a native speaker. The burden of being so close to his brother in Germany, without being able to join him, torments Abi. He has not given up on moving westward one day, so his zeal to learn the German language is undiminished. After graduating from elementary school, he struggled to choose a career path and signed up for an advanced school of computing and informatics, spawned by his family's advice to choose a profession with good financial prospects. He hated it and had a hard time keeping up with the curriculum. Obývačka found a seemingly ideal volunteer for him, a former physics teacher who was eager to get Abi back on track, but his strict and authoritarian style of teaching made Abi despair even more and lose all confidence in his intellectual capabilities. "Don't you want to swap heads?" he asked me with a desperate smile after a particularly challenging tutoring session in Obývačka's community center. I wanted to reply that I am an anthropologist and that a swap of brains would most probably block his advancement in mathematics altogether, but I stopped myself just in time. I sensed that the implications of this thought experiment were more profound. Abi was longing to be someone else, or maybe himself, but transformed.

During his time in Slovakia, Abi managed to build an extraordinary network of influential supporters: he was friends with the chair of the church council of the *Cirkev Bratská* (Church of Brethren), an evangelical free church that exists only in the Czech Republic and Slovakia, the curator of the modern art museum *Kunsthalle*, and the director of the library of the Bratislava *Goethe Institut*. Abi was even invited to the president's palace to meet Andrej Kiska when he was president of the Slovak Republic. He was a familiar face in the entire Bratislava nonprofit scene, not least because he was a potent ally in the struggle against refugee hostility and xenophobia: his case, that of an underage orphan who had endured terrible hardships during his journey to Slovakia and after, is bound to wake the empathy of even the most skeptical refugee opponents. He is a "morally legitimate suffering body" in the truest sense.

Friends and supporters were worried about Abi. Radovan, the head of the church council, explained to me that minors who make it to Europe suffer a severe loss of identity and self-confidence, not least connected to their previous social standing: only relatively wealthy families have sufficient means to enable the journey. "Then they come here and see that they cannot maintain their status and lifestyle, that they are nobodies and have to start from zero. That is a really frustrating experience." Martina from Obývačka told me that Abi is in a phase of his life where he needs to start thinking and acting independently. She thinks he did not receive enough guidance in the formative years of his young life: no one was there to show him the ropes when he most needed it. She thinks that this is why he is having such a hard time making crucial decisions about his future life all by himself. There are no specific guidelines on how to deal with children and adolescents in the integration project. It is common sense that they need more attention, but there is barely any time or resources for the special care they need.

When the situation at the computing school became unbearable for Abi, Martina set up a meeting with everyone in Slovakia who plays a part in Abi's life—his NGO social worker, volunteers, and Radovan. They discussed Abi's situation and decided to make him consider a different path of education. He is good with languages, and his motivation to improve his German is especially high, so they suggested trying to get him into a secondary school with a language profile. Abi was relieved that interrupting his computer science education was framed as a conceivable option, but he was still anxious about his future job prospects and the fact that he would lose time by changing trajectories.

Abi is a young man who spent a considerable amount of his life in utter insecurity. Although very resilient and eager to socialize and make the best of adverse situations, the fatigue and frustration of these years linger on him. In his new surroundings, he has not only encountered a lot of friendliness, but also hostility and harassment. Martina and the others are faced with the question of whether letting-be was really the morally correct way to deal with the situation.

Being a young unaccompanied teenage refugee when entering Slovakia, it is rather obvious that Abi has to become a subject of a different kind of care, outside the anonymous care protocol. What is deemed appropriate is care in its most existential sense, as nourishing and nurturing human beings who are not yet or not anymore capable of taking care of themselves, like children or the elderly (Buch 2014). A kind of care that is personalized in that it takes the recipient's whole being into account and responds compassionately to individual handicaps and needs. One could call it 'attuned' in the sense of being-with—although definitely not letting-be in Zigon's sense because it involves nudging the protégées onto the path that *is best* for them.

The personal care I have described in this example is a mode of attention akin to child-rearing. It indeed takes on the quality of a ground project in caregivers' lives, coming with an emotional commitment to get it right and the fear of causing lasting damage. There is an enduring tension between strictness and laissez-faire.

A child is the "archetypical figure of innocence" because it "reflects this search for purity in the secular world, this deep yearning for a time before corruption, a space beyond social norms" (Ticktin 2017, 579). Many studies have shown the absurdity of the abruptness with which underage refugees lose this status when they come of age. From one day to the next, young people are not seen as needing any sort of special or preferential treatment anymore. They lose access to the welfare infrastructures that took care of them. They are expected to secure their own accommodation and subsistence or face deportation (Plann 2019). Ticktin maintains that the politics of innocence work according to a certain logic of expansion, of looking for new, even more innocent subjects that become beneficiaries of care. White children fit the (Western) configuration of innocence better than children of color (ibid., 579). Animals are even more unsuspected (Ticktin 2017, 584). No one can hold on to the label of complete purity for long before being replaced, and thus previous claimants have to be expelled from the realm of innocence to make way for new archetypes. Politicians aiming at reducing the number of asylum seekers and increasing thresholds for asylum strive to dispel unaccompanied children or teens, denying them the status of innocent children more and more often. The tendency of authorities to declare children older than they actually are or their documents say is a common occurrence.

But there is also the opposite reasoning: to take the moral and emotional exceptionality of children as the template for the perception and treatment of all refugees. Some argue that refugees, by default, share characteristics that bring them closely into line with the 'innocent child' and make them occupy a subject position amenable to care in its existential sense. "We should be the eyes, ears and mouth of the refugee," said Navid, who together with theologian Milota had been in charge of an earlier integration project when the Migration Office's partner was the Catholic Charita. Navid continues, "They can hear, but they cannot understand; they can talk, but they don't know what to say; they can see, but they can't make sense of it." According to him, the purpose of an integration NGO is, first and foremost, to take care of all of that and then slowly and softly release refugees into independence. This portrayal of refugees not just as disadvantaged by lack of resources or structural discrimination, but bereft of bodily functions, or at least their expedient usage, inevitably leads to an entirely different conclusion about the ideal nature of care and responsible and sustainable integration.

Navid spent two years in prison in Iran for his political activities, and when he was released, he decided it was safer for him and his sister to go abroad. They both studied medicine in Košice, at their own expense. It took him a few years to convince himself that he could not go back to Iran. He applied for asylum and had to give up his studies soon thereafter. Since then, he has worked different jobs mainly in the social sector while twice applying for Slovak citizenship unsuccessfully. "I have given up on my personal life," he told me when he finished telling his story without seeming bitter. His life was just fully dedicated to helping others now.

Milota was born into a deeply religious Greek Catholic family. After studying theology, she went to Israel to volunteer and returned with a Kirgiz husband.

> I experienced the whole process foreigners in Slovakia go through first-hand (na vlastnej koži). Being married to a foreigner, my family not accepting that, then losing friends, then all the remarks, jokes, xenophobia and all. In the end, my husband couldn't take it anymore and left for London.

Milota and Navid were already close friends when Navid got a part-time position at the Roman Catholic Charita as a social worker in the integration project, and what he told her about the project did not please her at all: the team consisted of young women who, in her opinion, did not quite know what to do with themselves. They had no experience living abroad, so they tried to "tame" clients by intimidating them. Milota started making calls to the central office in Bratislava with her ideas and was finally offered the position of project manager. She immediately threw herself into her new role. Firstly, she replaced the whole team, employing only people with experience of living abroad or dealing with migrants. Then, she introduced an extensive Slovak language learning program. Clients received 12 hours of language training per week, six from a professional Slovak teacher who was hired, and six from volunteers.

Navid worked as a cultural mediator, but he was in the field most of the day, helping people with all tasks imaginable. They were both available twenty-four hours a day. Milota's approach to integration is consensus-based, but also very proactive: she is convinced that integration only happens from within when the person is really ready for it and motivated. It is impossible to be integrated against one's own will. Yet they did offer very specific support. "You have to understand their culture. They won't ask for anything. But if advice is properly communicated, they are very happy."

Generally, Milota finds a three-year trajectory feasible for integration. If willing, anyone can learn the language and navigate everyday life independently after three years. "It's like with a kid: he gets born, and after three years he is capable of being a social being in society. And it is the same with clients. Coming here is like going through birth again." She stressed that their goal was also the ultimate independence and self-sufficiency of clients. When a mother tried to emotionally blackmail her into offering help which she did not deem justified, by claiming "But you are my family," she reacted quite harshly by telling her that she was mistaken in this respect. Their love and support were neither aimless nor unconditional.

Milota recalled one case where one of their teenage clients, a half-orphan, was accused of something his friend had done: bullying a girl. The father of the girl came to school and screamed at him, which left a lasting impact on the boy. He had visibly changed his behavior when he came to Charita's office; the formerly cheerful boy seemed quiet and intimidated. His mom suffered but did not know what to do. Milota and Navid got in contact with the school's director, learned that the boy had been unrightfully accused, and decided to step in. They set up a meeting with the girl's father and explained the misunderstanding. Then Milota told him:

I understand your reaction because your daughter came home crying and you wanted to protect her. But Farhad is here without a father to protect him, his mom doesn't speak enough Slovak, so we protect him instead. So please, if you could apologize to him so he sees how a good father should behave, he doesn't have a male role model here.

The appeal bore fruit, the father apologized indeed, which left a deep impression on the boy. "This is how we worked," Milota concluded with pride.

After the project moved to Refúgium, Milota and Navid maintained close bonds with their former clients without doing "anything professional," respecting the authority and role of their successors. Milota and Navid understand that the goal of Refúgium's efforts is to prevent people from getting dependent on help from the start, but they believe that overzealousness in this respect is doing more harm than good. Refugees are oftentimes severely traumatized and disoriented, they are *vyvrátení z koreňov* (torn away from their roots), as Navid phrased it. As Charita's team, they were deeply involved in people's lives and offered them as much support as they needed until they were steady and settled. Asked what the goal of successful integration was, Navid simply answered "that they are not *zablúdený*" (lost; *zablúdiť sa* = wander, go astray, go lost).

Being a substitute father for a newborn child, the eyes and ears and minds of disoriented people, someone mending the wounds of loss and uprooting, all the images Milota and Navid use to characterize their relationship to refugees are highly hierarchical: they entail knowing what *is best* for clients and having the authority to pursue exactly that. The subject position foreseen for refugees in this case is a passive one; they are not expected to take initiative because they are still unable to do so. As could be expected, this approach yields a lot of criticism: especially those organizations that have taken over clients from Charita complain that its staff "taught them the position of the client," as Sofia phrased it, which was why they were now struggling with clients' passivity and ingratitude.

On the other hand, many clients were really impressed by Charita's approach. They told me they missed Charita's care, and years after changing organizations, still had to get used to the very different tone they heard in Refúgium's and ASPR's premises. Abi felt outright betrayed by the sudden change of guards and was nostalgic for Charita's care. "ASPR is not doing anything," he told me with a bitter tone.

Displaced persons in Georgia constantly claim that the humanitarian organizations do 'nothing' for them although they verifiably receive financial and other forms of support, as Elizabeth Cullen Dunn (2018) observed. Dunn explains that humanitarian organizations reproduce and copy-paste ready-made solutions with restricted time and means whenever a humanitarian crisis demands quick intervention, often relying on the assumption that "something" is always better than "nothing" (Dunn 2018, 66 and 84). By contrast, the recipients often feel that something is indeed worse or more painful than nothing: donated items only point to the personal possessions that they lost; activities such as theater workshops make people more acutely aware of their paralyzing purposelessness, the macaroni they are provided with is only a faint reminder of *real* food. According to Dunn, "(n)othingness is thus not merely the result of violence, but also the result of care; not merely the remnant of destruction but also an effect of construction" (Dunn 2018, 111).

As a consequence, the 'soft power' approach that humanitarian aid often employs, expecting cooperation and compliance in exchange for the help received, proves ineffective: clients do not see any benefit, and thus do not feel indebted either. It may thus be deduced that under certain circumstances, those who are being cared for have become immune against the constraining force of the gift of care, against the expectation of reciprocation subtly constructing assemblages of hierarchy and power. Therefore, many refugees experience what is meant to be empowerment as abandonment. Personalized care, by contrast, which is more binding and constraining, is often perceived as more meaningful. Clients seek this level of support very consciously. To them, it is a form of help that can be appreciated to such an extent that one is willing to sacrifice something in return.

Is Integration Obsolete?

Anonymous care is largely believed to be the morally superior approach to fostering autonomy, but sometimes givers and receivers prefer personal or paternal care, producing, potentially, similar results in terms of long-term satisfaction and independence. As in the previous chapters, we see a juxtaposition between the structural constraints emerging from integration policies (that aim at abstracting care) and the individual approach of refugee supporters (who try to make room for personalized care). Again, a closer look reveals that the situation is more complex than this, as the contradictions that occur are not fully congruous with the opposition between state and non-state actors or paradigms. Refugee care practices oscillate between both poles: NGO workers who strongly believe in the appropriateness of equal and detached care sometimes care very individually, or they have difficulties figuring out what the most sustainable path to independence is. Refugee supporters who see refugees in analogy to children sometimes cut ties and deny support.

Looking closely at the momentary shifts and changing frameworks of legitimation, the answers to questions to do with the good vary: Is 'the good' in care a methodological approach, a systematic pursuit of a goal that has been established rationally? This tendency is apparent in the commitment of social workers to 'fashion themselves' according to the emancipatory paradigm of integration policies through forms of (mutual and self-) control. Or does good care require an intuitive approach, a reliance on compassion and an authentic connection to (irreplaceable) persons, in other words, is it a virtue to be cultivated through repeated engagement with others who have come to matter? The emotional comittment and passionate pursuit of the clients' best stands in stark contrast to the adherence to discipline and self-imposed rules. Yet, in everyday practice, they take turns determining refugee supporters' moral behavior, supporting my claim that these two forms of thinking about moral practice are complementary rather than mutually exclusive, and are equally necessary to understand the continuity of both *bordel* and *riešiť* in refugee care.

Anonymous care and personal/paternal care create different trajectories for those who are to be integrated (and those who integrate), and both of them suit certain individuals while others are uncomfortable with them. Both positions have their inherent logic, and both can involve subtle forms of violence and harm recipients. The emancipation imperative rests on the assumption that eventually, all refugees would consider it not only logical and beneficial but also moral to prioritize their independence and detach from institutional help. Yet the assumption that these ideals of autonomy and self-sufficiency are shared is flawed, as it glosses over a variety of racial, gendered, bodily, emotional, and sociocultural specifics. For unaccompanied minors, clients of old age, with a handicap, with mental illness, or for those who grew up in a society with strict role expectations that leave less space for individual choice and autonomy, it is very difficult, if not impossible, to assume the subject position that is expected of them. Clients like Salma, Abi, or Paolo do not consider becoming independent a desirable goal at all, nor do they necessarily recognize an ethical obligation to do so. They and many other refugees are craving support and companionship and gladly accept any guidance offered to them in building a calm and peaceful existence in Slovakia.

Similarly, many supporters struggle to assume the subject position of anonymized carer and long for a real connection and meaningful impact instead. These circumstances are not sufficiently acknowledged in many critiques of the integration paradigm in policy and science: there is both supply and demand for the more comprehensive, adaptive integrative measures. Furthermore, the explicit or implicit suggestion in integration critiques that a self-confident 'migrants and allies'—lobby could disrupt the one-sided, mainstreaming integration paradigm, promoting 'radical diversity' and 'de-integration' instead (Czollek 2018) is not universally applicable. There are places, like Slovakia, where the conditions for subversive migrant subjectivities are (still) very unfavorable—because migrants lack the strength that is in numbers, and because migrants' security and life chances depend disproportionately on their ability to integrate. It is all but clear if Slovakia will ever enter a postmigrant (and postintegration) era if it continues along the political paths it has unwaveringly followed in the past decade, and which comes to be accepted even by many traditional immigration societies in Europe at the time I am writing this—namely one in which limiting or even reducing migrant numbers is paramount.

Those who want to do away with integration question whether there should be any institutionalized integration as a practice of care. It is certainly necessary to develop utopian scenarios in which integration has become obsolete, but as long as they are very far removed from reality, acknowledging a fundamental need for services, help, and support remains crucial for migrants' safety and well-being.

Chapter 8

CONCLUSION

Riešiť Despite the Mess

"We stand in between the different parties, but in the end, we are the ones who have to *riešiť* despite all the nice slogans and catchphrases." This statement is key to my understanding of refugee supporters' positionality. Sofia said this when she came out of the meeting Marginal had organized with Abed and the Migration Office, which led to the decision to let Abed have his will and go to India for a diploma. The social worker from the Migration Office had concluded the meeting by saying that refugees "can achieve anything" and should be encouraged to "fulfill their potential." In Sofia's view, these were just romantic platitudes, making everyone feel righteous and comfortable while obfuscating the fact that this 'achievement' was really a kind of scam.

At the same time, refugee supporters still face other (more disturbing) slogans, the rallying cries of extremists and xenophobes who claim that refugees are "parasites" or "terrorists" who "threaten our culture" and "cannot be integrated." 'Slogans' refer here to the grand proclamations of principles and normative judgments—which may be naïvely simplistic and dangerously ignorant of the messiness of real life. The practice of refugee care in Slovakia is diametrically opposed to the logic of slogans: it lacks the clarity and unambiguity, the claims to truth and comprehensiveness encompassed in snappy catchphrases. Their work also eschews the reductionist, essentialist, manipulative quality of populist slogans. By distancing herself from other people's moral statements and fearmongering, encapsulated in pointed catchphrases, Sofia downplays the role of principles, making it secondary to the short-term, inescapable logic of riešiť. She suggests a realm beyond moral commitments, where the goal is not to find the best but just *good enough* solutions.

This realm consists of expectations, experiences, norms, lessons, and emotions. They all have the potential to direct action. They are methodically, meticulously, or spontaneously weighed, negotiated, appropriated, prioritized, neglected, or forgotten. Refugee supporters find themselves in a moral laboratory, for instance, when testing and shifting the boundaries between tolerance and accommodation. They go through moral breakdowns that trigger, among other things, leaps to trust or distrust. All these operations belong to a fundamentally ephemeral and unstable situation in which moral sentiments and emotional judgments constantly mix. Addressing this situation requires engaging in an 'ordinary ethics' that is realized through practice rather than the mere application of preexisting principles.

When I started to reflect on these impressions that stayed with me after my ethnographic fieldwork, and on what significance they may carry beyond the small-scale field

I studied, I couldn't help but notice that their scope of applicability had likely grown. The parameters for refugee care in the EU had fundamentally shifted since I started fieldwork, making other places—arguably—more like Slovakia. In this conclusion, I want to briefly sketch this development. Before this backdrop, I add some thoughts on what conclusions might be drawn from this study both politically and for further research.

Recent Political Developments and Implications

Shifts in asylum policy

I started to be interested in refugees in Slovakia when I was doing fieldwork for another project in Prešov, a town in the East of the country, in the autumn of 2015 and was struck by the urgency with which the 'refugee crisis' was debated in all four Visegrád countries. When I first started thinking about this project, I had a diachronic angle in mind. This was more a semiconscious assumption than a confident statement, but I felt that I was looking at a country suddenly thrown into events and debates that most Western European states had faced decades ago. The interpretations of local experts bolstered this reading. In the early phase of my fieldwork, when I interviewed predominantly researchers and activists, I latched onto the frequent mentions of Slovakia's 'tolerance deficit.' My collocutors referred to the homogeneity of Slovakia's population, which had "no experience with diversity," assuming that being more accepting of difference and more welcoming toward strangers was a learning process that Slovakia had to go through in a globalized world.

In this early stage, I was convinced that the 'social situation' I was about to explore through ethnographic fieldwork was particular to the Slovak setting. Parallels were to be expected with other Visegrád states that pursued a very similar agenda in 2015, but all in all, the relevance of my inquiry seemed to be geographically confined. As I argued in previous chapters, the vast critical literature on migration and refugee policies is only applicable to the Central and Eastern European case to a limited degree. Sensible approaches to asylum policy and integration need to take the local cultural, social, and historical specificities into account and develop tailor-made solutions for contexts which may be vastly different from, let's say, in Britain or Germany.

However, the applicability of my observations is now as broad as never before. This is because the public perceptions of refugees and asylum have changed dramatically in the years leading up to the completion of my book. In 2024, we are confronted with an entirely different picture than a few years ago, and the strong anti-refugee sentiments in the Visegrád countries have spread across the continent. Of course, the German AfD, the French Front National, or the British Defence League have already been around for a while, but their signature rhetoric of national purity, scapegoating migration for social tensions and job market problems, and inciting fear of criminality and terrorism has gradually made its way into mainstream discourse and politics. The consequences of this shift toward the right are all too familiar: in the past years, a consensus has emerged that the topic of refugees can only be approached with great caution. Most EU member states have introduced more restrictive asylum regimes, right-wing nationalist parties enjoy consistent or rising approval rates, hate speech against refugees has risen to alarming levels both online and offline, and violent incidents with racist motives have multiplied. The flagrant indifference toward inhabitants of the Moria refugee camp in Greece during the onset of the COVID-19 pandemic has shown that the responses to humanitarian crises have radically altered.

Ever since 2015, the EU has quarreled over the very touchy topic of a reform of the Common European Asylum System (CEAS)—primarily with the sensible goals of defining a unitary approach to asylum in the EU, providing better help for the most challenged countries at the borders of the Schengen zone, and deploying effective crisis mechanisms. At the time I am writing this, the reform is still highly controversial but hoped to be completed before the EU elections in June 2024. It has been clear throughout the negotiations that most member states, some more, some less transparently, want the reform to signal one thing to their respective populations: their governments' efforts to restrict refugees' numbers. This also entails measures which are hoped to have mainly a deterring effect. Persons without a long-term perspective of staying in the EU, that is, from countries with low protection rates, are supposed to undergo asylum trials at the border—in detention-like border camps. According to new crisis regulations, the standards for accommodation and welfare—which have often not been met in the past—will be lowered even further if the numbers of arriving refugees surge. Urgent demands to criminalize sea rescue also fit into this frame. Countries with a right-wing administration, like Italy, are of course leading voices in these negotiations. It is telling, however, that during these consultations, Germany with a coalition government of Social Democrats (*Sozialdemokratische Partei Deutschlands*, SPD), Green Party (*Die Grünen*) and Liberals (*Freie Demokratische Partei*, FDP) has also debated a more restrictive national asylum policy, aiming to increase the number of deportations and curtailing rights of foreigners who are subject to deportation.[1]

The bewildered observations of Central and Eastern Europe's xenophobia, which could be found in journalistic and scholarly accounts just a few years ago, now seem misplaced, since we hear a very similar vocabulary from leaders across Europe and across the political spectrum. One could almost say that in popular understanding, the reading of asylum as a favor has been replaced by a reading as an unbearable imposition and as a threat—even in countries that used to pride themselves as beacons of humanitarian aid and human rights. The effects of this comprehensive shift on local providers of refugee care—and whether it might boost their 'messiness' to the levels observed in Slovakia—remain to be studied.

This does not mean that Slovakia and its neighboring countries appear more moderate in comparison. The topic of refugees and asylum has gained steam during Russia's war on Ukraine. After a remarkable and coordinated display of solidarity when Ukrainian refugees started arriving in Slovakia, almost two years later, Ukrainians are

---

1. For comprehensive surveys of the EU's asylum policies since 2015, see: Bousiou and Schleyer 2023; De Nunzio 2023. For recent developments in German asylum policies, see Thränhardt 2023; Ayoub 2023.

increasingly labeled as culturally 'other' and as a burden on the Slovak welfare system. The Visegrád states have also remained very skeptical toward the CEAS reform and any movement toward a more unitary approach to migration and asylum in the EU. They strictly reject any proposal entailing a redistribution of refugees. Alternative compensation payments to the border states have been labeled by Poland as a 'fine' for not accepting refugees.

Political recommendations

Before these developments, the question of how to maintain minimum standards of refugee care and protect the right to asylum poses itself with renewed urgency in Slovakia and beyond. It would be negligent and cynical of me to write this conclusion without spelling out the obvious systemic flaws that have appeared throughout the ethnography and discuss possible solutions. From the start, I made it clear that this is not a piece of activist or militant research, and this remains true insofar as I claim no intellectual property of the political recommendations that follow. I only relay and organize ideas, wishes, and conclusions which come from my NGO, Migration Office, and refugee interlocutors. They should be neither new nor surprising to anyone working in the field, and indeed many of them have already been suggested and negotiated.

Pomoc a Nádej and Refúgium agree that the 'frictional' cooperation between NGOs and the Migration Office is problematic, to say the least. For years now, they have suggested a model in which state welfare and social work are kept separate: according to this, the Migration Office would create offices in which refugees receive their benefits and deal with matters concerning their legal status. In this way, NGOs could function as independent consultants: clients' relationships with their social workers would be untainted by material and financial anxieties. Ideally, the rates would have to be raised as well to give new arrivals a realistic chance to settle in before becoming self-reliant and provide the elderly and infirm with financial security.

Refugee supporters would not have to navigate the delicate terrain of representing the 'hostile' state of Slovakia while being nongovernmental at the same time, and having to defend and implement policies they do not (necessarily) endorse. The separation of state and social work domains would have to be paired with de-projectization: NGOs would work in the field permanently and on their own terms. They would adapt the parameters of their work according to their own needs. Most importantly, the constant loss of expertise and social capital that occurs whenever project partners change could be avoided. It would also be a first (albeit insufficient) step toward solving a crucial problem, the acute shortage of funding. NGOs should be able to raise sufficient funding from a broad range of sources, like Obývačka already does, and employ more interpreters and cultural mediators, improving communication and creating favorable conditions for the emergence of trust and for adjusting levels of care to individual clients' needs. They would also be able to dedicate more time and effort to enjoyable social activities like trips, picnics, barbecues, kids' summer camps, women's circles and the like—occasions which are experienced as particularly meaningful for all involved.

A second necessary step would be a broad educative campaign aimed at systematically equipping anyone who comes into contact with refugees with the necessary skills and knowledge. It would be good to gradually raise and regularly update the Migration Office and NGO workers' competencies in social work methodology, intercultural communication, and language proficiency. Also, institutions refugees inevitably get in touch with sooner or later, like job centers, social security authorities, municipalities, hospitals, and schools, would benefit from information on the legal ramifications of their dealings with refugees. This would significantly unburden NGO workers who regularly have to instruct all of these institutions about their duties and the requirements vis-à-vis refugees and foreigners. Ideally, competencies would have to be relegated directly to the segments of society and everyday life where integration is actually taking place. It would help to de-informalize and institutionalize refugee care and to create new default support mechanisms relating to education, work, and housing, bringing relevant organizations and institutions on board.

As a consequence, cooperation and mutual communication between different NGOs and public authorities should be intensified. Both refugees and refugee supporters are affected by the unclear allocation of competencies. It would help each organization to make their tasks manageable, and develop and elaborate their routine, so they know exactly what refugees can expect from them. In addition, a lot of potential for synergies and collaboration is wasted because of the prejudices and reservations organizations have toward each other. The common ground is usually much larger than the disagreements, and platforms to communicate regularly openly and transparently would certainly lift one or another blockade.

Finally, a more coordinated and empathetic approach from the EU would be needed to combat the causes why the previous suggestions, although widely approved of, have still not been implemented. As long as the refugee question continues to be a focal point of East–West confrontation, provoking assertions of national autonomy and sovereignty toward the Unions' presumed dictate, an improvement of internal refugee policies remains unlikely. Efforts to offer payments as an alternative to the acceptance of relocated refugees is a step in the right direction, but, as mentioned above, it does little to reject the underlying animosities.

From the Slovak perspective, the EU's concern with distribution is neither understandable, nor expedient. A functioning system of refugee care is needed independently of the situation in other member countries. The number of refugees arriving in Slovakia through a redistributive mechanism is minuscule and will likely remain negligible as opposed to the number of those who arrive in Slovakia in other ways. In this regard, the EU would hence be well-advised to prioritize the unification of standards regarding asylum procedures and reception—if it is to take its commitment to human rights and its status as a role model in the rule of law seriously. In the (very) long run, this will also affect the distribution of refugees across the EU by widening the field of desired target countries.

Contribution to the Study of Refugee Care

The developments I have outlined above mean that asylum and refugee care should and will remain important fields of study in anthropology and neighboring disciplines, as many of the complications and challenges that have been identified in recent research have amplified. The purpose of this book has been to contribute to this vibrant field a novel approach that goes beyond political and structural dichotomies and the diffusion of power through migration regimes—by focusing on the interpersonal, emotional, and moral interactions between the various actors. I want to conclude the book by summarizing what we can learn from this venture for the study of refugees and humanitarianism in Central Eastern Europe and beyond—which are the most relevant insights, and which questions posed by this study deserve further scrutiny.

The unwitting impact of political narratives

Sofia distanced herself from other actors' use of simplifying slogans, but despite (or partly because of) this rejecting attitude, the 'knowledge' that is condensed in widespread narratives on refugees impacts refugee supporters' work extensively. According to the theories I apply in this study, both emotion and morality entail evaluations that draw on a person's entire cultural embeddedness and experiential knowledge. The conventional pearls of wisdom, catchphrases, and tropes about refugees and refugee care certainly belong to this repertoire.

Throughout the book, I have analyzed and problematized the workings of some of the most influential 'systems of knowledge' concerning refugees: how asylum is cast as an exclusive right of 'morally legitimate suffering bodies'; how the ideal refugee is envisioned as a 'worthy guest'; how refugees appear as 'storytellers,' 'profit-seeking,' or, on the other side of the political spectrum, as 'helpless children'; how integration is understood as the efforts of a 'deviant' group to emulate a national 'cultural mainstream'; and so on. The faults and omissions of these narratives are obvious and generally known to refugee supporters. In my ethnography, however, we have seen multiple times how this vocabulary affects even those who do not use it and how these evaluations appear in practices even of those who do not approve of them.

The ethnography also shows *why* these narratives unwittingly surface in the practice of refugee supporters who otherwise resolutely reject them: namely, for the same reasons that make them attractive as political catchphrases. They appeal to the foundations of emotional well-being and moral integrity, like purpose, self-worth, self-efficacy, and community. In public and political discourse, negative and abridged bits of knowledge about refugees often appeal to fears of loss of status, financial precarity, disintegration of societal cohesion, and changes to the fabric of one's lifeworld.

While refugee supporters do not believe in any grand narratives in which refugees or migrants are the scapegoats, they remain responsive to such explanations on the level of individual offenses against them: when they feel that their hard work is not sufficiently acknowledged; when they fear failing in their ground projects; when they get the impression that their trust, effort, or affection is not valued or reciprocated. These are basically situations in which their moral and emotional embodied appraisal of the situation amounts to a negative conclusion. In such states, simplified and biased explanations provide temporary relief; of course, they remain in constant competition with the benevolent beliefs toward refugees they also hold. Hence, refugee supporters' moral lives are arguably more complicated than those of people who believe these narratives without reservations. In other instances, refugee supporters recur to these narratives very consciously because it is the only way to rebut accusations and counter common prejudices.

I believe great potential lies in studying how narratives work to shape relationships and behavior by latching onto moments of moral and emotional offense. These questions could be the subject of ethnographic, statistical, or sociolinguistic studies. This is an important contribution to studying the political discourse on refugees and asylum at large, especially in times when, as argued in the previous subchapter, nationalist-protectionist positions are increasingly held by parties and voters identifying as centrist or even leftist, and misinformation and hateful content regarding refugees spreads faster than ever, particularly on social media and through direct messenger services.

Exposing the illusion of permanence

The messiness of refugee care in Slovakia is evolving dynamically: in the beginning, I stated how efforts to establish more orderly conditions are doomed to fail because so many aspects of refugee care are characterized by a certain fleetingness, impermanence, and precarity. The project circles lead to a high fluctuation of staff and skills; sustainable political solutions are absent, necessitating constant improvisation; current national and European events regularly upend the political climate and other framework conditions. Additionally, each chapter has introduced a simultaneity of two maxims or paradigms that are very hard to reconcile seamlessly. And yet, from the sidelines, refugee care in Slovakia seems remarkably permanent: the provision of (good enough) services is consistent, conditions seem unchanging, and support is unwavering.

The focus on individual moral and emotional practice reveals the forces that tear on this permanence from all sides; it shows that rather than with orderly circumstances, we are dealing with delicate balances. Indeed, some elements remain static exactly because they are held in place by equal pressures exerted from all sides. It is the very nature of a dilemma that there are two or more options with the same validity or urgency. Throughout the book, we have seen that refugee supporters and refugees react to this by practicing strategic indeterminacy: they dwell between trust and mistrust, balance emancipating and paternal care, oscillate between intervention and acceptance, and navigate compliance and resurgence toward state authorities.

What is being consolidated, then, are the strategies and methods to maintain this inconclusiveness. They are trained and learned practices which nevertheless need constant adapting and perfecting in a 'moral laboratory'-mode. I have also shown that even this predicament of indeterminacy is inherently ambivalent: while it entails straining emotional and communicative labor to always 'invent' new solutions, it is also perceived as creative and meaningful.

In other words, the focus on these practices is crucial for confounding the illusion of permanence and order and reveals the dense web of processes that is necessary to 'carry on,' which poses the question of which other hidden dynamics could be rendered visible when putting individuals and their relationships in the center of one's inquiry.

Blurring the boundaries between categories of actors

A point I have made in the book, starting in the Introduction, is that path dependencies between structural positions and inclinations toward specific opinions and behaviors in refugee care are less pronounced than one might expect.

To recapitulate, the literature on refugees and asylum that I introduced at the beginning of the book often engages with conflicts of interest in the political arena: geopolitical considerations, nationalist rhetoric, migrant agencies, humanitarian agendas, and so on. Concretely, certain non-liberal, restrictive, controlling, supervising impulses are associated with state authorities and their representatives while accommodating, empathetic, supportive, state-critical stances are expected from refugee supporters in or outside of NGOs. We have seen that this juxtaposition is at least partly true and at the root of many irresolvable conflicts and confrontations.

Yet many conflicts in refugee care do not arise between categories of actors, or between different opinions and worldviews. Instead, they may be engendered by more mundane, micro-scale, individual, and internal struggles. A focus on the moral and emotional trajectories of individual minds inevitably takes us to the conclusion that actors' responses and practices cannot be located along a spectrum, but rather move fleetingly up and down the scale. Approaching actors as conflicted individuals detaches them from their structural roles in a migration regime and the polarizations often associated with such positions: NGO workers are neither selfless heroes nor tacit henchmen of state power; refugees are neither helpless victims nor fully free to redeem their agency; and state migration authorities cannot be reduced to being either hostile or opportunistically hospitable.

I believe that examining the micro-dynamics of human interaction has the potential to provide an entirely different outlook on the topic of migration, or, more precisely, on the processes that arise when people who have been on the move settle down in new surroundings. These processes may take very similar shapes in any society that absorbs people on the move. They produce similar frictions, no matter whether one thousand or one million people arrive. As Anna Tsing argued in a liberating critique of metaphysical accounts of globalization—all frictions can ultimately be traced back to "encounters across difference" (Tsing 2005, 3). Taking these encounters seriously and studying them at close range contribute to a fuller and more differentiated understanding of modern immigration societies.

The systematic impact of emotional needs

If we take the previous observation one step further, one aspect that has shone through all chapters is how much refugee help is structured by the emotional requirements in interhuman contact. The emotional needs of individuals match and sometimes supersede other directives for action, like political ideals and moral standards.

Refugee supporters understand their commitment to refugees as a ground project that is closely connected to their sense of self-worth. They find purpose and validation in exchanging favors among a network of like-minded persons. Despite all calls for a professional and emancipating approach, they invest in their relationships with refugees, carefully nurturing mutual trust and intimacy, and develop friendships, accepting an increased exposure to pain, disappointment, and offense. Refugees also often feel that their presence in Slovakia is endowed with meaning and stability based on their bonds with Slovak mentors. Indeed, practices of personal care often shield both refugee supporters and refugees from feeling alienated from their jobs, respectively their new homes. Again, the ethnography has provided an ambivalent evaluation of this observation—next to purpose and orientation, the consequences also include mutual dependencies, the cementation of structures of power and influence, the risk of overwork, and the delay of political reform. However, it needs to be acknowledged that the emotional needs of individuals play an important role in the overall functioning of the Slovak refugee system.

The need for a human connection and an appraisal of other persons that is non-arbitrary shape the way refugee supporters understand their job (or voluntary engagement). This means it determines to a significant degree how organizations in refugee support operate. In the Slovak context, in which there are only a few organizations and few refugees, and relationships between carers and those cared for are close, it is particularly easy to point out how an individual's emotional needs and capacities shape the system as a whole. But I think this aspect is widely underestimated in other contexts as well—for instance, in refugee care systems in other countries.

Additionally, this focus may serve as protection against totalizing political or cultural explanations for problems that arise between refugees and those trusted with their care and thus contributes to de-exceptionalizing mobility (Dahinden 2016; Anderson 2019). Encounters between these two groups resemble, for instance, other engagements between providers of care and vulnerable or disadvantaged individuals or groups. I strongly encourage testing the applicability of the suggested approach to these fields.

Encouraging a constructive debate on migration

Finally, I think the perspectives and approaches suggested above yield advantages for the field of refugee studies beyond the scholarly community, for science communication and public discourse on the issue. They can, if communicated properly, offer a constructive and dispassionate contribution to heated public debates on asylum policy and integration programs, because they relay observations that are easily reproducible and experiences that most recipients will relate to—for instance, if a person one cares about displays behaviors one does not agree with, and one goes through the moral dilemma whether it is wiser to intervene or not. Bringing down the problems refugee care is faced with to such frictional encounters which are as mundane as they are ubiquitous can help transpose the controversies on asylum and migration onto the level of everyone's (introspective) experience (Rapport 2007) and put ideological quarrels on hold while addressing some of the most pressing issues of the present.

REFERENCES

Agamben, Giorgio. 2005. *State of Exception*. Chicago, IL: University of Chicago Press.

Alexeyeff, Kalissa. 2008. 'Are You Being Served? Sex, Humor and Globalisation in the Cook Islands.' *Anthropological Forum* 18, no. 3: 287–93.

Allan, Graham. 1989. *Friendship: Developing a Sociological Perspective*. Studies in Sociology. Boulder, CO: Westview Press.

Anderson, Benedict R. 2003 [1991]. *Imagined Communities: Reflections on the Origin and Spread of Nationalism*. London: Verso.

Anderson, Bridget. 2019. 'New Directions in Migration Studies: Towards Methodological De-Nationalism.' *Comparative Migration Studies* 7, no. 1: 1–36.

Andersson, Ruben. 2014. *Illegality, Inc: Clandestine Migration and the Business of Bordering Europe*. Oakland, CA: University of California Press.

Angenendt, Steffen, and Eduard Gnesa. 2018. *SWP Kurz gesagt: Gute Argumente für den Globalen Pakt für Migration*. Stiftung für Wissenschaft und Politik, 05.11.018. Accessed 05.08.2020. https://www.swp-berlin.org/kurz-gesagt/2018/gute-argumente-fuer-den-globalen-pakt-fuer-migration/.

Arendt, Hannah. 1996 [1955]. *Elemente und Ursprünge totaler Herrschaft: Antisemitismus, Imperialismus, Totalitarismus*. München: Piper.

Aydemir, Fatma, and Hengameh Yaghoobifarah, eds. 2019. *Eure Heimat ist unser Albtraum*. Berlin: Ullstein fünf.

Ayoub, Maysa Abbas. 2023. 'Understanding Germany's Response to the 2015 Refugee Crisis.' *Review of Economics and Political Science* 8, no. 6: 577–604.

Bangstad, Sindre. 2017. 'Doing Fieldwork among People We Don't (Necessarily) Like.' *Anthropology News* 58, no. 4: 238–43.

Bangstad, Sindre, Bjørn Enge Bertelsen, and Heiko Henkel. 2019. 'The Politics of Affect.' *Focaal* 2019, no. 83: 98–113.

Barcellos Rezende, Claudia. 1999. 'Building Affinity through Friendship.' In *The Anthropology of Friendship*, edited by Sandra Bell and Simon Coleman, 79–98. Oxford: Berg.

Bargerová, Zuzana, and Boris Divinský. 2008. *Integrácia migrantov v Slovenskej republike. Výzvy a odporúčania pre tvorcov politík*. Bratislava: IOM Medzinárodná organizacia pre migráciu.

Bargerová, Zuzana, Katarína Fajnorová, and Alena Chudžíková. 2011. *Stav integrácie cudzincov s doplnkovou ochranou do spoločnosti a návrhy odporúčaní pre tvorcov verejných politík*. Bratislava: Stimul.

Beck, Ulrich. 1995 [1988]. *Gegengifte: Die organisierte Unverantwortlichkeit*. Frankfurt am Main: Suhrkamp.

Beger, Paula. 2018. 'Par ordre du mufti? Kontestation der Visegrád-Gruppe gegen den europäischen Umverteilungs- und Neuansiedlungsmechanismus für Flüchtlinge.' *Zeitschrift für Vergleichende Politikwissenschaft* 12, no. 1: 247–62.

Belák, Andrej, Andrea Madarasova Geckova, Jitse P. van Dijk, and Sijmen A. Reijneveld. 2017. 'Health-Endangering Everyday Settings and Practices in a Rural Segregated Roma Settlement in Slovakia: A Descriptive Summary from an Exploratory Longitudinal Case Study.' *BMC Public Health* 17, no. 1: 128–43.

Berliner, David, Michael Lambek, Richard Shweder, Richard Irvine, and Albert Piette. 2016. 'Anthropology and the Study of Contradictions.' *hau* 6, no. 1: 1–27.

Bognitz, Stephanie. 2018. 'Mistrusting as a Mode of Engagement in Mediation. Insights from Socio-Legal Practice in Rwanda.' In *Mistrust. Ethnographic Approximations*, edited by Florian Mühlfried, 174–67. Bielefeld: transcript.

Böhnisch, Lothar, and Christian Lösch. 1973. 'Das Handlungsverständnis des Sozialarbeiters und seine institutionelle Determination.' In *Gesellschaftliche Perspektiven der Sozialarbeit*, edited by Hans-Uwe Otto and Siegfried Schneider, 21–40. Neuwied: Luchterhand.

Borárosová, Ingrid, and Ondřej Filipec. 2017. 'Europeanization of Slovak Migration Policy and its Consequences: From Modernization to Fortification?' *The Polish Migration Review* 2, no. 2: 55–71.

Bosáková, Lucia, Andrea Madarasova Geckova, Jitse P. van Dijk, and Sijmen A. Reijneveld. 2020. 'School Is (Not) Calling: The Associations of Gender, Family Affluence, Disruptions in the Social Context and Learning Difficulties with School Satisfaction Among Adolescents in Slovakia.' *International Journal of Public Health* 65, no. 8: 1413–21.

Bousiou, Alexandra, and Linnea Schleyer. 2023. 'Consolidating the Fortress Europe: Conceptualizations of Solidarity in the EU Asylum System Governance Post-2015.' In *The EU Under Strain? Current Crises Shaping European Union Politics*, edited by Mechthild Roos and Daniel Schade, 213–32. Berlin/Boston: Walter de Gruyter.

Brah, Avtar. 1996. *Cartographies of Diaspora: Contesting Identities*. London, New York: Routledge.

Brand, Melanie. 2018. 'When Stories Seem Fake. Tacit Mistrust in Domestic Violence Counselling in South Africa Mistrust.' In *Mistrust. Ethnographic Approximations*, edited by Florian Mühlfried, 71–92. Bielefeld: transcript.

Brković, Čarna. 2017. *Managing Ambiguity: How Clientelism, Citizenship and Power Shape Personhood in Bosnia and Herzegovina*. New York: Berghahn.

Brnula, Peter. 2008. *Sociálna práca so žiadateľmi o azyl a azylantmi*. Prešov: Akcent print.

Bruner, Edward M. 1993. 'Epilogue: Creative Persona and the Problem of Authenticity.' In *Creativity/Anthropology*, edited by Smadar Lavie, Kirin Narayan, and Renato Rosaldo, 321–34. Ithaca, NY: Cornell University Press.

Bucci, Mauro. 2016. *Hotel Splendid*. Cesenatico: Mauro Bucci Ethnographic Films.

Buch, Elena. 2014. 'Troubling Gifts of Care: Vulnerable Persons and Threatening Exchanges in Chicago's Home Care Industry.' *Medical Anthropology Quarterly* 28, no. 4: 599–615.

Burawoy, Michael, and Katherine Verdery. 1999. 'Introduction.' In *Uncertain Transitions: Ethnographies of Change in the Postsocialist World*, edited by Michael Burawoy and Katherine Verdery, 1–18. Lanham, MD: Rowman and Littlefield.

Bürge, Michael. 2018. 'Mis(sing) Trust for Surviving. Confronting Complexity and the Un/Known in Makeni, Northern Sierra Leone.' In *Mistrust. Ethnographic Approximations*, edited by Florian Mühlfried, 105–28. Bielefeld: transcript.

Burnett, Kari. 2015. 'Policy Vs. Practice: The Effectiveness of Refugee Integration Policies in the Czech Republic.' *European Spatial Research & Policy* 22, no. 1: 121–33.

Bútorová, Zora, and Oľga Gyárfášová. 2011. *Language Competence of Slovak Population: German Language in Comparison with Other Languages*. Bratislava: Institute for Public Affairs. Accessed 22.06.2020. http://www.ivo.sk/6546/en/news/language-competence-of-slovak-population-german-language-in-comúarison-with-other-languages.

Cabot, Heath. 2014. *On the Doorstep of Europe: Asylum and Citizenship in Greece*. Philadelphia, PA: University of Pennsylvania Press.

Calhoun, Craig. 2004. 'A World of Emergencies: Fear, Intervention, and the Limits of Cosmopolitan Order.' *Canadian Review of Sociology/Revue canadienne de sociologie* 41, no. 4: 373–95.

Candea, Matei, and Giovanni Da Col. 2012. 'The Return to Hospitality.' *Journal of the Royal Anthropological Institute* 18: 1–19.

Carey, Matthew. 2017. *Mistrust: An Ethnographic Theory*. Chicago, IL: HAU.

Carpio, Glenda. 2008. *Laughing Fit to Kill: Black Humor in the Fictions of Slavery*. Oxford, New York: Oxford University Press.

Carrier, James. 1999. 'People Who Can Be Friends: Selves and Social Relationships.' In *The Anthropology of Friendship*, edited by Sandra Bell and Simon Coleman. Oxford: Berg.

Carty, John, and Yasmine Musharbash. 2008. 'You've Got to be Joking: Asserting the Analytical Value of Humor and Laughter in Contemporary Anthropology.' *Anthropological Forum* 18, no. 3: 209–17.

Casas-Cortes, Maribel, Sebastian Cobarrubias, Nicholas de Genova, Glenda Garelli, Giorgio Grappi, Charles Heller, Sabine Hess et al. 2014. 'New Keywords: Migration and Borders.' *Cultural Studies* 29, no. 1: 55–87.

Chambers, David W. 2016. *Building the Moral Community*. Lanham, Boulder, New York, London: Lexington Books.

Chouliaraki, Lilie. 2010. 'Post-Humanitarianism.' *International Journal of Cultural Studies* 13, no. 2: 107–26.

Chudžíková, Alena. 2016. 'Obraz utečencov v médiách na Slovensku.' In *Otvorená krajina alebo nedobytná pevnosť? Slovensko, migranti a utečenci*, edited by Miroslava Hlinčíková and Grigorij Mesežnikov, 95–111. Bratislava: Inštitút pre verejné otázky/Heinrich Böll Stiftung.

Cohen, Shari J. 1999. *Politics Without a Past: The Absence of History in Postcommunist Nationalism*. Durham, NC: Duke University Press.

Corsín Jiménez, Alberto. 2011. 'Trust in Anthropology.' *Anthropological Theory* 11, no. 2: 177–96.

Cuttitta, Paolo. 2017. 'Repoliticization Through Search and Rescue? Humanitarian NGOs and Migration Management in the Central Mediterranean.' *Geopolitics* 23, no. 3: 632–60.

Czollek, Max. 2018. *Desintegriert euch!* München: Carl Hanser Verlag.

Dahinden, Janine. 2016. 'A Plea for the "De-migranticization" of Research on Migration and Integration.' *Ethnic and Racial Studies* 39, no. 13: 2207–25.

Damasio, Antonio R. 2005 [1994]. *Descartes' Error: Emotion, Reason and the Human Brain*. New York, NY: Penguin Books.

Daniel, E. Valentine, and John C. Knudsen, eds. 1995. *Mistrusting Refugees*. Berkeley, CA: University of California Press.

Davies, Thom, Arshad Isakjee, and Surindar Dhesi. 2017. 'Violent Inaction: The Necropolitical Experience of Refugees in Europe.' *Antipode* 49, no. 5: 1263–84.

De Certeau, Michel. 1984. *The Practice of Everyday Life*. Berkeley, Los Angeles, London: University of California Press.

De Genova, Nicholas. 2002. 'Migrant "Illegality" and Deportability in Everyday Life.' *Annual Review of Anthropology* 31, no. 1: 419–47.

———, ed. 2017. *The Borders of "Europe": Autonomy of Migration, Tactics of Bordering*. Durham, London: Duke University Press.

De Genova, Nicholas, Glenda Garelli, and Martina Tazzioli. 2018. 'Autonomy of Asylum?' *South Atlantic Quarterly* 117, no. 2: 239–65.

de Haas, Hein. 2008. 'The Myth of Invasion: The Inconvenient Realities of African Migration to Europe.' *Third World Quarterly* 29, no. 7: 1305–22.

de Jong, Sara. 2011. 'False Binaries. Altruism and Selfishness in NGO Work.' In *Inside the Everyday Lives of Development Workers: The Challenges and Futures of Aidland*, edited by Anne-Meike Fechter and Heather Hindman, 21–40. Sterling, VA: Kumarian Press.

Di Nunzio, Paola. 2023. 'The Crisis of the Common European Asylum System: Rethinking Solidarity in Light of Human Rights.' *UNIO – EU Law Journal* 8, no. 2: 40–50.

Derrida, Jacques. 2001. *On Cosmopolitanism and Forgiveness*. London, New York: Routledge.

———. 2005. 'The Principle of Hospitality.' *Parallax* 11, no. 1: 6–9.

Derrida, Jacques, and Anne Dufourmantelle. 2000. *Of Hospitality*. Stanford, CA: Stanford University Press.

Dijstelbloem, Huub, and Lieke van der Veer. 2019. 'The Multiple Movements of the Humanitarian Border: The Portable Provision of Care and Control at the Aegean Islands.' *Journal of Borderlands Studies* 27, no. 1: 1–18.

Divinský, Boris. 2007. 'Slovakia.' In *European Immigration. A Sourcebook*, edited by Anna Triantaphyllidu and Ruby Gropas, 291–305. Aldershot: Ashgate.

Donert, Celia. 2017. *The Rights of the Roma: The Struggle for Citizenship in Postwar Czechoslovakia*. New York, NY: Cambridge University Press.

Douglas, Mary. 1968. 'The Social Control of Cognition: Some Factors in Joke Perception.' *Man* 3, no. 3: 361–76.

———. 2002 [1970]. *Natural Symbols*. Hoboken: Taylor and Francis.

Duijzings, Ger. 2020. 'Perpetrators as "Victims" in Eastern Bosnia (1992–1994): Towards an Anthropology of Dark Emotions.' In *Opfer. Dynamiken der Viktimisierung vom 17. Bis zum 21. Jahrhundert*, edited by Harriet Rudolph and Isabella von Treskow, 259–79. Heidelberg: Winter.

Dunn, Elizabeth Cullen. 2018. *No Path Home: Humanitarian Camps and the Grief of Displacement*. Ithaka, NY: Cornell University Press.

Dunn, John. 1988. 'Trust and Political Agency.' In *Trust. Making and Breaking Cooperative Relations*, edited by Diego Gambetta, 73–93. Oxford: Blackwell.

Durkheim, Émile. 1965 [1912]. *The Elementary Forms of the Religious Life*. New York: Free Press.

———. 1973 [1925]. *Moral Education: A Study in the Theory and Application of the Sociology of Education*. New York: Free Press.

Dyring, Rasmus. 2018. 'From Moral Facts to Human Finitude: On the Problem of Freedom in the Anthropology of Ethics.' *hau* 8, no. 1–2: 223–35.

Dyson, Jane. 2010. 'Friendship in Practice: Girls' Work in the Indian Himalayas.' *American Ethnologist* 37, no. 3: 482–98.

Dzenovska, Dace. 2018. *School of Europeanness: Tolerance and Other Lessons in Political Liberalism in Latvia*. Ithaca, NY: Cornell University Press.

EF EPI. 2019. *EF English Proficiency Index. A Ranking of 100 Countries and Regions by English Skills*. E.F. Education First, 12.11.2019. Accessed 22.06.2020. https://www.ef.com/__/~/media/centralefcom/epi/downloads/full-reports/v9/ef-epi-2019-english.pdf.

El-Mafaalani, Aladin. 2018. *Das Integrationsparadox: Warum gelungene Integration zu mehr Konflikten führt*. Köln: Kiepenheuer & Witsch.

European Commission. 2014. Eurobarometer 75.3. 2011. TNS Opinion and Social, Brussels [Producer]. GESIS Data Archive, Cologne. ZA5481 Data file Version 2.0.1. doi:10.4232/1.11852.

———. 2018a. Eurobarometer 83.3. 2015. TNS Opinion, Brussels [producer]. GESIS Data Archive, Cologne. ZA5998 Data file Version 2.0.0. doi:10.4232/1.13133.

———. 2018b. *Civil Society Monitoring Report on Implementation of the National Roma Integration Strategy in Slovakia. Focusing on Structural and Horizontal Preconditions for Successful Implementation of the Strategy*. Publications Office of the European Union, 26.07.2019. Accessed 21.11.2020. https://op.europa.eu/en/publication-detail/-/publication/6a8a35c1-b1aa-11e9-9d01-01aa75ed71a1/language-en/format-PDF#.

European Council. 2015. *Council Decision. Establishing Provisional Measures in the Area of International Protection for the Benefit of Italy and Greece*. European Council, 22.09.2015. Accessed 30.04.2019. https://eur-lex.europa.eu/legal-content/EN/TXT/HTML/?uri=CELEX:32015D1601andfrom=DE.

Faist, Thomas. 2014. 'Brokerage in Cross-Border Mobility: Social Mechanisms and the (Re) Production of Social Inequalities.' *Social Inclusion* 2, no. 4: 38–52.

Farías, Ignacio. 2014. 'Die Improvisation einer Politik. Katastrophenbewältigung, neoliberale Experimente und die Grenzen ökonomischen Wissens.' In *Formationen des Politischen. Anthropologie politischer Felder*, edited by Asta Vonderau and Jens Adam, 153–82. Bielefeld: transcript.

Fassin, Didier. 2005. 'Compassion and Repression: The Moral Economy of Immigration Policies in France.' *Cultural Anthropology* 20, no. 3: 362–87.

———. 2011. 'Hierarchies of Humanity.' In *Humanitarian Reason: A Moral History of the Present Times*, edited by Didier Fassin and Rachel Gomme, 223–42. Berkeley, CA: University of California Press.

————. 2016. 'From Right to Favor. The Refugee Question as Moral Crisis.' *The Nation*, 05.04.2018. Accessed 23.03.2018. https://www.thenation.com/article/archive/from-right-to-favor/.

Faubion, James D. 2001. 'Toward an Anthropology of Ethics: Foucault and the Pedagogies of Autopoiesis.' *Representations* 74, no. 1: 83–104.

————. 2011. *An Anthropology of Ethics*. New Departures in Anthropology. Cambridge: Cambridge University Press.

Fedele, David. 2014. *The Land Between*. Canberra: Ronin Films. DVD.

Feischmidt, Margit, and Ildiko Zachariás. 2019. 'Politics of Care and Compassion: Civic Help for Refugees and Its Political Implications in Hungary—A Mixed Methods Approach.' In *Refugee Protection and Civil Society in Europe*, edited by Margit Feischmidt, Ludger Pries, and Celine Cantat, 59–99. Cham: Palgrave Macmillan.

Ferguson, James, and Akhil Gupta. 2005. 'Spatializing States. Toward an Ethnography of Neoliberal Governmentality.' In *Anthropologies of Modernity. Foucault, Governmentality, and Life Politics*, edited by Jonathan X. Inda, 105–31. Malden, MA: Blackwell Pub.

Fiddian-Qasmiyeh, Elena. 2016. 'Representations of Displacement from the Middle East and North Africa.' *Public Culture* 28, no. 3: 457–73.

Filadelfiová, Jarmila, Oľga Gyárfášová, Martina Sekulová, and Miroslava Hlinčíková. 2011. *Migranti na slovenskom trhu práce: Problémy a perspektívy*. Bratislava: Inštitút pre verejné otázky.

Filčák, Richard, Marek Szilvasi, and Daniel Škobla. 2017. 'No Water for the Poor: The Roma Ethnic Minority and Local Governance in Slovakia.' *Ethnic and Racial Studies* 41, no. 7: 1390–407.

Fisher, William F. 1997. 'Doing Good? The Politics and Antipolitics of NGO Practices.' *Annual Review of Anthropology* 26, no. 1: 439–64.

Follis, Karolina S. 2012. *Building Fortress Europe: The Polish-Ukrainian Frontier*. Philadelphia, PA: University of Pennsylvania Press.

Foucault, Michel, and Daniel Defert. 1999. *Dits et écrits: 1954–1988*. Paris: Gallimard.

Foucault, Michel, and Paul Rabinow. 1984. *Essential Works of Foucault 1954–1984*. New York, NY: New Press.

Gallová Kriglerová, Elena. 2016. 'Integrácia migrantov na Slovensku.' In *Otvorená krajina alebo nedobytná pevnosť? Slovensko, migranti a utečenci*, edited by Miroslava Hlinčíková and Grigorij Mesežnikov, 61–77. Bratislava: Inštitút pre verejné otázky.

Gallová Kriglerová, Elena, and Alena Chudžíková. 2016. *Nórsky vzor. Integrácia utečencov v Nórsku*. Bratislava: Centrum pre výzkum etnicity a kultúry.

Gambetta, Diego. 1988. 'Can We Trust Trust?' In *Trust. Making and Breaking Cooperative Relations*, edited by Diego Gambetta, 213–37. Oxford: Blackwell.

Garelli, Glenda, and Martina Tazzioli. 2013. 'Challenging the Discipline of Migration: Militant Research in Migration Studies, an Introduction.' *Postcolonial Studies* 16, no. 3: 245–49.

Gažovičová, Tina, ed. 2011. *Vzdelávanie detí cudzincov na Slovensku. Potreby a riešenia*. Bratislava: Centrum pre výzkum etnicity a kultury, Nadácia Milana Šimečku.

Geiger, Martin, and Antoine Pécoud. 2013. *Disciplining the Transnational Mobility of People*. London: Palgrave Macmillan UK.

Giddens, Anthony. 1990. *The Consequences of Modernity*. Stanford, CA: Stanford University Press.

————. 1992. *The Transformation of Intimacy: Sexuality, Love and Eroticism in Modern Societies*. Cambridge: Polity Press.

Goldstein, Donna M. 2003. *Laughter Out of Place: Race, Class, Violence, and Sexuality in a Rio Shantytown*. Berkeley, CA: University of California Press.

Górak-Sosnowska, Katarzyna. 2016. 'Islamophobia without Muslims? The Case of Poland.' *Journal of Muslims in Europe* 5, no. 2: 190–204.

Graham, Mark. 2002. 'Emotional Bureaucracies: Emotions, Civil Servants, and Immigrants in the Swedish Welfare State.' *Ethos* 30, no. 3: 199–226.

Grätz, Tilo. 2004. 'Friendship Ties Among Young Artisanal Gold Miners in Northern Benin (West Africa).' *Afrika Spectrum* 39, no. 1: 95–117.

Grenčíková, Adriana, Ilona Skačkauskienė, and Jana Španková. 2018. 'The Features of Labor Emigration from the Slovak Republic.' *Business: Theory and Practice* 19: 271–77.

Griffiths, Melanie. 2012. '"Vile Liars and Truth Distorters"; Truth, Trust and the Asylum System.' *Anthropology Today* 28, no. 5: 8–12.

Grill, Jan. 2018. 'Re-learning to Labor? "Activation Works" and New Politics of Social Assistance in the Case of Slovak Roma.' *Journal of the Royal Anthropological Institute* 24, no. 1: 105–19.

Gusterson, Hugh. 2017. 'From Brexit to Trump: Anthropology and the Rise of Nationalist Populism.' *American Ethnologist* 44, no. 2: 209–14.

Gyárfášová, Oľga. 2018. 'The Fourth Generation: From Anti-Establishment to Anti-System Parties in Slovakia.' *New Perspectives* 26, no. 1: 109–33.

Gyárfášová, Oľga, and Martin Slosiarik. 2016. *Voľby do NR SR 2016: Čo charakterizovalo voličov. (Working Papers in Sociology)*. Sociologický Ústav SAV Bratislava, 11.2016. Accessed 14.08.2020. http://www.sociologia.sav.sk/pdf/Working_Papers_in_Sociology_012016.pdf.

Haas, Bridget M. 2017. 'Citizens-in-Waiting, Deportees-in-Waiting: Power, Temporality, and Suffering in the U.S. Asylum System.' *Ethos* 45, no. 1: 75–97.

Haggerty, Kevin D., Dean Wilson, Gavin J. D. Smith, and Katja Franko Aas. 2011. '"Crimmigrant" Bodies and Bona Fide Travelers: Surveillance, Citizenship and Global Governance.' *Theoretical Criminology* 15, no. 3: 331–46.

Hallam, Elizabeth, and Tim Ingold. 2007. 'Creativity and Cultural Improvisation. An Introduction.' In *Creativity and Cultural Improvisation*, edited by Elizabeth Hallam and Tim Ingold, 1–23. Oxford: Berg.

Hamann, Ulrike, and Serhat Karakayali. 2016. 'Practicing Willkommenskultur: Migration and Solidarity in Germany.' *Intersections* 2, no. 4: 69–86.

Han, Clara. 2012. *Life in Debt: Times of Care and Violence in Neoliberal Chile*. Berkeley, CA: University of California Press.

Hann, Chris. 2006. 'The Gift and Reciprocity: Perspectives From Economic Anthropology.' In *Handbook for the Economics of Giving, Altruism, and Reciprocity*, edited by Serge-Christophe Kolm and Jean Mercier Ythier, 207–23. Amsterdam: Elsevier.

———. 2012. 'Faltering Dialogue? For a Doubly Rooted Cosmopolitan Anthropology.' *Focaal* 2012, no. 63: 39–50.

———. 2015. 'The Fragility of Europe's Willkommenskultur.' *Anthropology Today* 31, no. 6: 1–2.

Hann, Chris, Caroline Humphrey, and Katherine Verdery. 2001. 'Introduction: Postsocialism as a Topic of Anthropological Investigation.' In *Postsocialism. Ideals, Ideologies and Practices in Eurasia*, edited by Chris Hann, 1–28. London, New York: Routledge.

Hannerz, Ulf. 2003. 'Being There… and There… and There! Reflections on Multi-Site Ethnography.' *Ethnography* 4, no. 2: 201–16.

Hanzelka, Jan, and Ina Schmidt. 2017. 'Dynamics of Cyber Hate in Social Media: A Comparative Analysis of Anti-Muslim Movements in the Czech Republic and Germany.' *International Journal of Cyber Criminology* 11, no. 1: 143–60.

Haraway, Donna. 1988. 'Situated Knowledges: The Science Question in Feminism and the Privilege of Partial Perspective.' *Feminist Studies* 14, no. 3: 575–99.

Harvey, David. 2005. *A Brief History of Neoliberalism*. Oxford: Oxford University Press.

Henig, David, and Nicolette Makovicky. 2017. *Economies of Favour After Socialism*. Oxford: Oxford University Press.

Herzfeld, Michael. 1997. *Cultural Intimacy: Social Poetics in the Nation State*. London, New York: Routledge.

Hess, Sabine, Lisa-Marie Heimeshoff, Stefanie Kron, Helen Schwenken, and Miriam Trzeciak. 2014. 'Migration – Kontrolle – Wissen. Transnationale Perspektiven. Einleitung.' In *Migration,

Kontrolle, Wissen: transnationale Perspektiven, edited by Lisa-Marie Heimeshoff and Sabine Hess, 9–40. Berlin: Assoziation A.

Hess, Sabine, Bernd Kasparek, Stefanie Kron, Mathias Rodatz, Maria Schwertl, and Simon Sontowski, eds. 2017. *Der lange Sommer der Migration*. Berlin, Hamburg: Assoziation A.

Hirschkind, Charles. 2006. *The Ethical Soundscape: Cassette Sermons and Islamic Counterpublics*. New York, NY: Columbia University Press.

Hitzer, Bettina. 2011. 'Emotionsgeschichte – ein Anfang mit Folgen.' *H-Soz-Kult Forschungsberichte*, 23.11.2011. Accessed 10.11.2020. https://www.hsozkult.de/literaturereview/id/forschungsbe richte-1221.

Hlinčíková, Miroslava. 2015. 'The Social Integration of Vietnamese Migrants in Bratislava: (In) Visible Actors in Their Local Community.' *Central and Eastern European Migration Review* 4, no. 1: 41–52.

Hlinčíková, Miroslava, Alena Chudžíková, Elena Gallová Kriglerová, and Martina Sekulová. 2014. *Migranti v meste. Prítomní a (ne)viditeľní*. Bratislava: Inštitút pre verejné otázky and Centrum pre výzkum etnicity a kultúry.

Hlinčíková, Miroslava, and Martina Sekulová. 2015. *Integrácia ľudí s medzinárodnou ochranou na Slovensku. Hľadanie východísk*. Bratislava: Inštitút pre verejné otázky.

Hochschild, Arlie Russell. 2016. *Strangers in Their Own Land: Anger and Mourning on the American Right*. New York, NY: New Press.

Holmes, Seth M. 2013. *Fresh Fruit, Broken Bodies: Migrant Farmworkers in the United States*. Berkeley, CA: University of California Press.

Holmes, Seth M., and Heide Castañeda. 2016. 'Representing the "European Refugee Crisis" in Germany and Beyond: Deservingness and Difference, Life and Death.' *American Ethnologist* 43, no. 1: 12–24.

Hörlin, Sinje. 2015. *Figuren des Misstrauens*. Konstanz: Konstanz University Press.

Horváth, Pavol, and Vojtech Kopčan. 1971. *Turci na Slovensku*. Bratislava: SPN.

Hosking, Geoffrey. 2005. 'The Intelligentsia and Russia's Twentieth-century Crisis of Trust.' *Slavica Lundensia* 22: 229–52.

Howard, Marc Morjé, ed. 2003. *The Weakness of Civil Society in Post-Communist Europe*. Cambridge: Cambridge University Press.

Huizinga, Johan. 2016 [1955]. *Homo Ludens: A Study of the Play Element in Culture*. Ranchos de Taos: Angelico Press.

Humphrey, Caroline. 2002. *The Unmaking of Soviet Life: Everyday Economies After Socialism*. Ithaca, NY: Cornell University Press.

———. 2012. 'Favors and "Normal Heroes": The Case of Postsocialist Higher Education.' *hau* 2, no. 2: 22–41.

Jacobsson, Kerstin, and Steven Saxonberg. 2013. *Beyond NGO-ization: The Development of Social Movements in Central and Eastern Europe*. Farnham/Surrey: Ashgate Publishing Limited.

Jelínková, Marie. 2019. 'A Refugee Crisis Without Refugees: Policy and Media Discourse on Refugees in the Czech Republic and Its Implications.' *Central European Journal of Public Policy* 13, no. 1: 33–45.

Josephides, Lisette. 2005. 'Resentment as a Sense of Self.' In *Mixed Emotions: Anthropological Studies of Feeling*, edited by Kay Milton and Maruška Svašek, 7–90. Oxford: Berg.

Kalb, Don. 2001. 'Afterword: Globalism and Postsocialist Prospects.' In *Postsocialism: Ideals, Ideologies, and Practices in Eurasia*, edited by Chris Hann, 317–33. London, New York: Routledge.

Karakayali, Serhat, and Olaf Kleist. 2015. *Strukturen und Motive der ehrenamtlichen Flüchtlingsarbeit. (EFA) in Deutschland*. Berliner Institut für empirische Integrations- und Migrationsforschung, 08.08.2016. Accessed 01.12.2016. https://www.bim.hu-berlin.de/media/Studie_EFA2_BIM_ 11082016_V%C3%96.pdf.

Karakayali, Serhat, and Vassilis Tsianos. 2007. 'Movements that matter. Eine Einleitung.' In *Turbulente Ränder*, edited by Transit Migration Forschungsgruppe, 7–17. Bielefeld: transcript.

Kasparek, Bernd, and Marc Speer. 2015. 'Of Hope. Hungary and the Long Summer of Migration.' *Bordermonitoring.eu*, 02.09.2016. Accessed 31.08.2020. https://bordermonitoring. eu/ungarn/2015/09/of-hope-en/.

Kazharski, Aliaksei. 2019. 'Frontiers of Hatred? A Study of Right-Wing Populist Strategies in Slovakia.' *European Politics and Society* 26, no. 2: 1–13.

Khosravi, Shahram. 2010. *"Illegal" Traveller: An Auto-Ethnography of Borders.* London: Palgrave Macmillan.

Kissová, Lenka. 2018. 'The Production of (Un)deserving and (Un)acceptable: Shifting Representations of Migrants within Political Discourse in Slovakia.' *East European Politics and Societies* 32, no. 4: 743–66.

Klarenbeek, Lea M. 2018. 'Relational Integration: A Response to Willem Schinkel.' *Comparative Migration Studies* 7, article 20: 1–8.

Kleinman, Arthur. 2012. 'Caregiving as Moral Experience.' *The Lancet* 380, no. 9853: 1550–51.

Kluknavská, Alena. 2015. 'A Right-Wing Extremist or People's Protector? Media Coverage of Extreme Right Leader Marian Kotleba in 2013 Regional Elections in Slovakia.' *Intersections* 1, no. 1: 147–65.

Kluknavská, Alena, and Matej Hruška. 2019. 'We Talk about the "Others" and You Listen Closely: The Extreme Right Communication on Social Media.' *Problems of Post-Communism* 66, no. 1: 59–70.

Kluknavská, Alena, and Josef Smolík. 2016. 'We Hate Them All? Issue Adaptation of Extreme Right Parties in Slovakia 1993–2016.' *Communist and Post-Communist Studies* 49, no. 4: 335–44.

Kováts, András, Marta Miklušáková, and Vera Rangelová. 2006. *Praktická sociálna práca s utečencami. Prístup cez ľudské práva.* Budapešť: Menedék.

Kozubík, Michal, Daniela Filakovska Bobakova, Rastislav Rosinsky, Martina Mojtova, Miroslav Tvrdon, and Jitse P. van Dijk. 2020. 'Social Structure in a Roma Settlement: Comparison over Time.' *International Journal of Environmental Research and Public Health* 17, no. 19: 1–13.

Krajčová, Nadežda. 2015. 'Current Issues in Slovak Higher Education.' *Procedia - Social and Behavioral Sciences* 174: 2481–88.

Krastev, Ivan, and Stephen Holmes. 2018. 'Explaining Eastern Europe: Imitation and Its Discontents.' *Journal of Democracy* 29, no. 3: 117–28.

Krzyżanowski, Michał. 2018. 'Discursive Shifts in Ethno-Nationalist Politics: On Politicization and Mediatization of the "Refugee Crisis" in Poland.' *Journal of Immigrant & Refugee Studies* 16, no. 1–2: 76–96.

Kusá, Zuzana, Bohumil Búzik, Robert Klobucký, Silvia Miháliková, Marianna Mrva, Katarína Strapcová, Mária Suríková, Miroslav Tížik, and Milan Zeman. 2017. *Naše európske hodnoty 2017. Hodnoty v dynamike spoločenských zmien na Slovensku a v Európe. Komentár k zisteniam slovenskej časti výskumu európskych hodnôt EVS 2017.* Sociologický Ùstav SAV Bratislava, 18.07.2017. Accessed 01.05.2019. http://www.sociologia.sav.sk/cms/uploaded/2786_attach_EVS_SK_ 2017_tlacova_sprava%20final.pdf.

Kusiak, Joanna. 2012. 'The Cunning of Chaos and Its Orders: A Taxonomy of Urban Chaos in Post-Socialist Warsaw and Beyond.' In *Chasing Warsaw: Socio-Material Dynamics of Urban Change since 1990*, edited by Monika Grubbauer and Joanna Kusiak, 291–320. Frankfurt, New York: Campus Verlag.

Laclau, Ernesto. 2005. *On Populist Reason.* London, New York: Verso.

Lahno, Bernd. 2002. *Der Begriff des Vertrauens.* Paderborn: Mentis.

Laidlaw, James. 2002. 'For an Anthropology of Ethics and Freedom.' *Journal of the Royal Anthropological Institute* 8, no. 2: 311–32.

———. 2014. *The Subject of Virtue: An Anthropology of Ethics and Freedom.* Cambridge, New York: Cambridge University Press.

Lambek, Michael, ed. 2010. *Ordinary Ethics: Anthropology, Language, and Action.* New York, NY: Fordham University Press.

Lang, Kai-Olaf, and Eva-Maria Walther. 2020. *SWP-Aktuell 2020/ A21 Slowakei: Neuanfang mit Unbekannten: Nach der Abwahl der Sozialdemokraten ist eine brüchige Regierungskoalition zu erwarten.* Stiftung für Wissenschaft und Politik, 17.03.2020. Accessed 19.11.2020. https://www.swp-berlin.org/10.18449/2020A21/.

Larson, Jonathan L. 2013. *Critical Thinking in Slovakia After Socialism.* Woodbridge: Boydell & Brewer.

Ledeneva, Alena V. 1998. *Russia's Economy of Favours: Blat, Networking, and Informal Exchange.* Cambridge: Cambridge University Press.

Ledeneva, Alena V. 2018. 'Preface.' In *The Global Encyclopaedia of Informality, Volume 1: Towards Understanding of Social and Cultural Complexity.* Edited by Alena V. Ledeneva, Anna L. Bailey, Costanza Curro, Elizabeth Teague, and Sheelagh Barron, vii–x. London: UCL Press.

Lenč, Jozef, and Monika Zaviš. 2018. 'Islamophobia in Slovakia. National Report 2017.' In *European Islamophobia Report 2017,* edited by Enes Bayrakli and Farid Hafez, 563–76. Istanbul: Seta Foundation for Political, Economic and Social Research.

Leško, Marián. 1996. *Mečiar a mečiarizmus: Politik bez škrupúľ, politika bez zábran.* Bratislava: VMV.

Lévi-Strauss, Claude. 1966. *The Savage Mind.* Chicago, IL: University of Chicago Press.

Lewis, J. David, and Andrew Weigert. 1985. "Trust as a Social Reality." *Social Forces* 63, no. 4: 967–85.

Lipset, David, and Eric Kline Silverman, eds. 2019. *Mortuary Dialogues: Death Ritual and the Reproduction of Moral Community in Pacific Modernities.* New York, NY: Berghahn Books.

Lisle, Debbie, and Heather L. Johnson. 2018. 'Lost in the Aftermath.' *Security Dialogue* 50, no. 1: 20–39.

Loizos, Peter. 1994. 'Confessions of a Vampire Anthropologist.' *Anthropological Journal on European Cultures* 3, no. 2: 39–53.

Luhmann, Niklas. 2009 [1968]. *Vertrauen: Ein Mechanismus der Reduktion sozialer Komplexität.* Stuttgart: Lucius & Lucius.

Lutz, Catherine. 1986. 'Emotion, Thought, and Estrangement: Emotion as a Cultural Category.' *Cultural Anthropology* 1, no. 3: 287–309.

MacIntyre, Alasdair C. 2003. *After Virtue: A Study in Moral Theory.* Notre Dame, IN: University of Notre Dame Press.

Mahmood, Saba. 2005. *Politics of Piety: The Islamic Revival and the Feminist Subject.* Princeton, NJ: Princeton University Press.

Makovicky, Nicolette, Jonathan Larson, and Juraj Buzalka. 2020. 'Common Decency in the Populist Era.' *Anthropology News,* 11.06.2010. Accessed 20.07.2020. https://www.anthropology-news.org/index.php/2020/06/11/common-decency-in-the-populist-era/?utm_source=rssandutm_medium=rssandutm_campaign=common-decency-in-the-populist-era.

Malkki, Liisa H. 1995. 'Refugees and Exile: From "Refugee Studies" to the National Order of Things.' *Annual Review of Anthropology* 24, no. 1: 495–523.

———. 2015. *The Need to Help: The Domestic Arts of International Humanitarianism.* Durham: Duke University Press.

Martin, Luther H., ed. 1988. *Technologies of the Self: A Seminar with Michel Foucault.* Amherst, MA: University of Massachusetts Press.

Massumi, Brian. 2002. *Parables for the Virtual. Movement, Affect, Sensation.* Durham, London: Duke University Press.

Mattingly, Cheryl. 2013. 'Moral Selves and Moral Scenes: Narrative Experiments in Everyday Life.' *Ethnos* 78, no. 3: 301–27.

———. 2014. *Moral Laboratories: Family Peril and the Struggle for a Good Life.* Oakland, CA: University of California Press.

Mauss, Marcel. 1990 [1954]. *The Gift: Form and Reason for Exchange in Archaic Societies.* New York, NY: Norton.

Mavelli, Luca. 2017. 'Governing Populations Through the Humanitarian Government of Refugees: Biopolitical Care and Racism in the European Refugee Crisis.' *Review of International Studies* 43, no. 5: 809–32.

Mayblin, Lucy, and Joe Turner. 2020. *Migration Studies and Colonialism.* Cambridge: Polity.

Mazzarella, William. 2019. 'The Anthropology of Populism: Beyond the Liberal Settlement.' *Annual Review of Anthropology* 48, no. 1: 45–60.

Meissner, Fran, and Tilmann Heil. 2020. 'Deromanticising Integration: On the Importance of Convivial Disintegration.' *Migration Studies* 42, no. 1: 1–19.

Mesežnikov, Grigorij, and Oľga Gyárfášová. 2017. 'Heutiger Rechtsextremismus und Ultranationalismus in der Slowakei: Stand, Trends, Unterstützung.' *Institute for Public Affairs Bratislava.* Accessed 15.07.2020. http://www.ivo.sk/8082/sk/aktuality/heutiger-rechtsextremismus-und-ultranationalismus-in-der-slowakei-stand-trends-unterstutzung.

Mezzadra, Sandro, and Brett Neilson. 2012. 'Between Inclusion and Exclusion: On the Topology of Global Space and Borders.' *Theory, Culture & Society* 29, no. 4–5: 58–75.

———. 2013. *Border as Method, Or, the Multiplication of Labor.* Durham: Duke University Press.

Miciukiewicz, Konrad. 2011. 'Migration and Asylum in Central Eastern Europe. The Impacts of European Integration.' In *(Post)transformational Migration. Inequalities, Welfare State, and Horizontal Mobility,* edited by Marek Nowak and Michal Nowosielski, 177–200. Frankfurt: Peter Lang GmbH Internationaler Verlag der Wissenschaften.

Ministerstvo práce, sociálnych vecí a rodiny Slovenskej Republiky. 2009. *Koncepcia integrácie cudzincov v Slovenskej Republike,* 06.05.2009. Accessed 19.02.2024. https://www.employment.gov.sk/files/slovensky/ministerstvo/integracia-cudzincov/dokumenty/koncepcia-integracie-cudzincov-v-slovenskej-republike.pdf

———. 2014. *Integračná politika Slovenskej republiky,* 10.01.2014. Accessed 19.02.2024. https://www.employment.gov.sk/files/slovensky/uvod/informacie-cudzinci/integracna-politika.pdf

Misztal, Barbara A. 2000. *Informality: Social Theory and Contemporary Practice.* London, New York: Routledge.

Moffitt, Benjamin. 2016. *The Global Rise of Populism: Performance, Political Style, and Representation.* Palo Alto, CA: Stanford University Press.

Moffitt, Benjamin, and Simon Tormey. 2014. 'Rethinking Populism: Politics, Mediatisation and Political Style.' *Political Studies* 62, no. 2: 381–97.

Mol, Annemarie, Ingunn Moser, and Jeannette Pols, eds. 2010. *Care in Practice: On Tinkering in Clinics, Homes and Farms.* Bielefeld: transcript.

Möllering, Guido. 2001. 'The Nature of Trust: From Georg Simmel to a Theory of Expectation, Interpretation and Suspension.' *Sociology* 35, no. 2: 403–20.

Montaigne, Michel de. 2004 [1580]. *On Friendship.* London: Penguin.

Mudde, Cas. 2007. *Populist Radical Right Parties in Europe.* Cambridge: Cambridge University Press.

Mudde, Cas, and Cristóbal Rovira Kaltwasser. 2017. *Populism: A Very Short Introduction.* Oxford: Oxford University Press.

Muehlebach, Andrea. 2012. *The Moral Neoliberal: Welfare and Citizenship in Italy.* Chicago, IL: University of Chicago Press.

Mühlfried, Florian. 2018. 'Introduction. Approximating Mistrust.' In *Mistrust. Ethnographic Approximations,* edited by Florian Mühlfried, 7–22. Bielefeld: transcript.

———. 2019. *Misstrauen. Vom Wert eines Unwertes.* Stuttgart: Reclam.

Nicolaysen, Kristin. 2016. *A Song for Mursal.* Alta: Filmverkstedet. DVD.

Nietzsche, Friedrich. 1954 [1887]. *Werke in drei Bänden, Band 1.* München: Carl Hanser.

Nussbaum, Martha C. 2001. *Upheavals of Thought: The Intelligence of Emotions.* Cambridge: Cambridge University Press.

———. 2011 [1986]. *The Fragility of Goodness: Luck and Ethics in Greek Tragedy and Philosophy.* Cambridge: Cambridge University Press.

Nyers, Peter. 2006. *Rethinking Refugees: Beyond States of Emergency*. London, New York: Routledge.

Oltmer, Jochen. 2012. 'Einführung. Migrationsverhältnisse und Migrationsregime nach dem Zweiten Weltkrieg.' In *Das "Gastarbeiter"-System*, edited by Jochen Oltmer, Axel Kreienbrink und Carlos Sanz Díaz, 9–22. München: Oldenbourg Wissenschaftsverlag.

Ong, Aihwa. 2004. 'The Chinese Axis: Zoning Technologies and Variegated Sovereignty.' *Journal of East Asian Studies* 4, no. 1: 69–96.

Ortner, Sherry B. 1984. 'Theory in Anthropology Since the Sixties.' *Comparative Studies in Society and History* 26, no. 1: 126–66.

Ostiguy, Pierre. 2017. 'Populism: A Socio-Cultural Approach.' In *The Oxford Handbook of Populism*, edited by Cristóbal Rovira Kaltwasser, Peter Taggart, Paulina Ochoa Espejo, and Pierre Ostiguy, 73–97. Oxford: Oxford University Press.

Paine, Robert. 1969. 'In Search of Friendship: An Exploratory Analysis in "Middle-Class" Culture.' *Man* 4, no. 4: 505–24.

———. 1999. 'Friendship: The Hazards of an Ideal.' In *The Anthropology of Friendship*, edited by Sandra Bell and Simon Coleman, 39–58. Oxford: Berg.

Pažitný, Peter, Tomáš Szalay, Angelika Szalayová, Karol Morvay, Roman Mužik, Mária Pourová, Daniela Kandilaki, Peter Balík, and Tomáš Sivák. 2014. *Modernizácia Slovenských Nemocníc; Základné Rámce Zdravotnej Politiky 2014–2016*. Bratislava: Health Policy Institute. Accessed 25.09.2020. http://hpi.sk/cdata/Publications/hpi_zakladne_ramce_2014.pdf.

Pelkmans, Mathijs. 2018. 'Doubt, Suspicion, Mistrust … Semantic Approximations.' In *Mistrust: Ethnographic Approximations*, edited by Florian Mühlfried, 169–78. Bielefeld: transcript.

Penninx, Rinus. 2019. 'Problems of and Solutions for the Study of Immigrant Integration.' *Comparative Migration Studies* 7, article 13: 1–11.

Perényi, János. 1972. 'Wirtschaftliche und soziale Umgestaltung in Ungarn unter der Türkenherrschaft im XVI.–VII. Jahrhundert.' *Historický časopis* 20, no. 4: 629–63.

Perl, Gerhild, and Sabine Strasser. 2018. 'Transnational Moralities: The Politics of Ir/ Responsibility of and against the EU Border Regime.' *Identities* 25, no. 5: 507–23.

Petriska, Šimon. 2019. *Pokrytie protestov "Za Slušné Slovensko" slovenskými alternatívnymi médiami*. Bachelor thesis in Political science at the Department for social studies, Masaryk University, Brno, 24.05.2019. Accessed 06.08.2020. https://is.muni.cz/th/q2fgl/Petriska_BP_2019 .pdf.

Pilkington, Hilary. 2016. *Loud and Proud: Passion and Politics in the English Defence League*. Manchester: Manchester University Press.

Pirický, Gabriel. 2013. 'The Ottoman Age in Southern Central Europe as Represented in Secondary School History Textbooks in the Czech Republic, Hungary, Poland, and Slovakia.' *Journal of Educational Media, Memory, and Society* 5, no. 1: 108–29.

Pitt-Rivers, Julian A. 2012 [1977]. 'The Law of Hospitality.' *hau* 2, no. 1: 501–17.

Plamper, Jan. 2010. 'Wie schreibt man die Geschichte der Gefühle? William Reddy, Barbara Rosenwein und Peter Stearns im Gespräch mit Jan Plamper.' *WerkstattGeschichte* 19, no. 54: 39–69.

Plann, Susan Joan. 2019. *Coming of Age in Madrid: An Oral History of Unaccompanied Moroccan Migrant Minors*. Brighton, Chicago, Toronto: Sussex Academic Press.

Podolinská, Tatiana, and Tomáš Hrustič, eds. 2015. *Čierno-biele svety: Rómovia v majoritnej spoločnosti na Slovensku*. Bratislava: Ústav etnológie SAV; Veda vydavateľstvo SAV.

Polese, Abel, and Jeremy Morris. 2015. 'My Name is Legion. The Resilience and Endurance of Informality beyond, or in Spite of, the State.' In *Informal Economies in Post-Socialist Spaces*, edited by Jeremy Morris and Abel Polese, 1–21. London: Palgrave Macmillan.

Popper, Karl R. 2003 [1945]. *Die offene Gesellschaft und ihre Feinde: Band 1; Der Zauber Platons*. Tübingen: J.C.B. Mohr (Paul Siebeck).

Pott, Andreas, Christoph Rass, and Frank Wolff, eds. 2018. *Was ist ein Migrationsregime? What Is a Migration Regime?* Migrationsgesellschaften. Wiesbaden: Springer VS.

Priebus, Sonja, and Paula Beger. 2017. 'Die Asyl- und Flüchtlingspolitik Ungarns in der Krise.' *Südosteuropa Mitteilungen* 57, no. 2: 30–47.

Pries, Ludger. 2018. 'Introduction: Civil Society and Volunteering in the So-Called Refugee Crisis of 2015—Ambiguities and Structural Tensions.' In *Refugee Protection and Civil Society in Europe*, edited by Margit Feischmidt, Ludger Pries, and Celine Cantat, 1–23. Cham: Palgrave Macmillan.

Prinz, Jesse. 2003. 'Emotion, Psychosemantics, and Embodied Appraisals.' *Royal Institute of Philosophy Supplement* 52: 69–86.

Pytlas, Bartek. 2013. 'Radical-right Narratives in Slovakia and Hungary: Historical Legacies, Mythic Overlaying and Contemporary Politics.' *Patterns of Prejudice* 47, no. 2: 162–83.

———. 2014. *Radical Right Parties in Central and Eastern Europe*. London, New York: Routledge.

Qadim, Nora El. 2014. 'Postcolonial Challenges to Migration Control: French–Moroccan Cooperation Practices on Forced Returns.' *Security Dialogue* 45, no. 3: 242–61.

Radcliffe-Brown, A. R. 1940. 'On Joking Relationships.' *Africa* 13, no. 3: 195–210.

Rajaram, Prem Kumar. 2016. 'Whose Migration Crisis? Editorial Introduction.' *Intersections* 2, no. 4: 5–10.

Rapport, Nigel. 2007. 'An Outline for Cosmopolitan Study.' *Current Anthropology* 48, no. 2: 257–83.

Reckwitz, Andreas. 2002. 'Toward a Theory of Social Practices.' *European Journal of Social Theory* 5, no. 2: 243–63.

Reddy, William M. 2001. *The Navigation of Feeling: A Framework for the History of Emotions*. Cambridge: Cambridge University Press.

Rivkin-Fish, Michele. 2011. 'Learning the Moral Economy of Commodified Health Care: "Community Education", Failed Consumers, and the Shaping of Ethical Clinician-Citizens.' *Culture, Medicine and Psychiatry* 35, no. 2: 183–208.

Robbins, Joel. 2004. *Becoming Sinners: Christianity and Moral Torment in a Papua New Guinea Society*. Berkeley, CA: University of California Press.

———. 2007. 'Between Reproduction and Freedom: Morality, Value, and Radical Cultural Change.' *Ethnos* 72, no. 3: 293–314.

Rosaldo, Michelle Z. 1984. 'Toward an Anthropology of Self and Feeling.' In *Culture Theory: Essays on Mind, Self, and Emotion*, edited by Richard A. Shweder and Robert A. LeVine, 137–57. Cambridge [Cambridgeshire]/New York: Cambridge University Press.

Rose, Nikolas. 2000. 'Community, Citizenship, and the Third Way.' *American Behavioral Scientist* 43, no. 9: 1395–411.

Rose-Ackerman, Susan. 2001. 'Trust and Honesty in Post-Socialist Societies.' *Kyklos* 54, no. 2: 415–44.

Rosenberger, Sieglinde, and Jakob Winkler. 2014. 'Com/passionate Protests: Fighting the Deportation of Asylum Seekers.' *Mobilization: An International Quarterly* 19, no. 2: 165–84.

Rosenwein, Barbara H. 2007. *Emotional Communities in the Early Middle Ages*. Ithaca, NY: Cornell University Press.

———. 2010. 'Problems and Methods in the History of Emotions.' *Passions in Context: International Journal for the History and Theory of Emotions* 1, no. 1: 5–37.

Roubal, Petr. 2020. *Spartakiads. The Politics of Physical Culture in Communist Czechoslovakia*. Prague: Karolinum Press.

Rozakou, Katerina. 2012. 'The Biopolitics of Hospitality in Greece: Humanitarianism and the Management of Refugees.' *American Ethnologist* 39, no. 3: 562–77.

———. 2016. 'Socialities of Solidarity: Revisiting the Gift Taboo in Times of Crises.' *Social Anthropology* 24, no. 2: 185–99.

Rydza, Hana. 2020. 'Neues Personal, alte Probleme. Die Parlamentswahlen in der Slowakei und die Folgen.' *Osteuropa* 70, no. 1–2: 3–16.

Sampson, Steven. 2003a. 'From Forms to Norms: Global Projects and Local Practices in the Balkan NGO Scene.' *Journal of Human Rights* 2, no. 3: 329–37.

————. 2003b. 'Trouble Spots: Projects, Bandits and State Fragmentation.' In *Globalization, the State and Violence*, edited by Jonathan Friedman, 309–42. Lanham, MD: AltaMira Press.

Sandri, Elisa. 2018. '"Volunteer Humanitarianism": Volunteers and Humanitarian Aid in the Jungle Refugee Camp of Calais.' *Journal of Ethnic and Migration Studies* 44, no. 1: 65–80.

Santos-Granero, Fernando. 2007. 'Of Fear and Friendship: Amazonian Sociality Beyond Kinship and Affinity.' *Journal of the Royal Anthropological Insitutet* 13, no. 1: 1–18.

Scheer, Monique. 2012. 'Are Emotions a Kind of Practice (And Is That What Makes Them Have a History)? A Bourdieuian Approach to Understanding Emotion.' *History and Theory* 51, no. 2: 193–220.

Scheper-Hughes, Nancy. 1995. 'The Primacy of the Ethical: Propositions for a Militant Anthropology.' *Current Anthropology* 36, no. 3: 409–40.

Schillaci, Rossella. 2011. *Other Europe/Altra Europa*. Turin: AzulFilm. DVD.

Schinkel, Willem. 2018. 'Against "Immigrant Integration": For an End to Neocolonial Knowledge Production.' *Comparative Migration Studies* 6, article 31: 1–17.

Schiocchet, Leonardo. 2014. 'Suspicion and the Economy of Trust among Palestinian Refugees in Lebanon.' *The Cambridge Journal of Anthropology* 32, no. 2: 112–27.

Schulze Wessel, Martin. 2018. *Der Prager Frühling: Aufbruch in eine neue Welt*. Stuttgart: Reclam.

Simmel, Georg. 1990 [1968]. *The Sociology of Money*. London, New York: Routledge Classics.

Smart, Alan. 1999. 'Expressions of Interest: Friendship and Guanxi in Chinese Societies.' In *The Anthropology of Friendship*, edited by Sandra Bell and Simon Coleman, 119–36. Oxford: Berg.

Smart, J. J. C., and Bernard Williams. 1973. *Utilitarianism: For and Against*. Cambridge: Cambridge University Press.

Smith, Andrea L. 2004. 'Heteroglossia, "Common Sense," and Social Memory.' *American Ethnologist* 31, no. 2: 251–69.

Solomon, Robert C. 1988. 'On Emotions as Judgments.' *American Philosophical Quarterly* 25, no. 2: 183–91.

Sorge, Antonio. 2009. 'Hospitality, Friendship, and the Outsider in Highland Sardinia.' *Journal of the Society for the Anthropology of Europe* 9, no. 1: 4–12.

Speer, Marc. 2016. 'Ungarn: Gänzlich unerwünscht. Entrechtung, Kriminalisierung und Inhaftierung von Flüchtlingen in Ungarn.' *bordermonitoring.eu*, 05.07.2016. Accessed 19.11.2020. https://bordermonitoring.eu/ungarn/2016/07/gaenzlich-unerwuenscht-entrechtung-kriminalisierung-und-inhaftierung-von-fluechtlingen-in-ungarn/.

Spencer, Liz, and Ray Pahl. 2006. *Rethinking Friendship: Hidden Solidarities Today*. Princeton, NJ: Princeton University Press.

Stan, Sabrina. 2012. 'Neither Commodities Nor Gifts: Post-socialist Informal Exchanges in the Romanian Healthcare System.' *Journal of the Royal Anthropological Institute* 18, no. 1: 65–82.

Štatistický úrad Slovenskej republiky. 2018. *Štatistická Ročenka Regiónov Slovenska 2018*. Štatistický úrad Slovenskej republiky Bratislava, 31.01.2019. Accessed 21.11.2020. https://www7.statistics.sk/PortalTraffic/fileServlet?Dokument=67d47a1b-2e80-4b02-bab1-f0ed548b893b.

Stephen, Lynn. 2017. 'Creating Preemptive Suspects: National Security, Border Defense, and Immigration Policy, 1980–Present.' *Latin American Perspectives* 45, no. 6: 7–25.

Stevenson, Lisa. 2014. *Life Beside Itself: Imagining Care in the Canadian Arctic*. Berkeley, CA: University of California Press.

Stewart, Michael, ed. 2012. *The Gypsy "Menace": Populism and the New Anti-Gypsy Politics*. London: Hurst and Company.

Stolle, Dietlind. 2002. 'Trusting Strangers – The Concept of Generalized Trust in Perspective.' *Österreichische Zeitschrift für Politikwissenschaft* 31, no. 4: 397–412.

Sutter, Ove. 2017. 'Welcome! The Emotional Politics of Voluntary Work with Refugees.' In *Journal of European Ethnology and Cultural Analysis* 2, no. 1: 5–25.

Svašek, Maruška. 2005. 'Introduction: Emotions in Anthropology.' In *Mixed Emotions: Anthropological Studies of Feeling*, edited by Kay Milton and Maruška Svašek, 71–90. Oxford: Berg.

Szczepanikova, Alice. 2011. 'From the Right of Asylum to Migration Management: The Legal–Political Construction of "a Refugee" in the Post-Communist Czech Republic.' *Europe-Asia Studies* 63, no. 5: 789–806.

Szombati, Kristóf. 2018. *The Revolt of the Provinces: Anti-Gypsyism and Right-Wing Politics in Hungary.* New York, Oxford: Berghahn.

Sztompka, Piotr. 1999. *Trust: A Sociological Theory.* Cambridge: Cambridge University Press.

Tazzioli, Martina. 2019. 'The Politics of Migrant Dispersal. Dividing and Policing Migrant Multiplicities.' *Migration Studies* 48, no. 3: 1–20.

Ther, Philipp. 2014. *Die neue Ordnung auf dem alten Kontinent: Eine Geschichte des neoliberalen Europa.* Berlin: Suhrkamp Verlag.

Thorleifsson, Cathrine. 2017. 'Disposable Strangers: Far-right Securitisation of Forced Migration in Hungary.' *Social Anthropology* 25, no. 3: 318–34.

———. 2019. *Nationalist Responses to the Crises in Europe: Old and New Hatreds.* London, New York: Routledge.

Thränhardt, Dietrich. 2023. 'Welcome Culture and Bureaucratic Ambiguity: Germany's Complex Asylum Regime.' In *Migration Control Logics and Strategies in Europe: A North-South Comparison*, edited by Claudia Finotelli and Irene Ponzo, 267–81. Cham: Springer International Publishing.

Throop, C. Jason. 2012. 'Moral Sentiments.' In *A Companion to Moral Anthropology*, edited by Didier Fassin, 150–68. Chichster: Wiley-Blackwell.

Ticktin, Miriam I. 2012. *Casualties of Care: Immigration and the Politics of Humanitarianism in France.* University of California Press.

———. 2017. 'A World without Innocence.' *American Ethnologist* 44, no. 4: 577–90.

Tize, Carola. 2020. 'Living in Permanent Temporariness: The Multigenerational Ordeal of Living under Germany's Toleration Status.' *Journal of Refugee Studies* 37, no. 4: 1–20.

Torsello, Davide. 2003. *Trust, Property and Social Change in a Southern Slovakian Village.* Münster: Lit Verlag.

Transit Migration Forschungsgruppe, ed. 2007. *Turbulente Ränder: Neue Perspektiven auf Migration an den Grenzen Europas.* Bielefeld: transcript.

Tsing, Anna Lowenhaupt. 2005. *Friction: An Ethnography of Global Connection.* Princeton, NJ: Princeton University Press.

Turner, Victor. 1974. *Dramas, Fields, and Metaphors: Symbolic Action in Human Society.* Ithaca, NY: Cornell University Press.

Tužinská, Helena. 2009. 'Communication in Asylum Courts. Limits of Inquiry.' *Slovenský národopis* 57, no. 5: 560–78.

———. 2019. 'Doing Things With Questions. Interpreting in Asylum Settings.' *Lud* 103: 81–99.

———. 2020. *Medzi riadkami. Etnografia tlmočenia azylových súdnych pojednávaní.* Bratislava: Akamedia.

UNHCR Slovensko. 2006. *Počet žiadateľov o azyl od roku 2001 poklesol na polovicu*, 17.03.2006. Accessed 01.04.2024. https://www.unhcr.org/sk/470-sknovinky2006pocet-ziadatelov-o-az yl-od-roku-2001-poklesol-na-polovicu-html.html.

van Baar, Huub. 2012. 'Socio-Economic Mobility and Neo-Liberal Governmentality in Post-Socialist Europe: Activation and the Dehumanisation of the Roma.' *Journal of Ethnic and Migration Studies* 38, no. 8: 1289–304.

Vandevoordt, Robin. 2017. 'The Politics of Food and Hospitality: How Syrian Refugees in Belgium Create a Home in Hostile Environments.' *Journal of Refugee Studies* 30, no. 4: 605–21.

Vašečka, Michal. 2009. *Postoje verejnosti k cudzincom a zahraničnej migrácii v Slovenskej republike.* Bratislava: International Organisation for Migration.

Vigoda-Gadot, Eran, Aviv Shoham, and Dana R. Vashdi. 2010. 'Bridging Bureaucracy and Democracy in Europe: A Comparative Study of Perceived Managerial Excellence, Satisfaction with Public Services, and Trust in Governance.' *European Union Politics* 11, no. 2: 289–308.

Vries, Leonie Ansems de, and Elspeth Guild. 2019. 'Seeking Refuge in Europe: Spaces of Transit and the Violence of Migration Management.' *Journal of Ethnic and Migration Studies* 45, no. 12: 2156–66.

Vrzgulová, Monika. 2016. *Nevyrozprávané susedské histórie: Holokaust na Slovensku z dvoch perspektív.* Bratislava: VEDA; Ústav etnológie Slovenskej akadémie vied.

Walters, William. 2015. 'Reflections on Migration and Governmentality.' *Movements: Journal for Critical Migration and Border Regime Studies* 1, no. 1: 1–25.

Walther, Eva-Maria, and Steven Jobbitt. 2022. 'Narrating Crisis and Continuity in Migration Debates in the Visegrád States.' *Hungarian Studies Review* 49, no.1: 1–10.

Weber, Max. 2015. 'Bureaucracy.' In *Max Weber's Rationalism and Modern Society*, edited by Tony Waters and Dagmar Waters, 73–127. New York, NY: Palgrave Macmillan.

Weick, Karl E. 1998. 'Introductory Essay—Improvisation as a Mindset for Organizational Analysis.' *Organization Science* 9, no. 5: 543–55.

Weizman, Eyal. 2009. *Sperrzonen: Israels Architektur der Besatzung.* Hamburg: Edition Nautilus.

Wimmer, Andreas, and Nina Glick Schiller. 2002. 'Methodological Nationalism and Beyond: Nation-State Building, Migration and the Social Sciences.' *Global Networks* 2, no. 4: 301–34.

Zaun, Natascha. 2018. 'States as Gatekeepers in EU Asylum Politics: Explaining the Non-adoption of a Refugee Quota System.' *Journal of Common Market Studies* 56, no. 1: 44–62.

Zigon, Jarrett. 2007. 'Moral Breakdown and the Ethical Demand: A Theoretical Framework for an Anthropology of Moralities.' *Anthropological Theory* 7, no. 2: 131–50.

———. 2008. *Morality: An Anthropological Perspective.* Oxford, New York: Berg.

———. 2011. *Multiple Moralities and Religions in Post-Soviet Russia.* New York: Berghahn Books.

———. 2018. *A War on People: Drug User Politics and a New Ethics of Community.* Oakland, CA: University of California Press.

Žúborová, Viera, and Ingrid Borárosová. 2017a. 'Migration Discourse in Slovak Politics. Context and Content of Migration in Political Discourse: European Values versus Campaign Rhetoric.' *Journal of Nationalism, Memory & Language Politics* 11, no. 1: 1–19.

———. 2017b. 'The Myth of the Angry Voters: Parliamentary Election in Slovak Republic.' *Slovak Journal of Political Sciences* 17, no. 1: 34–48.

Zückert, Martin, Jürgen Zarusky, and Volker Zimmermann, eds. 2017. *Partisanen im Zweiten Weltkrieg: Der Slowakische Nationalaufstand im Kontext der europäischen Widerstandsbewegungen. Vorträge der gemeinsamen Tagung des Collegium Carolinum und des Instituts für Zeitgeschichte München-Berlin in Bad Wiessee vom 6. bis 9. November 2014.* Göttingen: Vandenhoeck & Ruprecht.

INDEX

Milton Keynes UK
Ingram Content Group UK Ltd.
UKHW010647310524
443344UK00003B/21